THE MAN WHO WOULD BE BING

THE MAN WHO WOULD BE BING

The Life Story of Michael Holliday

Ken Crossland

The Book Guild Ltd
Sussex, England

First published in Great Britain in 2004 by
The Book Guild Ltd
25 High Street
Lewes, Sussex
BN7 2LU

Typesetting in Times by
Keyboard Services, Luton, Bedfordshire

Printed in Great Britain by
CPI, Bath

A catalogue record for this book is available from the
British Library

ISBN 1 85776 841 8

For Linda

Contents

Foreword

It has been well documented that the origins of the most significant popular music of the twentieth century emanated from and had its roots in American culture. From the great creative influences of the jazz age in the Twenties and Thirties, to the big orchestras and their crooners such as Bing Crosby and Frank Sinatra in the Forties and Fifties, so it was to America during the early Fifties that most of our own recording artists, guided by their producers, looked for inspiration and songs, usually a cover of a big hit.

To a fourteen-year-old in 1956 like myself, growing up in Newcastle-on-Tyne with my school friend Hank Marvin, we would listen open-mouthed to the new sounds and new music that was to change our lives forever – rock'n roll.

Prior to the advent in the UK in 1956 of our own Tommy Steele and the great skiffle craze led by Lonnie Donegan, this country had a wealth of hit-making crooners such as Dickie Valentine, Frankie Vaughan, David Whitfield and of course Michael Holliday. All had paid their dues singing with the famous big bands of the day.

The Shadows' career began in October 1958, as the backing group for the new rock'n roll sensation, Cliff Richard. It was at Abbey Road studios around the end of 1958 that we first met Michael, who by then was a very big star from his huge hit records, 'The Story Of My Life' and 'Stairway Of Love' as well as his many television appearances.

Norrie Paramor, who was the producer of Mike's records, as well as guiding Cliff and The Shadows' recording career, introduced us. Norrie had also had an incredible run of success as the producer for Ruby Murray, who at one time had five singles in the top twenty, and Eddie Calvert with 'Oh Mein Papa'.

Mike immediately made us feel welcome with his big smile and we, the new kids on the block, felt at ease. Nothing breeds confidence like success and Mike and Norrie were a winning team in their biggest year.

After that, our paths were only to cross a couple more times as our respective careers took different directions. The last time I saw him was in his dressing room in a London theatre not long before he died. Once again a warm welcome, a drink or three and he introduced me to two beautiful young ladies for which I was truly grateful.

Forty years on we live in an age where everyone is a 'celebrity'. People have their fifteen minutes of fame when the fridge door opens and are then quickly forgotten. Michael Holliday's stay in the spotlight lasted but a few short years, but I hope you will enjoy the story of his life.

Bruce Welch
London
September 2003

Acknowledgements

Many people over many years have contributed to the writing of this book.

I have known Mike Milne, Michael Holliday's son, for a number of years and must thank him for his forbearance in the face of my constant requests for 'more'. I am particularly indebted to Mike for providing me access to his archive of his father's papers, plus a wealth of photographs, private recordings and personal scrapbooks.

I owe a particular debt to David Stuckey, who first helped me shape the idea for telling the story of Michael Holliday's life in the early 1990s, and indeed it was David who came up with the undeniably accurate title. It was with David that I first made contact with John Ammonds, whose patient willingness to plumb the depths of his memory banks for names and recollections has been invaluable. My thanks to you, John.

In similar vein, I owe a lot to Stan White. Stan was one of the first to encourage my interest in Mike over 25 years ago and his gift to me of the original letter tapes that Mike sent to him was truly the beginning of my research. I am grateful to Stan for his permission to quote so freely from them.

I met Stephen Pattinson in 1993 when he was commissioned to write the script for a BBC Radio 2 feature on Mike. Steve's friendship and encouragement since then has been a delight and I am grateful to him for sharing with me the detailed material that he gathered as part of his research for that, and other programmes that he scripted for the BBC.

Margaret Bonakdar has been an invaluable source of memories of Mike, as well as an unstinting researcher. Without her relentless internet pursuit of anything and everything to do with Mike, I never would have succeeded in joining up so many of the dots.

I am especially grateful to Bruce Welch of The Shadows for contributing such an insightful foreword.

A full list of interviewees and other sources is provided at page 305 and I am indebted to all of those who freely gave their time. It would also be remiss of me not to offer my thanks to the following people:

Michael Collins; George Halliwell; Michael Kenefick; Malcolm Macfarlane (International Club Crosby), plus other ICC members Ron Bosley, John Joyce, Keith Parkinson, Jim Reilly and Fred Reynolds; Spencer Leigh (BBC Radio Merseyside); Michael Adams (BBC Radio Shropshire); Colin Brown; Eddie Hope; Harry Hodnet; and Alex Young.

I am grateful for the help provided by Neil Somerville, Tracy Weston and other staff at the BBC Written Archives Centre, Jaki Faulkner at the BBC Photo Library, Greg Burge at EMI Archives, Kate Calloway at the EMI Photo Archive, Cary Anning at Abbey Road Studios, Steve Woof at EMI Records, staff at the Croydon Coroner's office, and Carol Biss, Joanna Bentley and other staff at The Book Guild.

I cannot let my first book pass without thanking so many friends who offered interest and encouragement along the way, not least Karen McInerney, my friend and personal assistant, who offered me so much help and support. We all miss you, Karen.

Last and by no means least, my heartfelt love and thanks go to my wife Linda and my sons, Russell and Howard, whose tolerance knows no bounds, and to my parents, each of whom taught me how to dream and how to make dreams come true.

Ken Crossland
Dorridge, UK
November 2003

Chapter 1

The Land Of Nod

London, 28th October 1963. Almost midnight. The blue Ford Galaxie edged its way up the driveway and out through the gates. At the end of the private road, it turned right and made its way quietly and unnoticed through the deserted streets. It was heading for town.

The Galaxie was unashamedly American. Big, brash, loud. Twice the width and twice the length of the average British saloon, it was a symbol of success. Anyone who owned a Ford Galaxie had made it big.

'MH 811' said the plate. It was the only clue to the identity of the singer inside. He was late, but that was nothing new. He'd always been unreliable, never more so than when he had things on his mind. His friends knew it, and made allowances. And boy, did he have things on his mind now.

The Galaxie glided effortlessly towards the West End, guzzling petrol greedily as it gobbled up the miles. Through the streets of south London until it reached the Embankment, then across Waterloo Bridge and into Charing Cross Road. Finally, they reached the edge of Soho. They were almost there. The car made a left turn into Goslet Yard, a dark and dingy cul-de-sac just south of Oxford Street. It pulled up quietly by the kerb and the singer went inside the doors of his friend's club.

The boxer had all but given him up. He'd known him long enough to realise that he was nothing if not unpredictable. If he didn't come into the club tonight, well, there was always tomorrow, or the day after or the day after that. They'd been friends since 1957 and the days of *6.5 Special*. It was the BBC's first attempt to bring rock'n roll to television, the first time that the Beeb had set out to appeal directly to teenagers.

The singer had been a big star even then and he was a catch for the new programme. The boxer was just the opposite. A household name from his epic fights with Gus Lesnevich, he'd been the first Briton to hold the World Light Heavyweight Championship for over 50 years. But once his fighting days were over, he had needed something new to keep his name in the spotlight. He'd found it in television, fooling around and playing the role of the amiable buffoon. His name was Freddie Mills.

The boxer and the singer couldn't have been less alike, but they'd become friends in the way that opposites often do. Mills was the archetypal street fighter: rough, tough and depending on his nightclub for a living now that the fight days were over. Even his novelty value on TV was starting to wear thin. He liked having 'names' in his club and didn't seem to care what sort of names they were.

But the singer had the world at his feet – or so it seemed. He was a child of the Mersey, long before it had been fashionable. Four kids from The Cavern had changed all that. He was a product of the river and the docks. He grew up in the shadow of the Liver Building, watching the boats sail in and out of a vibrant and thriving port. He'd expected nothing more than a life at sea until he found out that he could sing like Bing Crosby. *Exactly* like Bing Crosby.

It had been eight years since the sultry August afternoon when he'd carried his battered old guitar case into EMI's Abbey Road studios. His recording test. It had been his big break. He'd been nervous, really nervous, but it didn't show. It never showed. Norrie Paramor, the producer who would later usher a raw teenager called Cliff Richard onto the British pop stage, signed him there and then.

The hit records had come fast and free. 'Nothin' To Do', 'Hot Diggity', 'Gal With The Yaller Shoes' and then the one that

2

sealed it, 'The Story Of My Life'. It hit number one in February 1958 and the singer never looked back. There were more big sellers – 'Stairway Of Love', 'In Love', even another number one with 'Starry Eyed'. Then the hits dried up.

He was already a star on television before the hit records came along, and an even bigger one after. The BBC gave him a regular TV series, he topped the bill on *Sunday Night At The London Palladium*, and was first on the lists of guests for the likes of the Beverley Sisters and Vera Lynn. In 1958, he made his first film appearance in a comedy with the soon-to-be *Goldfinger* girl, Shirley Eaton, and the ageing Crazy Gang. He was in demand in Europe and South Africa and there were signs of interest from the USA. It seemed too good to be true.

The success brought wealth that he never dreamed of in his days at sea. Some weeks, he would gross over £1,000, a king's ransom at a time when the average weekly wage was nearer £10. With his wife Margie and their 14-year-old son, he lived in luxury in a mansion in the Surrey hills. He had a paddock for his beloved horses and an orchard where he could hide when he needed to. He seemed to have it all.

The public lapped up his easygoing style – 'in tune with life, in tune with song', the TV announcers said. The relaxed ex-sea dog, the casual crooner who sang his songs in a rocking chair and fooled around singing duets with himself on a tape recorder. Life was a breeze. Or so it seemed.

But behind the public façade, the singer was a different man. The urbane TV star gave way to an insecure, neurotic individual, uncertain about who he was and who he could trust. One minute he loved the limelight, the next he hated the intrusion. He wanted the adulation of the fans, then he wished they would leave him alone. He never understood how he had come to be so successful. And anyway, it wasn't a real job, singing a few songs and fooling around. Real jobs were about chopping wood or stoking fires. He should never have left the sea. 'I'm not cut out for this, boss,' he told his TV producer in the quick, Scouse accent that was part and parcel of his off-screen persona.

3

The TV and radio bookings were still there but he knew they were getting harder to come by. EMI Columbia had just signed him to a new three-year recording contract, fighting off a rival bid from Decca, but he needed a hit. They said he was still a big name, but it was harder and harder to convince him. As if to prove his point, he'd started turning down work.

And where had the money gone? There'd always been plenty of people around to 'advise' and help him spend his handsome earnings, but now they were telling him he couldn't afford things. He had taxes to pay on his big earnings of a year or two back, as well as other debts to settle. The accountants said he needed to set aside 50 per cent of every pound that he earned, just to start getting the debts down.

It was past midnight when he made his way down the stairs into the basement that housed the club. The doorman recognised the famous face and knew that his boss regarded him as a friend. He disappeared to fetch Mills from the back room to greet him.

'Michael,' he said, throwing his arms around him in the way he used to embrace his vanquished opponents, 'I'd given you up.'

The singer smiled the soft, lop-sided grin that endeared him to his public. 'Sorry boss,' he said, 'got caught up in something.'

They shared a few drinks and the boxer persuaded his friend to sing. Lennie Peters, the blind pianist later to become one half of the Seventies singing duo of Peters & Lee, was at the keyboard. The singer sang 'I Can't Believe That You're In Love With Me', an old Crosby song, the type he liked best. By now the club was almost empty, but he still raised a few laughs with his Jimmy Cagney impression. He seemed happy.

'Look,' said Mills, 'come back tomorrow night and see the show.'

His friend looked him in the eye. 'There won't be a tomorrow night,' he said. 'This is my last night. I'm gonna finish it tonight.'

The boxer thought at first that he was joking – some black humour, he thought, brought on by another of his friend's many moods. But then he realised that he was serious. He'd heard this

4

kind of talk before. He lived his own life to the full and believed that everyone else should do the same, so much so that he devoted some of his spare time to taking calls for the Samaritans. Now he had a caller standing next to him at the bar.

Mills took his friend behind the plush, velvet curtain and into the corridor that ran behind the main room. He found a table and a couple of chairs and the two men sat down. They talked for the best part of an hour. Mills's wife, Chrissie, joined them. Mills enlisted her help.

'Go and talk to Margie, you'll see, it'll be fine,' he told him. 'Tell him, Mummy,' Mills said to his wife, 'Margie'll sort it out, won't she?'

But that was part of the problem too. Margie had gone. The sweetheart he'd met at a Liverpool dance hall in 1946 had finally had enough. She'd been the one who was always there, the crutch that he leant on in his darkest, most doubt-ridden moments.

He was talking more and more about suicide and those who were close to him knew that there had been overdoses already. The psychiatrists said they were pleas for help, demands for attention, and anyway, Margie had always been there. Margie would get help, Margie would start to pick up the pieces once again.

Each time, he promised he would never do it again, but they were the same promises he made about the girls. Girls, girls, girls. He couldn't resist anything in a skirt, especially the young ones. It had become too much, even for Margie. The singer thought he'd lost her for good.

'I've looked everywhere for her,' he said. 'And then there's the taxman. He wants his money by tomorrow or else. I don't know what to do. Give me one good reason why I should carry on.'

The boxer dug deep. 'Your life is not yours to take,' he told the singer. 'Your mother gave you your life. She carried you for nine months. Think what it would do to her.'

The talk – and the drink – seemed to do the trick. The lop-sided grin was back for the first time since he walked through the door. 'Well, it's a reason,' he said, 'even if it's not a good one.'

5

By 3 a.m., Mills thought he had changed his friend's mind, but he was still worried. He talked to Chrissie about taking him back to their home at Denmark Hill for the night, just so they could keep an eye on him. The singer would have none of it. He was nearly drunk by now from the brandies that the boxer had kept on pouring and he wanted to go home to Dailson, the home that he and Margie had bought five years ago. Five years ago. He'd been top of the charts then. It seemed like a lifetime.

The singer had a minder, a water-skiing instructor that he had met during the summer season in Jersey. The minder told Mills not to worry – he would keep an eye on his friend. And when they headed out of the club, there was a girl in tow. Normal service resumed.

The boxer and his wife came outside to see them on their way. With the ski instructor behind the wheel, the Galaxie retraced its steps into Charing Cross road and glided off towards the river.

The ambulance took him to Croydon General Hospital. The doctors started working on him as soon as he was brought in, somewhere around 7 a.m. It would be touch and go. The ski instructor knew that he always took sleeping pills but there was no way of knowing just how many he had taken. Flush them out and then just hope – that was all they could do.

They worked on him all day. Word had reached Margie and she was sitting by the phone, waiting for news. There had been a letter to her that had arrived the day before. 'By the time you read this, I'll be in the Land of Nod,' it said. Margie had heard it all before, but just the same she'd had it checked out. The police had been to Dailson and said he was fine.

Mills turned up at the hospital, grief-stricken, but there was nothing he could do. The singer's mother was back in Liverpool, waiting for news. At the private school where his son was being educated, they turned off the television to keep the drama from the boy. They waited. It was all they could do – wait.

The singer cut a small, frail figure, but he was strong somewhere. He had to be to hang on like this. The day went by. By the time dusk began to fall, with its winter chill, it seemed like he would make it. He was still unconscious, but the signs were good. He was stable. It looked like he would pull through, just like all the times before, but he'd never come as close as this.

At 5.15 p.m., the doctors said the worst was over.

At 5.50 p.m., Michael Holliday, television's gentle philosopher of song, slipped away to the Land of Nod.

Chapter 2

Bing

'The voice of Bing Crosby has been heard by more people than that of any other human being who has ever lived.'

Decca Records made that claim in 1945. Sixty years on, it seems absurd. Bing Crosby? The guy who sings 'White Christmas'? Bob Hope's sidekick? C'mon.

Absurd, audacious, outrageous perhaps – but true. By the end of the first half of the twentieth century, Bing Crosby had become the world's first global superstar. He owed it all to two things – talent and technology.

The technology started with Thomas Edison. The man who invented the light bulb was also the first human being to hear the sound of his own voice. 'Mary had a little lamb,' he said, peering into the inverted horn of his first phonograph in 1877. The words did not matter. What counted was that Edison could capture and reproduce them.

By 1903, the world had its first million-selling record. No one gave Enrico Caruso a gold disc when his RCA Victor recording of 'Vesti La Giubba' sold a million copies but it was a landmark just the same. The new invention didn't exactly spread like wildfire. By 1929, only 17 more records had passed the new gold standard. And then came the Wall Street Crash. Most people were quick to write the obituary of the music business. With people begging in the streets for food, who was ever going to come up with the money to buy records?

But they did. Together with another new invention – radio – gramophone records provided an escape route from the harsh realities of the Great Depression. Someone even wrote a song about it. 'Brother Can You Spare A Dime?' became the anthem of the Depression, and Bing Crosby was its cheerleader.

Crosby was born in Tacoma, Washington on 3rd May 1903. The family soon moved to nearby Spokane, where Crosby grew up. Christened Harry Lillis Crosby after his father, the kid with sticky-out ears became 'Bing', a nickname that he took from a character in the local comic strip, the *Bingville Bugle.*

Crosby's domineering mother had designs on a career as barrister for her fourth son, or even an entry into the priesthood. But Bing had other ideas. When he emerged from the rigours of a Jesuit education at the local Gonzaga University, Crosby was already a musician in the making. He spent his free time in local music groups, first as a drummer and then as the vocalist. It was enough to convince Bing that a future of 'shiftless vagabondage' might be fun, and in 1925 he and his close friend Al Rinker fired up Rinker's Model T Ford and headed for Hollywood.

Success came quickly. The duo made their first record in 1926. They had no billing and sales were desultory, but it was a start. Within a year, the pair had landed a prestigious position with America's leading dance band, the Paul Whiteman Orchestra.

'Two Boys and A Piano' soon became a trio when Harry Barris joined to form the Rhythm Boys, but from the start, Crosby was the one to watch. His made his first solo record in 1927, his first film in 1930 and his first solo radio broadcast in 1931. And the rest, as they say, is history.

Bing Crosby single-handedly invented the concept of the solo pop singer. Before Bing, singers were nothing more than adjuncts to a dance band. They even had to pretend to play an instrument, to maintain the pretence that they were legitimate artistes. Crosby changed the mould and made it legit to just turn up and sing.

Bing Crosby soon became the role model for all the singers who followed. 'No singer who came after Crosby would ever approach a microphone or song without passing through his shadow,' Dean Martin's biographer, Nick Tosches wrote. Frank Sinatra called him the 'father of my career'. Tony Bennett said that in the early 1930s, 'Bing Crosby was bigger than Elvis and the Beatles combined'. Even a generation on, the young Elvis himself took some of his early phrasing from Crosby and ended up covering 31 of Crosby's records.

It was a classic case of the right man being in the right place at the right time. Electrical recording, the microphone and radio were transforming the business of popular singing. Singers no longer needed to shout – or 'project' as the professionals called it. Crosby realised that as long as the microphone could hear him, so could everybody else. He sang soft, sweet and gentle. They called it crooning, said he had a 'bedroom voice'. Some of the hoi polloi treated crooning like a social disease, but who cared? It was the path to the future, the road to romance. Bing Crosby was to crooning what Elvis was to rock.

So, the cosy crooner who sang 'White Christmas'? A pop icon? A musical revolutionary? Yes. You need to get used to the idea, because it's true.

Every would-be singer tried to sound like Crosby. His secret, they said, was that he sounded the way everyone thought *they* sounded when they sang in the bath. A more highbrow critic said that Crosby's art was the art that concealed the art. Whatever. For a quarter of the century, everyone tried to sing like Bing.

The only man who could was a sailor from Liverpool.

Chapter 3

Sunday, Monday Or Always

Liverpool, 26th November 1924. When Cissie Milne gave birth to her second son, Norman Alexander Milne, Bing Crosby was a name known only in the speakeasies of Spokane. Music, records and the world of show business were somewhere on a different planet.

Cissie and her husband Robert Milne lived at 55 Haigh Street in the shadow of the Mersey docks. Liverpool had once been the biggest port in the world and the sea still provided a living for most families. Robert Milne was a steamship fireman, although other than imparting some seafaring genes to his three sons, he made little contribution to their upbringing. In later years, Michael Holliday seldom if ever spoke of his father. Those who knew the Milne family speak only of Cissie as a single parent.

Cissie soon moved to St Agnes Road in Kirkdale and set about the task of bringing up three sons. She faced a constant battle to keep her sons' heads above the poverty line. A fiercely independent woman, she was determined to avoid the stigma of reliance on the state. 'They might not have had much,' recalled one schoolmate of Michael Holliday, 'but you never saw them in "police clothes"'. 'Police clothes' was the euphemism for handouts from the poorhouse. The smell of the chemicals that were used to eliminate traces of previous occupants – human and insect – was a social stigma; it told the world that the child inside came from a family unable to support itself.

It was a tough life and the Milne family lived hand to mouth.

13

Money went on food and clothes. There was no question of any being left over for a gramophone. Even a radio set seems to have been beyond Cissie Milne's reach. Young Norman found his entertainment elsewhere. With his schoolmate Harry Reeves, he got up to the usual and not-so-usual kids' pranks, although in a BBC radio interview in 1993, Reeves recalled that young Norman had one overriding interest – girls. Whilst Harry and his mates would talk about the fortunes of Liverpool's football teams, Norman's eyes would be elsewhere.

By the age of 13, he already seemed to be widely experienced. Reeves recalled that it was Norman who provided him with his sex education. His schoolmate would point out the prostitutes on the street corners and explain graphically to his friends that the discarded pieces of rubber they kept finding were condoms, not carnival balloons. The obsession with sex would stay with Norman Milne, aka Michael Holliday, for the rest of his life.

Harry Reeves's real contribution to this story is that he introduced Michael Holliday to the voice of Bing Crosby. It was a chance encounter. The two boys attended the St Alphonsus RC School in Kirkdale and Norman's regular routine was to stop by Harry's house on the way home. One afternoon, somewhere around 1935, Norman overheard a record playing in the next room. The gramophone belonged to Harry's elder brother but the voice belonged to Bing Crosby.

'Who's that singin'?' asked Norman.

'It's Bing Crosby, of course,' said Harry, amazed that his schoolpal had never heard what was already the most famous voice in the world.

'Wow!' said Norman. 'What a fantastic voice.'

From that moment on, his life would never be the same again. It was soon a regular routine for Norman to turn up early on the morning walk to school and beg Harry to 'put that record on again'.

Norman Milne wasn't the only one to be smitten with the voice of Bing Crosby. As Crosby's popularity spread, a host of singers took up the Crosby style and competed for the label of

'Britain's Bing Crosby'. It was both an accolade and a millstone, as Michael Holliday would eventually discover.

Al Bowlly was the first, despite being neither British nor sounding anything remotely like Crosby. Bowlly was born in Mozambique and started his career in South Africa. His lighter voice and stilted delivery were a million miles away from Crosby's relaxed baritone. But Bowlly was the first singer in Britain to establish an identity for himself that was separate from a dance band, just as Crosby had done in the States. The tag came from there.

When Bowlly died in an air raid in the early days of the Second World War, a young singer from Derby acquired the mantle. Denny Dennis found fame initially as the vocalist with the Roy Fox Band before launching a solo career. After the war, he moved to the States as the resident singer with the Tommy Dorsey Orchestra, treading the path that a young Frank Sinatra had followed a few years before. The American experience didn't last. Denny Dennis was soon back home, covering Perry Como's 1950s hits on Woolworth's half-price Embassy label, before retiring to become a pub landlord.

It wasn't just in Britain that singers copied the Crosby style. American crooners such as Frank Sinatra, Dean Martin and Perry Como all pitched their earliest recordings in an unmistakeable Crosby style. They each went on to develop their own separate identities but others remained forever as Crosby copyists. The most famous North American imitator was a Canadian, Dick Todd, 'The Canadian Crosby'.

The one thing that all the Crosby disciples had in common was that whilst they sounded *like* Bing, no one would ever mistake them *for* Bing. Michael Holliday was different, more a clone than a copyist. He grew up idolising Crosby to such an extent that he knew no other way of singing. Added to that, he had an almost identical tessitura to that of his idol. The tonal quality of his voice, especially in the lower register, was so like that of Bing's that it was uncanny. Even Crosby himself was struck by it. 'Sometimes I have to pinch myself to realise that it's not me singing,' he once said.

15

Crosby's long-time film partner Bob Hope was quick to see the potential for some new gags. When he and Bing arrived in London to film *Road To Hong Kong* in 1961, Hope was soon into his stride. 'Bing's getting so old,' he told the press, 'that the studio has arranged for Michael Holliday to do the singing parts.'

There were times when it was genuinely hard to tell the two voices apart. Even diehard Crosby collectors had to stop and think. Was that a new Bing recording or was it Michael Holliday? It soon became a national guessing game. The Shell Corporation even went as far as having both Mike and Bing record identical jingles for their television commercials, and left the viewer to decide which was which.

Singing songs to sell petrol was the last thing on Norman Milne's mind when he left school in 1938.

'I could sing a bit, but whoever heard of anyone singing for a living? Not a kid from Kirkdale anyway!' Mike said in an interview in 1958.

Norman's first job was as a cutter with a Liverpool tailoring firm. The intention was that he would serve a full apprenticeship but the job lasted all of two weeks. 'All I learned was how to make tea and cheek the girls when I had to carry the bundles of sleeve-linings down to the workshop,' Mike later recalled. Milkman, butchers' boy, market trader jobs followed – but young Norman never took any of them seriously. 'I just wanted to clown about and fool around,' he said. Norman was already discovering the side of his personality that liked to be in the spotlight. Clowning, imitating Charlie Chaplin, doing impressions or singing a few songs. It didn't matter what it was, but Norman enjoyed being the centre of attention.

The Milne family had the sea in their blood. When Norman's elder brother Bob joined the Merchant Navy, his younger brother liked the look of the faraway places that he saw on his brother's postcards. He decided it was time to follow in his footsteps. The idea of a career on land was put firmly to one side as Norman Milne headed for the docks and signed on for the Merchant Navy Pool.

16

His first posting was to a tanker, the *Congonian*, which made a regular run to the West African coast. The life on the ocean wave might have not meant anything more than washing dishes and peeling spuds, but the young Liverpudlian felt at home. There was something about the solitude of the sea that made him feel comfortable with himself. In years to come, when the pressures of show business were almost driving him out of his mind, he would find himself longing for those days at sea when he could just be himself.

Norman and his brother Bob soon found themselves in a very different sort of naval setting. The outbreak of war in 1939 and the German attempts to isolate Britain from its supply lines put the Merchant Navy in the front line. Bob Milne's ship, the *Aracataca* was torpedoed and Bob was one of only 15 survivors, spending eight days adrift in an open boat. When the news came that Bob was safe, Norman Milne decided that ships with guns were a better bet. In December 1942, he joined one of the Royal Navy's signals units.

Like all new recruits into the signals core, Norman underwent a period of training in Plymouth. One fellow recruit was a young pianist named Trevor Stanford. Stanford – who would later build a showbusiness career as Russ Conway – always kept an eye out for a piano. When he found one, he would sit down and start to play. One night, Norman Milne wandered over and started to sing.

'He had a lovely relaxed voice, even then,' Conway later recalled, 'but he was very nervous about his singing and always insisted on sitting down – I think he thought it took him out of the limelight.'

As their training progressed, Stanford and Norman Milne formed a voice and piano combination that entertained their colleagues in the evenings in the canteen. Stanford went on to join the Minesweeping Base at Lowestoft, whilst Norman found himself on a destroyer. His first posting was to HMS *Norfolk* where he was engaged in one of the biggest battles of the war in December 1943 – the sinking of the notorious German cruiser *Scharnhorst*.

Norman Milne returned to civilian life in 1946 and resumed

17

his quest for some fun and female company. It wasn't long before an evening's dancing in Liverpool began the metamorphosis of Norman Milne into Michael Holliday.

Norman was 22 years of age and soon flitting from job to job again. A local cleaning firm, Spic'n Span Cleaners, took him on as a driver. Norman had use of his Spic'n Span van for the evenings and took off in it for a night's girl-chasing at the Grafton Dance Hall in West Derby, not far from his mother's house in Kirkdale. Norman had been quick to develop some lines about his 'wheels' and was keen to try them out.

The first girl that Norman met that night was Margaret Barker. Margaret – Margie to her friends and family – was a young bank clerk from Toxteth. As Norman and Margie jived to the swing sound of the resident dance band, Margie's flared skirt revealed two shapely legs as Norman spun her around the floor. They chatted about this and that until Norman asked what else Margie was interested in apart from dancing. Without much thought, Margie replied 'Bing Crosby!'

Norman was delighted. 'Oh boy, have we got something in common,' he said.

In the years since he had first heard the Crosby record at Harry Reeves's house, Norman Milne had become a fan of everything and anything to do with Bing. So too was Margie. They talked non-stop for two hours – Bing's films, his records, and the different photographs of their idol that each of them possessed. The time flew by, so much so that Margie realised she had missed the last bus home. 'Don't worry, I'll drive you home,' said Norman.

The relationship survived its first challenge when Margie was led to the 'car' – the old van with 'Spic'n Span' in big letters down both sides. When they arrived at the top of Harlow Street, Norman stopped the van for them to say their goodnights.

'You don't look at all like a "Norman",' said Margie with a hint of mischief.

'Okay, what do I look like?' he asked.

'Oh much stronger than that – more like a Mike,' she said.

18

'Okay,' he said, 'call me Mike from now on – and can I see you tomorrow?'

The two young lovers did indeed meet the day after, and true to her word, Margie called her new boyfriend Mike from then on. They spent the day at Southport. It was a hot and sunny day and they went to the funfair, walked on the beach, ate some fish and chips and then some ice cream. As they walked back to his van, Mike began to sing:

> 'Oh won't you tell me when
> We can meet again
> Sunday, Monday or always?'

Margie stopped dead in her tracks. The voice was instantly familiar – it was the warm, rich sound that she listened to every night on her gramophone; it was the voice of Bing Crosby – but it was coming from Norman Milne.

'Mike, you sound just like Bing!' she told her new beau. 'Sing some more.'

'Well okay, just as long as you don't look at me,' said Mike.

There may have been an element of poetic licence in Margie's recollection of first hearing her husband-to-be's singing voice. Others who recall Norman Milne's early vocals speak of him having a much lighter voice than the one that made him famous. Nevertheless, the roles of the soon-to-be Michael Holliday and his wife-to-be, Margie, were cast from that moment on. Margie was convinced that her new beau was gifted of a rare talent. It was one to be exploited and Margie would provide the encouragement and the drive to do just that.

Mike was full of doubt. A singer? Him? Singing wasn't something that you did for a living. It was just a lark. And who would want to listen to him? Even at the very height of his fame, Michael Holliday never had an answer to that question. Margie persevered, convinced that her boyfriend had genuine talent. She was equally convinced that despite his reluctance, there was a part of him that wanted to be a star.

It was a slow process. Margie struggled to get Mike to sing even to her, let alone turn up at anything that looked like an audition. She resorted to having Mike sing down the phone line to her in adjacent phone booths in Lime Street station. Mike would take the number of Margie's phone and sing from the next booth. 'How was I?' he would ask nervously as they stepped out onto the station concourse.

The young singer's confidence started to grow. With the help of Mike's long-time friend, Tommy McNamara, Margie persuaded him to enter the New Voices of Merseyside contest at Liverpool's Locarno Ballroom. It was a big event, with 250 entries taking part in a series of heats over several weeks. The four unlikely sounding finalists were Walter Hilton, Pat Downes, Olive Pughe and – Mike.

Mike sang 'Strange Music' from *The Song Of Norway*, and more particularly, a Bing Crosby recording from 1944. 'Merchant Navy Man wins "New Voices" contest,' said the *Liverpool Echo*, the first cutting in the scrapbook of Michael Holliday's career. The first prize was £10, but the boost in confidence that it gave him was even more significant.

By now, Mike had decided to return to the sea, rejoining the Merchant Navy and inevitably spending long spells away from home. One trip took Mike to New Zealand, and whilst he missed Margie, the money was good. And there were other benefits too. He returned from the New Zealand trip with a present for Margie – a pile of Bing Crosby records that he had come across in a sale. The records were Margie's on one condition – that she agree to marry him.

They were married in the Brougham Terrace Registry Office on 29th November 1947, three days after Mike's twenty-third birthday. Margie was 19. The newly-weds immediately moved in with Mike's mother in St Agnes Road. The house was split, giving Mike and Margie the parlour and one bedroom. With a shared kitchen and no bathroom, it was a tightly packed home, all the more so when Margie produced a baby girl. The joy of their first child soon turned into their first experience of genuine tragedy when their daughter Bonnee died at the age of only four months.

A part of Norman Milne still craved the bright lights of show business, but with a wife to support and another baby on the way, he needed money. After spells in a variety of jobs in Liverpool, interspersed with even longer spells on the dole, Mike once again returned to the sea. His first posting was as a waiter aboard the *Britannic* – an ironic turn around since it was the *Britannic*, then a troop ship, that had brought Mike home at the end of the war. Mike progressed from the *Britannic* to the *Queen Mary*, where he served as a third-class steward. The Cunard liner's regular run was to New York and it was during one visit there that Mike was press-ganged into entering a talent contest at the Radio City Music Hall.

His shipmates heard of the contest when they docked and virtually frogmarched Mike onto the stage. ''Ere' they shouted to the judges, 'this lad will beat the lot of you.' Amused by the English sailors, the judges agreed to let him enter. Mike ambled over to the orchestra, borrowed a guitar and sat down on the stairs at the side of the stage. A soft pink spotlight picked out the lantern jaw that would become such a trademark, the casual rolling of the eyes, and the slow, good-natured smile. He looked completely at ease, despite being so nervous that he could hardly move.

When Mike finally found the courage to sing, he chose a simple Irish song. The title was 'Where The River Shannon Flows' – a Crosby number, of course. It was a smart tactical move, knowing that a Murphy or an O'Toole would, like as not, be amongst the judges. When Mike's voice swept out across the famous theatre, a veil of silence fell over the audience, followed by deafening applause. The judges' decision was a formality.

The prize was 100 dollars but more importantly, the moment had whetted Mike's appetite for showbusiness. He returned home with presents for Margie and their baby son Michael. He also returned home with one clear thought in his head. He was going to be a star.

Chapter 4

'Michael Holliday – Vocalist'

Norman Milne had now become 'Mike' to his friends. The name sat easily with him. The experience in New York had fuelled his ambitions but Mike quickly learned that there is a difference between winning a talent contest and breaking into show business. It was not enough just to possess a great voice. He also needed to find the will to succeed. He might have overcome his stage fright for a bit of a lark in New York, but he had yet to discover if he could handle the same terror every night.

Meanwhile, he and Margie needed to live. Employment was hard to find. Mike knew that his best source of income was from the sea, but ships were few and far between. 'Skint?' he once said years later to guitarist Johnny Wiltshire. 'You don't know what skint is. Standing on the docks with no shoes, waiting for a ship. That's skint,' he added, displaying a rare moment of anger.

The scars from the long periods Mike spent at home on the dole were deeply formed. His dole money was a princely £3 10s a week. On the way home from the labour exchange, he would stop off at the fishmongers for the one luxury that he and Margie allowed themselves – a plate of kippers.

He would also pick up his copy of *The Stage*. The paper was the weekly journal of British show business and Mike hoped to find his future in it. There were plenty of advertisements and openings but all of them asked for the same thing – a track record. 'How do I get a start?' was the question he would constantly ask Margie. She later recalled that he thought of show business as a series of rings – break through the first and then gradually work your way into the centre. It sounded simple, but Mike was realistic enough to know that if he wanted to hit the bull's eye, he needed to serve an apprenticeship.

One day in 1950, Mike saw an ad from what sounded like a small touring company. It offered no pay other than living costs and it would mean travelling from town to town by caravan. He would need to leave Margie and Michael to fend for themselves or rely on handouts from the National Assistance. Mike and Margie talked it over long into the night and made the decision that it was worth a try.

Mike packed a suitcase and headed off to join the group. It comprised an elderly Shakespearian actor plus a supporting cast of music hall veterans. Aside from his singing, Mike's main job was driving the converted bus that doubled as their caravan. The group performed wherever they could gather a small crowd, usually in village and church halls. Audiences never exceeded double figures and takings just about paid for the petrol to the next village. Mike's big moment – his only moment – came with one song that divided a series of Shakespearian soliloquies.

After six weeks away, Mike returned home dirty and dishevelled, looking, in Margie's words, 'like a tramp'. Nevertheless, his time away had only strengthened his ambition. Mike had spent his nights talking with his fellow travellers about the world of show business. He came away in no doubt that it was a world he wanted to enter. More importantly, Mike's solo spot had also instilled a small piece of self-confidence. Perhaps he could perform regularly in public after all.

Mike's chance to break into the second ring of his show business circle came the following year. His elder brother Bob had also returned from the sea and was working as the catering manager at Butlin's Holiday Camp at Pwllheli in North Wales.

The Butlin's camps were just reaching their peak in the early Fifties. They were the brainchild of Billy Butlin, a rotund South African who had opened his first camp in Skegness in

1935. A second camp at Clacton followed in 1938 before the war interrupted his plans. After the war, Butlin resumed his programme and in 1947 Pwllheli was one of three camps to open in the late Forties.

By modern standards, the camps had more in common with an army barracks than a holiday resort. On arrival, each holidaymaker took up residency in an individual chalet, forerunners of the modern-day holiday apartment. The chalets, built in long single-storey terraces looked like cell blocks, whilst on the inside, they were spartan to say the least.

The great thing about the chalets, however, was their accessibility. Most British holidaymakers were accustomed to a seaside digs routine built on a mantra of 'bed and breakfast and don't come back until dark'. Even though Butlin's imposed its own regimentation to the week, with strict times for each of the two-sitting meal servings, holidaymakers still felt free to come and go as they pleased.

There was a symmetry about the Butlin's camps. Each one had a Gaiety Theatre, a Viennese ballroom and a 'house' system that formed the basis for competitions. Campers were encouraged to join in everything, from egg and spoon races to 'Glamorous Gran' and 'Knobbly Knees' competitions. The Butlin's radio station, broadcast from loudspeakers around the camp, kept people up to date with the daily programme of activities. Topping it all were the Butlin's 'redcoats', named for their red blazers, who became the enduring image of the camps. The emphasis on entertainment made Butlin's a breeding ground for anyone with aspirations for a career on the stage.

Bob Milne saw an opportunity for his talented younger brother. A week before the 1951 season was due to begin, Bob invited the resident bandleader from Pwllheli, Dick Denny, to come and stay at St Agnes Road. Margie knew that Bob had more than just a social visit in mind, but realised that Mike would never agree to a formal audition. Somehow, she needed to find a way for Dick Denny to hear her husband's voice.

With Denny's indulgence, Margie and Bob came up with a

25

scheme. Bob and Dick would noisily make a point of leaving for a night in the local pub. When Mike and Margie were left alone, she would encourage him to do a song or two. It worked. With Bob and Dick listening from the other side of the door, Mike rattled off four numbers before Margie called out, 'You'd better come in now, you two.'

At first, Mike was none too pleased at the trick, but his anger turned to delight when Denny offered him a job as resident singer for the season. The job paid £5 per week, not much more than Margie had received from the National Assistance Board whilst Mike had been away with the Shakespearian group. But in Mike's terms, he was into the second ring of the show business circle.

All Mike now needed to do was find a dress suit, turn up and sing. Margie came up with the suit from a local pawnshop and Mike headed off for North Wales. A week later, she packed her bag and with young Michael in tow, headed off to join her husband.

When they arrived, they found Mike all set to quit. 'I can't do it,' he told his wife. 'I sit there night after night like a stuffed dummy pretending to play the guitar. I'm not cut out for this.'

Fortunately, Dick Denny was a patient man. He realised that Mike's desire to be a star would eventually come through, but still tried everything to get his new singer out of the starting gate. Perhaps a drink or two would do the trick. Mike, never a serious drinker, firmly rebutted that idea. Next, Denny tried the camp's resident hypnotist – no expense spared at Butlin's in the Fifties! – but that died a death too.

Finally, it was Bing Crosby who came to the rescue – or to be more precise, a Bing Crosby song. 'I Promise You' was written by Johnny Mercer and Harold Arlen for Bing's 1944 film *Here Come The Waves* and was one of Mike's favourites. One night towards the end of Margie's first week in Pwllheli, the band started up the familiar melody. From the back of the ballroom she suddenly saw Mike stand up and move towards the microphone. He started to sing:

26

'I promise you
A faithful heart
One that will always be true...'

The words came effortlessly, ingrained on Mike's mind from the scratchy old 78 he had of the Crosby recording. By the time he came to the end, the dancers had stopped their dancing and formed a horseshoe around the bandstand.

Dick Denny heaved a sigh of relief and moved over to the microphone. 'This is Mike Milne, our new vocalist,' he said, 'and he's going to sing another song for you – aren't you, Mike?'

'I guess so,' stammered Mike. 'What would you like to hear?'

Someone called out for 'When I Take My Sugar To Tea' and Mike went into the vocal, even delivering a soft-shoe shuffle in the middle eight bars. Margie and Bob could hardly believe that the relaxed, confident performer was the same man who until then, had been glued to his chair.

It was the breakthrough that Mike needed. The next day, he was a celebrity around the camp. At the afternoon tea dance, the ballroom was crammed to capacity. The audience hadn't come to dance, though. After the band played their first number, the call went up for a song from Mike. Buoyed by his experience from the night before, Mike picked up his guitar and sauntered over to the microphone. 'How about giving the boys in the band a rest?' he asked.

Margie was struck by an immediate change that had come over her husband. The Scouse accent was gone and in its place was a new speaking voice. It had a slower delivery, with a touch of Crosby's lilt and traces of an American twang that was a Fifties vogue. Mike's natural speaking voice would always retain its pacey, Liverpool delivery, but that night the audience heard the more measured tones of Michael Holliday for the first time.

Mike's breakthrough sustained him through that first summer season. Gradually his confidence grew and as it did, so too did the level of his ambition. It wasn't long before he was making approaches to some of the better-known bands. Both Geraldo

27

and Joe Loss turned him down, but Mike persevered. He was starstruck and having beaten his nerves to get this far, he was never going to be satisfied with a low-profile role in a second-string Butlin's camp.

When the 1952 season ended, Mike and Margie headed back to Mike's mother's house in Liverpool. The Dick Denny arrangement was strictly a summer-only affair, and Mike was facing another winter on the dole. But before then, he had one final engagement to fulfil as part of his contract. Each year, the bands from the various Butlin's camps came together for one grand finale at the Albert Hall. For Mike, it was more than just an end-of-season get-together.

The best known of all the Butlin's bands was the one from Clacton. Eric Winstone was the bandleader and Mike saw the Albert Hall concert as a chance to make an impression. Winstone was a musician who had been in the business since the mid-Thirties and was the most famous of all the Butlin's bandleaders. Winstone had started out as an accordion player, an instrument that attracted more than its fair share of ridicule amongst professional musicians. Despite that, his first band, Eric Winstone's Accordion Quintet and Swing Quartet, had been a success and had established him as a band leader. The association with Butlin's began as soon as the war ended in 1945 and lasted for 20 years.

Mike geared himself up to make an impression on Winstone. He knew that without some prompting, Winstone was unlikely to hang around and listen to each of the bands from the other camps, so Mike's first job was to find his target and make sure that he would be on hand to hear his vocals. Mike scoured the Albert Hall for a sight of Winstone, and finally saw him disappearing into one of the auditorium's many bars. Rather than burst in, Mike hung outside. His plan was to enter the bar just as Winstone was coming out and 'accidentally on purpose' bump into him. It worked to perfection.

Mike introduced himself and paid homage. 'Mr Winstone, I've admired you and your music for so long,' he said.

Winstone was no stranger to the line or to would-be singers

28

wanting a job. Irritated at being set up, Winstone came straight to the point. 'What is it you want?' he asked.

Mike realised that the bandleader had called his bluff. 'I'd like a job with your band,' he said.

'So would a lot of other fellas,' said Winstone.

Mike's heart was beating fifty to the dozen but he knew that this was his chance. 'Please,' he said, 'I'm with the Dick Denny Band and I'm on in a few minutes. Just listen to me. Please.' When the Denny band has finished its performance, Mike went looking for Winstone to gauge his reaction. It was encouraging. 'I'll be in touch,' said Winstone.

Mike returned home to Liverpool and spent three anxious weeks waiting each day for the postman to arrive. Eventually he could wait no longer. His patience snapped. 'I've got to phone him,' he told Margie and headed off for the telephone box around the corner.

As Mike disappeared around one corner, a telegram rider arrived around another. The telegram was for her husband but Margie knew what it must be about. She ripped open the message. 'ASK THAT YOU MEET ME MONDAY MORNING, MY OFFICE – ERIC WINSTONE,' it said.

Mike travelled to London to keep the appointment although by the time he did, another very significant step in his show business career had taken place. The singer who turned up to meet his new boss was no longer Mike Milne. He had a new name. Michael Holliday.

The need to find a new name had been Mike's idea. Both he and Margie had become frustrated with the way that people confused the name 'Milne' with other names. At various times he had been called 'Mike Mills', 'Mike Milner' or 'Mike Miller'. Even in the years after Mike died, various badly researched album sleeves have come up with their own theories about Mike's given name. The commonest suggestion is usually that Mike's original surname was Miller and that he changed it to Milne by deed poll. All of that is a myth, as Mike's birth certificate clearly shows.

Mike was very clear, however, that the name 'Milne' would not get him to the top. And, just as there are myths about Mike's true name, there is no shortage of theories about how he came to take the name of Holliday. The most popular was that it was his mother's maiden name. Not so. Cissie Milne's maiden name was Johnston and the 'Holliday' name was in fact another of Margie's suggestions. It was the name of an old boyfriend. 'I always thought it was such a happy sounding name,' Margie later recalled.

Mike and Margie had experimented with several other names before Margie came up with the suggestion of 'Holliday'. Mike was immediately taken by it. 'Michael Holliday,' he said. 'Michael Holliday.' He said it aloud several times, like a musician getting comfortable with a new instrument. It was the name he needed. Within days, Mike was handing out his new cards: 'Michael Holliday – Vocalist'.

It turned out to be an inspired choice, although not everyone was taken by it. Liverpool bandleader Hall Graham was one of several who told Mike that he would 'never get anywhere with a name like that'. The doubters were wrong, although breaking in the new name was not always plain sailing. Mike's early correspondence with the BBC frequently has him correcting people on his name. Just as 'Milne' was easily confused with something else, 'Holliday' just as easily became 'Holloday' or 'Holloway'.

In time, of course, it caught on. Whilst there remained a persistent misspelling as 'Holiday' throughout Mike's career, the choice itself was a good one. 'Holliday' fitted easily with Mike or Michael and enabled Mike to link his stage name to the concept of a holiday – a time for fun, relaxation and enjoyment. *Holliday With Strings*, *Mike On Holliday*, *Happy Holliday From Michael* all became a part of the Holliday brand.

Mike's new name was announced in time to coincide with the news of his engagement by Winstone. 'Mike Milne, the young Liverpool vocalist who has been featured with Dick Denny for the past two years, is to join Eric Winstone on 30 March 1953.

He will henceforth be known as Mike Holliday,' said one music journal.

The Winstone Band was more than just a Butlin's fixture. Outside the summer season period, the band toured widely and were regular broadcasters for the BBC. Mike made his radio debut with the band on 21st April 1953. Winstone gave Mike two solos, the second of which, 'Nina Never Knew' survives from a rare acetate recording. The band's performance that night did not go down well with the critics, although Mike made a good start. 'Michael Holliday shows promise although he must avoid a tendency to sharpness,' said one newspaper reviewer. It was probably the only time that Michael Holliday was accused of delivering a 'sharp' vocal.

The band's programme was broad-based. Mike initially was the fourth-billed vocalist, behind the more established names of June Marlow, Colin Prince and Roy Marsh. He usually sang two solos in each performance plus duets with the other singers. One regular duet was 'Back the Old Routine' with Colin Prince. It was another of Mike's favourite songs and one that he later incorporated into his trademark tape recorder duet routine.

The surviving acetate of Mike's first broadcast supports the views of those who recalled Mike at this time as a pleasant vocalist, but not especially like Bing. If anything, the slight stiffness of phrasing is more reminiscent of Mike's predecessor, Denny Dennis. John Joyce, a Crosby stalwart who Mike had befriended around the time that he joined Winstone, remembers Mike in the Winstone days as a singer more in the mould of the American singer-dancer, Danny Kaye.

'Mike once gave me a private record that his brother made him record,' said Joyce. 'It was pleasant but I didn't think he was like Bing at all. His voice was much lighter in the early Winstone days. If there was any resemblance, I would have said it was to Danny Kaye.'

Others, however, saw the Crosby likeness immediately. Jim Brown, Winstone's saxophonist, recalled being struck by it from the very beginning.

Lifelong Irish fan Michael Kenefick said the same thing. He recalled hearing Michael Holliday for the first time on a Winstone broadcast and thinking he was listening to an American singer. 'What also struck me was how relaxed he sounded,' said Kenefick.

Whether like Bing or not, Mike's time with the Winstone band gave him the experience that he needed. The band was a much bigger and more professional outfit than Dick Denny's entourage and its bookings extended beyond the Butlin's camps. When the holiday season was over, the Winstone band played a regular series of one-nighters around dance halls in the Home Counties, plus regular radio spots. For Mike, it was a full apprenticeship.

Eric Winstone was a colourful character and all the more so because of his 'ticks' – a series of involuntary muscle spasms and mannerisms that struck at moments of nervousness and tension.

Jim Brown recalled his first experience of them. 'When we had a meeting to talk about the programme, I kept thinking that Eric was winking at me the whole time,' remembered Jim, 'but I didn't know why.' Finally, one of the other members of the band told Jim to take no notice – it was just 'Eric's tick'. Winstone's twitch reminded other people of the Alf Ippititimus character that comedian Jack Douglas created. Douglas himself was part of the Butlin's Clacton set.

Pianist Johnny Pearson worked with Mike on both radio and TV and remembered Mike's stories of how Winstone's tick would reach a peak just before the curtain went up. Some of it seemed to rub off on Mike and by the time he left the Winstone band, he had started to develop some ticks of his own. The mannerisms were an early indication that the relaxed singer on the bandstand and the intensely nervous young man off-stage were two quite different people.

Jack Douglas saw the distinction very clearly. In an interview with *Radio Times* in 1959, he recalled Holliday as the 'original Charley Nervous. He constantly asked me what I thought of his style,' said Douglas. 'I spent hours trying to dispel his nervousness.'

Mike's twitches never developed to the same extent as those

of his boss and like Winstone, he found a way of concealing them on stage, but only just. Mike had two strong mannerisms. One was to use his chin to try and brush an imaginary object off his shoulder; the other was to reach down and touch his shin. Even though relatively little television footage of Mike survives, what little there is clearly shows Mike fighting to contain both of these mannerisms from the camera's prying eye.

The twitching increased at times of stress. Guitarist Johnny Wiltshire recalled that it was particularly severe during the 1961 summer season that they spent together in Blackpool. 'He would be driving along in the big American car,' said Johnny, 'when he would start rubbing his chin, down his shoulder and onto the steering wheel. In the end, it got so bad that he used to ask me to drive the car.'

Mike spent his second season with Winstone at Clacton in 1954 but by the time it had finished, he was ready to move on. He was starting to get frustrated with his role in the band, dictated by Winstone's need to play the hits of the day. Mike's dream had always seen himself making the decisions about the songs he sang. As a dance band vocalist, such a luxury was not on offer.

The band's programme from a Sunday concert at Romford in December 1954 had Mike covering Johnnie Ray's 'Such A Night', a strong beat number that Elvis Presley would soon convert into a rock'n roll standard. Mike's other song was 'Cinnamon Sinner' ('a marshmallow mama with a jellyroll heart'). It might have been a US Top Ten hit for Tony Bennett but it wasn't Mike's idea of a good song.

Despite his unease, Mike knew that his money from Winstone was good. The £12 per week that he had started on had risen to £20 per week by the summer of 1954, a highly respectable weekly wage. Moving to another band was unlikely to offer more. If Mike wanted to go further, he knew it would mean going solo.

The question was how. When Bing Crosby had outgrown the Paul Whiteman band in the early Thirties, he had made his

33

breakthrough with a solo spot on radio, the new phenomenon of that decade. Mike chose a similar route, but on television not radio. The holidaymakers at Butlin's had filled his head with the notion that he was cut out for TV stardom and Mike decided to put it to the test. His approach was direct and simple. One evening in January 1955, he pulled out a piece of blue Lion stationery and composed a letter to the BBC.

Dear Sir

Can I apply to you for a TV audition. I am a proffessional [sic] singer, at present doing one-night stands and cabaret. I sing modern love songs to a guitar and I feel my act would be OK for television.

If, to save wasting time, you work on recommendations only, Mr Noel Hunter, entertainments manager, Butlin's Hotel, Brighton would be glad to give you a word on my work as I do several cabarets for him.

I also have 200 letters from Butlin holidaymakers asking me if I shall be appearing on TV.

Yours Respectfully

M. Holliday

Without a word to Margie, Michael Holliday popped the letter in the post and waited to see what would happen.

Chapter 5

'There's A Yellow Rose In Texas...'

Times were changing at Broadcasting House. The BBC had been formed in 1922 as a Government-funded body and, as such, had enjoyed a monopoly position in the radio industry for over 30 years. When television came along in 1936, it seemed natural that the BBC should extend its remit, although there was little in the BBC's approach that suggested that it saw TV as the medium of the future. At heart, the Corporation was a radio station, and with its non-commercial roots, one that was still dedicated to the concept of public service rather than commercial returns.

The Second World War put television on hold, but after the war the BBC took up where it had left off. Its stately routine of public education programmes was a stark contrast to the picture in the USA where the national networks had already got the message that TV was more about comedy than culture. Whilst American viewers were witnessing the birth of *I Love Lucy*, the best that the BBC had come up with was *Muffin the Mule*. 'British TV is small, dull, slow, poor, starved and amateurish,' said Ronnie Waldman, BBC Television's Head of Light Entertainment in 1953.

Not that it mattered a great deal. Post-war Britain was a world of austerity and ration books. To most people, a television set was a fantasy. And even if you were lucky enough to afford a TV, you could only watch it for a few hours each day. Even in 1950, the BBC transmitted only four hours of television per day.

To cap it all, television reception was limited to those who lived within hailing distance of the BBC's two solitary transmitters, at Alexandra Palace in north London and Sutton Coldfield near Birmingham.

The change began with the death of King George VI in 1952. The following year's Coronation of the new Queen provided a massive stimulus to sales of television sets. The event became the world's biggest outside broadcast and it was said that 20 million people watched – a ratio of more than ten people to every set in the country.

The BBC's monopoly ended in 1954 when legislation paved the way for the birth of the Independent Television Network (ITV). Not only did the commercial channel bring competition, it also brought a different approach. ITV depended on advertising revenue to survive and advertisers were interested in only one thing – viewing figures. ITV knew that it had to offer programmes that would capture – and keep – an audience. The ratings war was under way.

The new station took to the air on 21st September 1955. Its front-line offerings look tame by modern standards, but at the time, they were revolutionary. ITV offered drama in *Armchair Theatre*, adventure in *The Adventures of Robin Hood* and political comment in *What The Papers Say*. *Emergency Ward 10* became the first in a long line of hospital soap operas. The BBC responded by moving *Hancock's Half Hour* from radio to TV and launching *Dixon Of Dock Green* and *This Is Your Life*. By the end of 1955, television had been turned on its head. Everybody wanted a TV set and every performer wanted to be on it.

The BBC had always been committed to unearthing new talent. After the war, the Corporation fulfilled its commitment to give every returning serviceman a shot at stardom, mainly on radio but with an increasing focus on television. The first TV auditions were held at Alexandra Palace in the late 1940s, where Tony Hancock was one of many who took a ten-minute pitch at making the grade. Much of the focus was on comedy but by 1955, Ronnie Waldman had extended the auditions to any kind of

36

variety act. Waldman gave the job of running the auditions to producer Albert Stevenson.

Mike's reply to his speculative letter arrived on 17th April 1955. It offered him a place on one of the auditions at the BBC's Nuffield Centre on Thursday 28th April 1955. Other than a stipulation that his performance 'should not exceed ten minutes in length', it was up to him how he used the time.

Ronnie Waldman also chose that final week in April to introduce one of his trainee producers into the auditioning process. Ernest Maxin would later become one of the BBC's most celebrated producers, from his work with Morecambe and Wise in the Seventies. That, though, was for the future. The Nuffield Centre auditions in April 1955 marked Maxin's TV debut.

Mike's spot came amidst a procession of other acts. Comedians, jugglers, ventriloquists and at least a dozen other singers performed their routines for Stevenson and Maxin, each working on their ten-minute shot at fame. Mike sang a couple of songs, just accompanying himself on his guitar. 'He stood out straight away,' said Maxin, 'just because of his voice.'

Despite his obvious vocal talents, Mike didn't shine on all fronts. 'He was relaxed,' said Maxin, 'but almost too much. His personality didn't really come through. I knew that his voice would carry him through but also that we would have to work hard to get him to project himself.' Even when Mike had reached the pinnacle of show business, Maxin still felt that he never really gave full rein to his talents. 'I worked with him at Blackpool in 1961,' said Maxin, 'and he was still singing to the front row of the audience.' Maxin's solution in Blackpool, was to insist that Holliday build a strong 'production number' into his act – 'something that would hit the back row of the theatre,' he explained. Mike was reluctant but when it was suggested that 'Temptation' – a Crosby hit from 1933 – was just the song, he agreed.

Albert Stevenson concurred with Maxin's view of Holliday's potential. His BBC file note captured the essence of Michael Holliday's future image:

A pleasant young Irishman [sic] with guitar – a cross between Gary Cooper and Robert Beattie. He has a lazy style which, combined with his appealing manner and eminently suitable light baritone voice, should render him very suitable for a TV solo spot.

Stevenson set about the task of finding the right programme in which to launch the young singer. Eventually, he settled on *The Nuffield Centre Show* on 22nd July 1955. The show was a musical magazine programme, and with no linking theme it meant that Mike could do a couple of freestanding vocals. The show went out live, something that added to Mike's nervousness, but meant that he needed to be away from Clacton for just one night.

Mike's excitement about the booking was tempered by yet more confusion about his name. Stevenson's letter to him had been addressed to 'Michael Holloday'. Mike replied acknowledging the booking but couldn't resist adding a PS. 'My name is HOLLIDAY NOT HOLLODAY.' Just to reinforce the point, Mike added his name – 'HOLLIDAY, MICHAEL' – in block letters to the top of the letter.

Mike had still not got around to telling anyone about his upcoming TV debut, not even Margie. When he did, it came on the back of a very out-of-character incident. One of Mike's regular numbers in the Winstone's Band programme was the Johnnie Ray hit 'Cry'. That night, Mike performed the song in a highly theatrical and out-of-character way. As he sang the lyrics up to their emotional climax, he stripped off his shirt and his tie and dropped to one knee for the song's big finish. It was the kind of 'projection' that Ernest Maxin had in mind, although it was motivated more than anything by the mischievous side of Mike's character that was always keen to take the mickey.

Margie was both startled and amused, so much so that she sought out members of the audience to get a reaction. The response was good, except that most people added their own postscript. 'We like it,' they said, 'but not as much as when he sings "his songs" like River Shannon.'

Margie knew that the feedback would only add to Mike's frustration. He wanted to sing the songs that suited him best, not offer up cover versions of other people's hits (unless of course, they were Bing Crosby's). But even that knowledge didn't prepare Margie for Mike's reply.

'I know,' he said, 'but I've done something about it. I'm going to be on television next week.'

Margie was aghast – and delighted. A week later she watched her husband's first broadcast from the Butlin's TV lounge. 'I was a nervous wreck,' she later recalled, 'twice as bad as I had been when Mike had first been on the radio with the Winstone band.'

Mike sang two songs on *The Centre Show*. One was an obscure Crosby number, 'My Baby Said Yes', that both Mike and Margie adored and which had been played constantly at their wedding reception. The other was 'Marrying For Love', Irving Berlin's recent hit from the show *Call Me Madam*. Alongside 'River Shannon', 'Marrying For Love' was Mike's favourite song to sing just with guitar accompaniment. It suited his vocal range and tone to perfection.

Mike was hit by a massive attack of nerves at the thought of appearing live on television, but none of that came across to the viewers. Mike sang his songs perched on a lofty stool, with an easy and relaxed style. He looked a natural for the small screen.

Mike's performance had a big impact on two particular viewers. One was producer Richard Afton who immediately signed Mike to a regular spot on *More Contrary*, a monthly TV show hosted by singing star Joan Regan. The other was Columbia Records chief, Norrie Paramor.

Paramor was becoming one of the most influential figures in British pop music. He had begun life as a dance band pianist in the 1930s but soon concluded that performing didn't hold the same appeal as producing. He saw his future behind the scenes – arranging, conducting and producing. His first experience came during the war when he joined the Ralph Reader Gang Show as musical director. After a brief return to performing, he joined

EMI Records as a studio conductor and by 1952, was head of A&R (Artistes and Repertoire) for their Columbia label. It was one of EMI's most established brands, but its image was too staid for the 1950s market. Paramor's immediate task was to reshape the label to the needs of the emerging pop market. Out went the dull, black disc labels that were associated with Thirties acts such as Layton and Johnstone. The bright green Columbia 78s that replaced them became one of the features of 1950s British pop.

Paramor's first major hit came in 1953 with Eddie Calvert's – 'The Man With The Golden Trumpet' – 'Oh Mein Papa'. His discovery of Irish songstress Ruby Murray soon followed. Her recording of 'Softly Softly' topped the charts early in 1955 and further established Paramor. Over the next few years, he would add other new stars to the Columbia label, culminating in his discovery of Cliff Richard and The Shadows in 1958. By then, Paramor had established himself as the leading British pop producer of the pre-Beatles era.

It was a phone call from Albert Stevenson that caused Paramor to tune in to *The Centre Show*. After seeing Mike's relaxed performance on television, he wasted no time in inviting him for a record test with EMI Columbia. It took place in the first week of August 1955 at EMI's Abbey Road Studios in St John's Wood.

Mike knew that if he wanted to make it big as a solo singer, he needed a record contract. It was a part of the business where he lacked experience. His two years with Eric Winstone had given him plenty of experience of live performances and radio broadcasts, but he had not featured on any of Winstone's occasional forays into the recording studio. Two weeks after his television debut, Mike made the trip from Clacton to London once more. The Abbey Road studios worked to a three session per day schedule and Paramor had asked Mike come along at the end of the afternoon session.

The timing was far from ideal. Stuart Eltham, EMI's senior recording engineer, was there. 'We'd just finished a long session when Norrie asked us to stay on because he had a guy coming in for a test,' he said. With their adjournment to the nearby pub delayed, Eltham and his team were anything but enthusiastic about staying on for a test with someone who, like as not, would turn out to be another no-hoper.

When Mike walked into Abbey Road's Studio Two for the first time, his entrance was, as ever, understated. 'He just came in carrying an old guitar case,' said Eltham. 'He had nothing about him that would make you think that he was going to be a star.' Norrie Paramor's reaction was the same. He later recalled the test as a tense affair:

> It was a boiling hot day when he turned up, right at the end of the afternoon's recording session, and tempers were frayed. Right away, he said, 'Can I have a chair? I don't like singing standing up.' I got him a chair and went to the piano and asked what key. 'I – I don't want you to accompany me,' he blurted out, 'I'll do it myself.'

Paramor didn't take kindly to having the format of his recording tests dictated to him. 'Too cocky by half' was his immediate impression of Holliday. Stuart Eltham remembers Paramor coming into the control booth and apologising to his team for wasting their time. And that before Mike had even sung a note!

Paramor decided to get the test over and done with. He went into the control room and switched on the mike. Through the glass screen, he gave the new singer a thumbs-up. Mike strummed a chord on his guitar and started to sing:

> 'It's an old-fashioned idea
> Marrying for love...'

Paramor's initial resentment disappeared in an instant. 'I didn't need a crystal ball,' he said later, 'to tell me I'd got a winner.'

Eltham was of the same view. 'He just had this absolutely gorgeous voice,' he said. 'We couldn't believe it.'

Eltham was so taken with Mike's voice that he made a point of asking to work on Mike's first full session ten days later. Over the next eight years, he became a regular on Mike's sessions at Abbey Road.

'It wasn't just his voice,' Eltham recalled. 'He had the most wonderful microphone technique. A lot of singers get too close to the mike so that the final consonant on a lyric comes across too strong, but not Mike.'

Eltham illustrated the point by reference to 'The Lady Is A Tramp'. 'Very often, "tramp" comes out as "tramppp". Then when you point it out, on the next take you get "the lady is a tram".' Eltham singled out Mike along with Matt Monro as the two most naturally gifted microphone singers that he recorded. 'It was a total gift,' he said. 'His diction was just perfect.'

Within a week of the recording test, Mike signed a letter that gave EMI the option of taking him on an exclusive contract. Paramor had booked Mike into Abbey Road for his first session on 23rd August 1955 although the session almost didn't go ahead. Mike's elder brother Bob had never fully recovered from his wartime injuries at sea. In the early 1950s, he contracted tuberculosis and died two days before his younger brother's recording debut. Mike was devastated. His first thought was to call Paramor and cancel the session, but with Margie's encouragement – this was after all, the break that Bob had encouraged Mike to pursue, she said – he decided to go ahead.

Paramor chose 'The Yellow Rose Of Texas' as the A side for Mike's debut disc. The song was already a hit in the USA for Mitch Miller and Paramor knew that there would be a number of singers vying to make the hit version for Britain.

It would be unusual now for a hit record in the States to be taken up by another artist on this side of the Atlantic. In the Fifties, however, all recorded versions of the same song came out on the same date. The practice was a reflection of the power of the music publishers. In the mid-Fifties, the song rather than the artist or the record company was king. No singer could record a song without the publisher's agreement and their interest

42

was primarily in the promotion of sheet music sales. Record charts had been introduced in the UK in 1952 but still played second fiddle to the sheet music listings.

The consequence was that several different artists often recorded the top songs of the day. All the competing versions would be released on the same date. Sheet music copies regularly featured several different artistes on the same cover – Mike's biggest record, for example, featured him alongside Alma Cogan, Dave King and Marty Robbins on the sheet music. Sheet music sales of the big songs reached up to 10,000 copies per day, easily rivalling the number of records sold.

Mitch Miller was best known for his work in the USA as Columbia Records A&R man, responsible for the novelty hits recorded by Rosemary Clooney and Guy Mitchell, and for driving Frank Sinatra into the waiting arms of Capitol Records. With 'The Yellow Rose Of Texas', Miller had taken to making his own records, surrounded by a chorus badged as 'Mitch Miller And His Gang'. But as a little-known figure in the UK – at least as a performer – there was every chance that a good 'cover' would steal the prize.

The song itself was a curiosity – one of those songs that everybody knows but no one knows why. Its origins dated back to 1836 and the Texan war of independence from Mexico. Legend has it that the original 'Yellow Rose Of Texas' was a slave girl, Emily West Morgan, who seduced the Mexican general, Santa Anna, long enough for the Texans to launch a counter-attack. A century later, when Miller resurrected it, the song was already a part of American folklore. Miller's records were big choral, sing-along affairs, in the style later taken up with great success by Ray Conniff. 'The Yellow Rose Of Texas' was a perfect fit for that style, but hardly an obvious choice for a balladeer such as Mike.

These were the days when records were made live. Today's modern approach where seemingly each individual piece is captured separately and edited into a final composite master was still a decade or more away. In the mid-Fifties, a recording session required everyone – the singer, the band, the backing vocalists – to be in the studio at the same time. Each song was recorded through a series of complete takes, and only when the producer was satisfied that he had one or more takes that were good enough for a final master could the entourage move on to the next number.

The one exception to this in 1955 was the use of twin-track recording. It meant that the engineer could capture a vocal on one track and the backing on the other, providing he could get a clear separation of the sound. The approach meant that it was possible to record the vocal and backing tracks separately, with the vocalist over-dubbing the vocal at a later point. The technique is now the norm for vocal recordings, but in 1955 it was regarded as little more than a contingency plan in case something went wrong.

To mimic Miller's choral sound, Paramor surrounded Mike with six male and three female backing singers, with engineer Stuart Eltham adding an echo to create a 'bigger' sound. The result was engaging and commercial but hardly typical of the records that would come to be associated with Michael Holliday. And despite Mike's enthusiasm for his first solo recording, he was still in the same position he had been with the Winstone band – singing someone else's hit.

The backing singers posed some technical problems for Stuart Eltham. 'Mike always sang very softly,' said Eltham, 'and it was difficult to get the separation between him and the backing.' Eltham solved the problem by constructing a vocal booth on the studio floor. Dubbed as the 'garden shed', it screened Mike off totally from the orchestra and backing vocalists and left him peering through a small window to watch for Paramor's hand-signals from the studio floor. Even then, Eltham found it hard to get the separation that he wanted.

Vocal booths had been commonplace in American studios since the end of the war, but not always popular with singers. In the film *Jolson Sings Again*, one scene shows Al Jolson being reintroduced to the modern world of recording after a long

44

absence. When told that he should sit in the booth to make his vocal, Jolson's response was 'what's the point of coming into the studio if the orchestra is in Hawaii?' Thirty years later, when Bing Crosby made his final recordings in London, he eschewed the idea of being isolated into a booth. 'I'm a band singer,' he told his producer.

As the afternoon wore on, Eltham decided that he would get the best results by having Mike superimpose the vocal separately. But with Mike due back in Clacton the next day, Paramor needed the session concluding there and then. That meant running into the evening. By the time Eltham and Paramor were satisfied with the result, it was past midnight.

Despite the technical problems, Paramor also managed to get a B side in the can from the same session. His choice of song, though, was even stranger. 'The Stein Song' was a raucous drinking song made famous by Rudy Vallee in the 1920s. Vallee had briefly enjoyed a career as America's most famous crooner before being eclipsed by Bing Crosby.

Stuart Eltham explained the reason behind its choice. 'Norrie was stuck for a B side,' he said. 'I happened to mention an old song that I knew was out of copyright.' Doubtless, too, Paramor was influenced by the fact that 'Stein Song' also needed a choir. Having paid the session fee for the nine singers, he might as well get two songs out of them as one.

'The Yellow Rose Of Texas' faced stiff competition and not just from Mitch Miller's recording. Gary Miller, Ronnie Hilton and Billy Cotton and his Band all recorded the song, but it was Miller who surprisingly won the race. His version reached number two in the UK charts to give him his one and only UK hit. Mike's version sold well enough. Paramor had been shrewd in picking a song that he knew would be a big hit. He reckoned that even if Mike's version didn't turn out to be the most popular, he would gain from having a record out of a song that was on everyone's lips.

Exact sales details of EMI's records from that period have not survived but press releases claimed figures of 40,000 to 55,000 as Mike's sales. That was probably an overstatement, as EMI sought to boost their new signing, but nevertheless was a creditable enough result. By the time the record was in the shops, EMI had already taken up their one-year option on Mike. The contract paid him the princely sum of one old penny ($^{1}/_{2}$p) per side.

Michael Holliday took the train back to Butlin's scarcely able to believe how his world had changed. It was the stuff of fairytales. A TV audition, a TV debut, a recording test and then a recording contract under the guiding hand of Britain's most enterprising producer. The contract was chicken-feed when compared to the sums involved in today's mega-deals but money was the last thing on his mind as he headed back to Clacton.

Michael Holliday knew there and then that 1955 would be his last year with the Winstone Band. It was time to go solo. Butlin's would have to make way for the BBC.

Chapter 6

'Isn't he small?'

Life with the Winstone band had been three long years of living out of a suitcase. Mike and Margie's only permanent address was still 40 St Agnes Road, Kirkdale – Mike's mother's home back in Liverpool. They made frequent trips back there although the Winstone band worked almost entirely in the Home Counties. It was clear even before Mike had decided to leave the band that they needed a base in London.

Having endured the austere surroundings of a Butlin's chalet for their time at Pwllheli, Mike and Margie chose to live outside the camp for the three years at Clacton. They rented rooms in a large house in the town. Co-tenants included fellow Winstone musician Jim Brown, and his wife Jan, who became lifelong friends. Outside the summer months, the Hollidays rented a variety of flats and rooms, sometimes living with friends for spells. Mike took it all in his stride. His years at sea meant he could feel comfortable with a here today, gone tomorrow existence. But Margie longed for a permanent home of their own.

Househunting was not Mike's number one priority at the end of 1955. He had made his breakthrough and needed to exploit it. At the end of the year, he gave notice on his contract with Winstone and set about finding the mentor who would steer his new career. It came in the form of Richard Stone.

Stone was still in the early stages of a long career that would establish him as one of Britain's leading theatrical agents. Like many who take on that role, his first taste of show business had come as a fledgling actor before the war intervened. Stone was an unusual character for show business. His father was a well-to-do stockbroker and gave his son the public school education that was designed to take him into the same profession. For a while it did, before the lure of the greasepaint proved too much for him to bear.

As with Norrie Paramor, Stone eventually decided that he was more at home behind the curtain rather than out front. During the war, he and a fellow Army Entertainments Officer, Felix de Wolfe, talked about working together when the war was over. They formed their agency in 1946 and quickly established a list of Britain's leading comedians and actors, with names such as Benny Hill, Terry Scott, Hattie Jacques and later, Dave Allen and Victoria Wood. Mike was an unusual name for Stone's list in that he was the only out and out singer on it. Norrie Paramor had made the introduction and it was just what Mike needed.

As with many of his managers and mentors, Mike's relationship with Stone wasn't easy. Stone, in his autobiography *You Should Have Been In Last Night*, recalled his time representing Mike. It was his one and only contact with the pop world, he said, and initially it was a happy association. It didn't stay that way for long. 'Michael was a shy, complex but very lovable guy,' wrote Stone, 'but not easy to understand.'

The pattern of Mike's life had already demonstrated that he was a far more complex character than he appeared on the surface. Only Margie and a few close friends knew of the terrors that still haunted him when faced with singing to a live audience, and yet the image he created was one of total ease and relaxation. His decision to leave Margie whilst he headed off in search of his track record, together with his dogged pursuit of Eric Winstone, also demonstrated a fierce desire to be a star – yet Mike was already beginning to deny any ambition to make it to the very top.

Richard Stone's first problem came towards the end of 1956 when he found himself needing to rebut stories that Mike was all set to quit show business. Mike was, in many respects, a naïve figure. He never saw himself as a star and never understood why anyone should pay attention to him. That meant that he treated the press and his fans in much the same way as he treated his friends back in Liverpool – no angle, no edge, but equally no thought about how to build and sustain a public image.

Mike was the featured singer in a week's variety in Chatham and, killing time between the first and second Monday night shows, agreed to give an interview to a local journalist. Mike was alone in his dressing room, nursing a headache that was all too often a by-product of his off-stage nerves. He'd agreed to the interview as much out of boredom as anything else. How was he coping with his new found fame, the journalist asked.

Mike was frank and open. 'I'm in a perpetual state of fright,' he told the interviewer, going on to say that he would 'give it until Christmas' to see if he could come to terms with it. It was all the ammunition that the enterprising reporter needed for his story.

Before Mike knew what had happened, the national papers were carrying a story with the headline 'TOP DISC STAR QUITS'. Mike and Margie were pictured in apparent domestic harmony, seemingly agreed on the fact that the showbiz life wasn't for them. Placards in Liverpool carried the story further: the local boy made good was, it seemed, intent on a return to sea.

If that wasn't enough, Mike also found himself in hot water over his attitude to fans. The same reporter had commented on the queue of fans eager to see Mike backstage. Mike was quoted as saying that he 'hated seeing fans when he wasn't feeling well'. Discrete editing removed the last part of the sentence to create another story with a headline of 'MIKE HOLLIDAY HATES FANS'.

Mike issued a rebuttal. 'I AM NOT QUITTING', said the headline of the prepared press release. He explained how his remarks had been misquoted, although in doing so, he revealed more of the tension within.

'I came into show business because I enjoy singing – not

because I had any idea about being a star,' said Mike. He went on to say that he found it incredible that anyone would pay money to buy his records or watch him perform. The rebuttal, cleverly orchestrated by Stone, worked at least for a while, but the stories refused to go away. The notion that Mike had an antipathy towards fans would return a year or two later when Mike refused to sanction the establishment of a fan club.

Mike's inability to see what others saw in him was never cured. Disc jockey Pete Murray, who worked with him on BBC TV's *6.5 Special*, recalled a straightforward character who was mystified by the world of show business.

'But I haven't got an act,' Murray recalled him saying.

'With a voice like yours, you don't need an act,' Murray told him.

Guitarist Johnny Wiltshire recounted a similar conversation with Mike in Blackpool in 1961. 'Look,' said Mike to Wiltshire, 'you could sing like Bing Crosby if you wanted. That's all I do. I'm no different from you or anyone else.'

The conversation was bizarre enough even without the circumstances in which it took place – Wiltshire driving Mike to his booking as top of the bill at Blackpool's most prestigious summer show. The car alone was a clear status symbol – a loud, flash American Ford Fairlane. It seemed to count for nothing. Mike's inability to see and value his own talent was endearing to the people around him, but it held the seeds of his eventual demise.

Meanwhile, Richard Stone had set about the task of promoting Mike with gusto. He was keen to get some radio bookings to supplement Mike's television work. Despite the rapid rise of television, radio still offered a more regular source of income and work. The BBC's Light Programme and the Home Service were full of programmes that relied on live acts and Stone immediately set to the task of securing some spots for Mike.

Stone used copies of 'The Yellow Rose Of Texas' to support his pitches, but not everyone was impressed. One radio producer sent the record straight back, saying that he had found the performance 'pleasant, but not the entertainment value of his normal performances with the Eric Winstone band'. In the meantime, Mike's contract to appear on *More Contrary* on television stood him in good stead. His first appearance came on 16th November 1955. Mike sang the two songs that had sustained most of his key auditions – 'Marrying For Love' and 'River Shannon' – and looked very much at home. 'LIVERPOOL LAD MAKES VERY GOOD' said *Liverpool Echo*. 'He has a free 'n easy natural style,' said reviewer Norman Frisby, 'and the Bing Crosby voice.' The review was one of the first to highlight the similarity of sound between Mike and Crosby.

Mike appeared on the show again in December and by the time his third appearance came round in January 1956, he had another new record to promote. As a follow-up to 'The Yellow Rose Of Texas', Norrie Paramor again picked a song that was already high in the American charts.

'Sixteen Tons' was a US hit for Tennessee Ernie Ford even before Mike cut his own version. Merle Travis wrote the song in 1946, creating a lyric that told the story of a coalminer, toiling all day to deliver his daily quota of 'sixteen tons', yet still in debt to the mine owner. 'I owe my soul to company store,' the miner laments.

Paramor was again using the tactic of piggybacking on a sure-fire winner. From a promotional perspective it was a wise move, although the record itself did little for Mike's reputation as a singer. Despite his great sense of rhythm, Mike was never at home with the pace of the song. The lyric's heavy use of American colloquialisms didn't help either. 'If ya hear me a-comin' ya better step aside / a lotta men din't an' a lotta men died' sounded fine coming from the mouth of Tennessee Ernie, but sung with a touch of Scouse, the result wasn't quite the same.

EMI pushed the record hard. Publicity man Doug Geddes photographed Mike shovelling heaps of coal at a London power station. The shoot was set for a January morning. 'Not only was I freezing cold,' Mike said later, 'but no one told me what to

51

wear. I turned up in clothes that were much too good and ended up with them covered in coal dust.' Despite the publicity, Mike's offering was never a real threat to Tennessee Ernie. Frankie Laine recorded a version especially for the UK and it was these two who took the honours. Paramor's hope of getting Mike into the charts would have to wait – but not for long.

He had Mike back in the recording studios again early in 1956. This time, Paramor had two projects in mind – another single plus an extended play (EP) disc. For the single, Paramor came up with a song called 'Nothin' To Do'. It was a song that was much more suited to Mike's natural style. Its wistful lyric told of a rambler with 'nothin' to do and nowhere to go'. It was a perfect fit to the easy-going image that Mike was rapidly building.

The record sold well and with no real competition, clawed its way into the *New Musical Express* Top Twenty early in March 1956. The song became a regular part of Holliday's act. When the first series of his own radio shows came along soon after, the song was a natural choice as a theme. Even after the bigger hits came Mike's way, he opened each TV show with the song, singing the first line and adding, 'if you've nothing to do for the next half hour, why not join us'.

The EP project was the first attempt by EMI to market Mike with the songs that he wanted to sing. Extended play discs were still relatively new. In 1956, a gramophone record was still, to most people, a highly breakable piece of wax that hurtled round a turntable at 78 revolutions per minute. The 7-inch 45 rpm disc, however, was catching up fast. 'Sixteen Tons' had been Mike's first disc to appear in both formats and within four years, 78s would disappear all together.

Long-playing records were still an expensive luxury to most of the record-buying public and EPs were a means of filling the gap between the expense of a full album and brevity of a three-minute single. They offered two tracks per side on a 7-inch 45-rpm disc and came with a glossy cover and mini sleeve notes. They were, to all intents and purposes, a mini-LP. The format survived well into the Sixties before disappearing when record companies found themselves under pressure to add a third or fourth title to a single, but without the 50 per cent premium that they charged for EPs.

'My Guitar and Me' was recorded in February 1956 and was in the shops by April. EMI's growing confidence in their new signing was such that Norrie Paramor gave Mike the final say on the choice of material. The four songs he picked were all personal favourites. 'River Shannon' and 'Marrying For Love' were the two songs that had sustained many of Mike's early appearances, whilst the two other numbers were an Irish folk song plus a rare jewel. 'Darlin' Katie' was a love ballad, sung simply and with great sincerity. Mike's diction and handling of the lyric nears perfection and the song remains a firm favourite for any Holliday connoisseur.

When 'Nothin' To Do' hit the charts, it prompted Richard Stone to notch up his promotion of Mike another gear. His persistence with radio paid off and Mike made his first solo appearance on 11th March 1956 in *Say It With Music*. He followed this with appearances on *Midday Music Hall* and *Workers' Playtime*, together with stage and radio appearances across the channel in Holland. Stone also succeeded in getting Mike some high-profile bookings on ITV, not least of which was the *Jack Jackson Show*. Jackson was a former BBC radio presenter with some legitimate claims to being the first modern disc jockey. His ITV show was one of the first outlets for pop music on TV.

Stone knew, however, that radio, TV and records were not enough to push Mike all the way to the top. Variety might have been past its peak, but every town in Britain still supported its own theatre and served up a twice-nightly menu of dancers, jugglers, comics and singers. The stage was the heart of British show business. Stone booked Mike into several one-week shows, in both London and the provinces, before landing a slot in a ten-week summer touring show, presented by impresario Harold Fielding.

Mike appeared as part of Vic Oliver's top-of-the-bill piece.

53

Oliver had been the bandleader on *More Contrary* and his spot sought to recreate the TV show with several artistes each singing one or two songs. The tour brought home the reality of life in show business. Margate, Bournemouth, Aberdeen, Torquay, Shrewsbury and Ipswich were neither glamour spots nor exactly adjacent locations, and Mike and the rest of the cast spent hours travelling around Britain. Just to enrich the geographic mix further, Fielding threw in regular Sunday concerts in Blackpool.

The reviews were good if not great. Mike came across as ill at ease on stage. Reviewers seemed surprised that he didn't seem to be able to deal with some of the basics – what to do with his hands when he wasn't holding a guitar, and how to adjust the height of his microphone. All too often Mike performed with the mike set too low, with the result that he sang with what one reviewer called an 'ungainly stoop'.

That Mike should find any microphone that was too low for him was a surprise in itself. Of all the dragons and demons that dogged his appearances on stage, Mike's self-consciousness about his lack of height was the greatest. Even by the standards of the Fifties when an average man stood only 5 feet 8 inches tall, Mike was a couple of inches short of that, although suggestions that he reached only 5 feet 2 inches seem to be an exaggeration.

Part of the problem was television. The small screen, together with Mike's long face and jaw, created the impression of a tall, languid man. People seeing Mike in the flesh for the first time expected a six-footer. Mike was six inches shorter and the difference was very noticeable. His desire to do everything he could to hang on to the idea that he was tall only made it worse. John Ammonds, who produced most of Mike's BBC shows, quickly established a pattern of shooting Mike 'from down to up'. The effect was to give a false impression of height. Even when Mike's shows took on a greater production element, Ammonds maintained the disguise. Mike's final series for the BBC introduced four girl dancers. Mike placed one stipulation on his producer – none of the dancers should be more than five feet tall!

Mike's hang-up with his lack of height never went away. One

fan remembered eagerly waiting for Mike to make his entrance onto the stage at the Liverpool Empire in 1962. Mike was by now an established and experienced star, but his entrance was to say the least, subdued. Mike's first words were 'All together now – isn't he small?'

Mike would go to whatever lengths necessary to conceal his lack of height. In 1959, he appeared on BBC's *This Is Your Life* when former signals friend Russ Conway was featured. Mike almost cancelled because he suddenly realised that the format on the show would mean that he would have to walk on and say his piece standing next to host Eamonn Andrews. Andrews was, in Mike's terms, 'a big bugger' and he sought advice from John Ammonds on how to get round the problem. What they came up with was an arrangement that enabled Mike to make his entrance off camera and immediately sit down before the camera settled on him.

For Babs and Teddie Beverley, the twins in the Beverley Sisters singing trio, Mike's hang-up with his lack of inches was not just vanity. They saw first hand the way Mike dreaded facing an audience. 'He really took it to heart when someone came up to him and said, "Ooh, you're not very tall, are you?"' they said.

Mike's summer tour in 1956 cost him the chance to break through into the world of films. The opportunity came through none other than the legendary Charlie Chaplin. Chaplin was filming *A King In New York* at Shepperton Studios near London and the script called for a singer to perform a nightclub number. Stone booked the slot for Holliday who turned up and gave a typically relaxed performance on 'Willow Weep for Me'.

'No good,' said Chaplin's producer. 'He wants something with more life to it – more in the Johnnie Ray mould.' Holliday shrugged his shoulders and was preparing to leave when Chaplin appeared on the set. He listened to the playback of Mike's recording.

'Wonderful,' he said, 'you'll do for me.'

Mike was exhilarated at making such a breakthrough only to find that the filming schedule clashed with his appearance in

Torquay. The local theatre management refused to accept a substitute and Mike's chance was gone. Even a contingency plan to have Mike's voice on the soundtrack with another actor doing voiceover came to nothing.

Despite the disappointment, Mike pressed on with the tour. The schedule may have been gruelling but ten weeks of seven-days-a-week appearances, plus his TV and radio fees, were generating an income stream that Mike had never seen before. He was also discovering that a star's life away from home brought something more than just money – a long line of available girls.

Chapter 7

Girls, Girls, Girls

Whilst Mike was treading the boards on the Harold Fielding summer tour in 1956, he was also making his way up the UK hit parade. After the success of 'Nothin' To Do', Norrie Paramor reverted to having Mike cover another big US hit for his next release. This time the song was a bright novelty number called 'Hot Diggity'. An Al Hoffman/Dick Manning composition, it had already been a US number one for Perry Como by the time Mike recorded it in April 1956.

Hoffman and Manning were an established partnership and were responsible for many of Como's big hits. Their biggest had been 'Papa Loves Mambo' in 1954, a song that was typical of the partnership. Al Hoffman had a penchant for novelty lyrics that were ideal for Como's weekly show on American television. The pairing were also responsible for such 'classics' as Alma Cogan's 'I Can't Tell A Waltz From A Tango' and the even more absurd 'Gilly Gilly Ossenfeffer Katzenellen Bogen By The Sea' for Max Bygraves.

Perry Como was a big star in the UK even before his weekly TV show started its run on the BBC the following year. Paramor knew that the race for a British cover of 'Hot Diggity' was effectively one for second place. Once again his bet was that it was going to be a big song and worth having Mike on board, even running second. As with 'The Yellow Rose Of Texas', there was no shortage of British covers. Glen Mason and the emerging TV star Marion Ryan both cut rival versions. Como's release secured the UK number four spot, but Mike's disc followed closely in its wake, peaking at number 14 on the Hit Parade.

To Paramor's surprise, however, it was the B side that really made the impact. Paramor had picked another new song for the flip side of the disc, with lyrics by top Hollywood lyricist Sammy Cahn. 'Gal With The Yaller Shoes' might have been a relatively minor feature in the Dan Dailey/Cyd Charisse movie *Meet Me In Las Vegas*, but it proved to be the perfect vehicle for Michael Holliday.

The song was about a horseman galloping to a rendezvous with his girl – 'the gal with yaller shoes and the golden hair'. The fast tempo and cowboy feel suited Holliday's vocal perfectly. Although there was a lot of Crosby in the voice, more than any previous Holliday recording, the disc had a strong, modern feel to it. For the first time, Michael Holliday had a disc out that had the kids up dancing.

'Gal With The Yaller Shoes' proved to Norrie Paramor that Mike could make it as a pop singer. What's more, it gave him the formula for putting him high on the chart – a strong pace, a happy-go-lucky lyric and a bright vocal backing. The only surprise was that it would take Holliday and Paramor twelve months and five flops to repeat it. Forty years on, 'Gal With The Yaller Shoes' is still one of the first titles in any *Best Of Michael Holliday* compilation.

Reviews of both songs were good. *New Musical Express* singled out 'Michael Holliday's excellent diction and feel for the song' as well as Paramor's 'two great scores and backing'. It was, said *NME*, 'novel, wonderfully in character and very commercial'. *Melody Maker* echoed its rival's view. Holliday's vocal was, it said, 'a model of restrained delivery'.

With both sides of the disc in demand, the single became a double A-sided release. 'Gal With The Yaller Shoes' made the running first and entered the charts on 16th June 1956 at number 19. It reached number 13 before dropping away, only to return in August for a further three-week spell. 'Hot Diggity' meanwhile entered the chart in its own right on 23rd June 1956 for a five-week stay.

Double A sides were a problem for the chart compilers. With no national sales figures available, they relied on sales returns from a small number of record shops, mainly in and around the South-East. The weekly sales totals of the top-selling discs formed the basis for the charts.

This system worked fine for most discs except where shops reported a demand for both sides of the same record. A buyer who asked for 'Hot Diggity' got the same product as someone who came in for 'Gal With The Yaller Shoes', but the chart compilers needed to attribute sales to one or other of the two titles. Mike's disc sold in the region of 80,000 copies but the sales credit was almost evenly split between the two titles. It gave Mike two moderate hits, but if all the sales had been attributed to 'Gal With The Yaller Shoes', Mike would have chalked up his first Top Ten appearance.

The summer tour ended in mid-September 1956. Mike was relieved to discover that Richard Stone had lined up an autumn programme for him that, apart from a week at the Leeds Empire, would put most of the focus on television. The relaxed young man in the casual shirt was now a regular feature on the nation's 5 million television screens and Stone booked Mike heavily on both channels. On BBC, he appeared in *The Show Band Show*, *Crackerjack* and *Summer Serenade*, whilst ITV became the first network to feature Mike in a series of programmes. Stone had also firmly established a regular flow of radio appearances. *Workers' Playtime* and *Midday Music Hall* were anachronistic shows and a throwback to radio's pre-television days but whilst his records made him a pop star, these shows cemented Mike's appeal with the nation's housewives.

In June 1956, Mike appeared as the star of his own radio programme for the first time. He recorded three shows with the title *Take It Easy* – further evidence of how the concept of relaxation was becoming associated with Michael Holliday. *Take It Easy* were the kind of shows that Mike liked best. Pre-recorded and without a studio audience, Mike was able to perform and do what he loved most – just sing.

The shows were broadcast at 9.45 p.m. on Sunday evenings. The style was low-key, calm and relaxed. Mike chose songs that in the main fitted the mood. 'Amor', 'I Promise You' and 'I'll Be Seeing You' were standards from the Crosby repertoire and even the need to reprise hits like 'Gal With The Yaller Shoes' came across as a gentle canter rather than the full gallop of the commercial recording. The late evening spot suited Mike well and BBC Light Entertainment top brass started to think about where else they might use the casual crooner to close their daily schedules.

After completing the three *Take It Easy* shows, Mike went into two longer-term engagements. First was a series for the commercial station Radio Luxembourg called *Songs For The Millions*. It featured Mike alongside fellow Columbia artistes Marie Benson and Tony Brent, and ran for 13 weeks. Mike then found himself with a regular Monday night spot on the Home Service for the BBC. Comedian Ted Ray was still one of the top radio draws and Richard Stone negotiated Mike into the position of resident vocalist on Ray's *The Spice Of Life* weekly show.

Mike's autumn schedule in late 1956 provided him and Margie with a rare chance to spend some nights together at home. And for the first time since they were married, they now had a home which was truly their own. Between them, Richard Stone and Norrie Paramor had convinced Mike that he was no flash in the pan. Success bred success and he could now afford to invest, they told him. It gave him sufficient courage to take Margie house-hunting.

The house they settled on in the summer of 1956 was in Chipstead Way in the village of Woodmansterne, just south of Croydon. The purchase price was £2,800 and Mike financed almost all of it through a bank loan. The house was unexceptional – a modest semi-detached in a conventional middle class street but it enjoyed both a rural setting and plenty of adjacent land. Mike, Margie and Mike junior moved in during August 1956.

The press were quick to pick up the story-line potential of the Hollidays as the idyllic, young married couple in their first home. *TV Times* ran a feature under the headline 'NOT AT SEA ANY LONGER', portraying Mike as the sailor who had struck gold on dry land. It built Mike and Margie up almost as if they were newlyweds – conveniently setting aside the fact that they had already been married for almost ten years.

Photographs showed Mike busy in his garden, building a garden wall and polishing his new car, all things that probably fitted much more easily into Mike's definition of 'real work' than singing did. 'Singing a few songs isn't real work,' he said in one interview, contrasting his lifestyle with that of someone who chopped trees or stoked boilers. Mike also made a virtue of the house's small size. 'I don't want to get anything big just in case I ever give up singing,' he said. For a new arrival on the scene, it was an odd remark. What it revealed was that Mike was already struggling to come to terms with his success.

Mike's bewilderment was understandable. It was only six years ago that he had left Margie and young Michael to the National Assistance Board and set off with the roving Shakespeare group. Margie had survived on a handout of £3 10 shillings per week. Now he was laying out £2,800, with a queue of banks happy to lend him the money. It took some getting used to.

Stone's canny handling of Mike's progress had transformed his earnings. He made 23 BBC appearances on radio and TV during 1956 and received a total of £372. His EMI royalties were around £400, reflecting total sales in the year of 100,000. Add to that his ITV fees, his Luxembourg contract and variety income, and Mike's gross earnings for the year topped £2,500.

In the mid-1950s, £1,000 was a lot of money; £2,500 was a serious amount. Even though these were years of affluence and 'never had it so good' Conservatism, monetary values had changed little since the turn of the century. The high-inflation years of the Sixties and Seventies were still to come, and until then Britain remained a nation that went to work on a twopenny tram ride, smoked ten cigarettes for a shilling (5p) and regarded a wage of £20 per week as a small fortune.

Mike's earnings took him to the fringe of an elite class of

supertax payers. Average earnings across all social classes in the mid-1950s were in the region of £500–£800 per annum. Eminent positions in the professions seldom carried salaries in excess of £1,000 (Oxford University paid its professors £850 per year). The bulk of the country's working population took home wages of £10–15 per week.

The turnaround in Mike's fortunes in little over a year was gargantuan. Even at the peak of his career with Winstone, his earnings had been well short of £1,000 a year. On a good week, he would top £20 – but not 52 weeks of the year. Mike knew that he was earning big money but never got comfortable dealing with it. Setting aside enough to meet his future tax demands was always a problem – not because he was an extravagant spender, simply because he had no notion of earning money today and finding that it led to a big tax demand two years downstream.

Neither Mike nor Margie had any experience of managing sums of money like this. Nor did they realise that this was the tip of an iceberg. Within four years, Mike's earnings would be ten times the figure they were in 1956. A good accountant would have been invaluable but Mike was wary of the professions. Accountants, solicitors and bankers were hardly natural bedfellows for a Liverpool sailor whose school qualifications were about stealing apples and chasing girls.

It's not clear where Mike obtained financial advice during these early years. Eventually, he appointed London accountants Baker Todman as his financial advisers but until then, he relied on tips and tweaks from a variety of sources. Not all of it was sound. The formation of *Michael Holliday Productions* in January 1957 was a case in point.

Mike formed the company to finance some film projects that he hoped would give him a springboard to launch his career in the USA. He recorded a colour TV special with the Kaye Sisters at considerable cost and used the company to raise some of the funding. He also believed that the company would help him reduce his tax bills. To a point that was true, but only if he could demonstrate that 'expenses' that he recharged to his company were legitimate. Margie was already on the payroll of the company in 1957 but soon Mike found himself needing to justify Margie's salary as a legitimate company expense.

Mike also added a layer of complexity by only using the company as a vehicle for part of his business. He channelled income from TV, radio and film work through it but income from other sources – personal appearances, record royalties and advertising – was kept separate and accounted for it as direct personal income. This dual structure was unnecessarily complex. It meant he had to split his costs across the two sets of accounts and keep two sets of books. Worse still, it exposed him to two separate tax calculations. None of this mattered a great deal when Mike's career was on the up and up, but it created chickens that would come home to roost in the early 1960s.

Financial affairs were one thing. Affairs of a different variety were also a part of the Holliday scene by the end of 1956. Mike had been an inveterate girl-chaser virtually from his schooldays. Success and fame did nothing to change his behaviour, except perhaps to exaggerate it.

Friends of Mike and Margie maintain that they were a couple who loved each other deeply. The public image showed an idyllic young couple, enjoying fame and fortune in a rags-to-riches fairytale. They were young, in love and happy with the simple things in life. They strolled hand in hand through the garden of their new home and, with a young son, they looked the epitome of a happily married Fifties family.

Ironically, much of that was true. Mike's son recalls a happy early childhood and a father who liked to try and play the disciplinarian but was at heart, a soft-centred individual. Margie increasingly played a significant role in her husband's career, helping him with his TV scripts and handling much of his fan mail. When Mike heard Bing Crosby's revival of an old song called 'Margie', he immediately scheduled it for his next album. 'She was the only woman he ever loved,' said one close friend.

Yet despite the love and dependence that Mike placed on

Margie, his appetite for sex drove him down a path of promiscuity and infidelity. It was not something that came with stardom. Harry Reeves's stories from their schooldays revealed a sexual maturity beyond his years. His time at Butlin's, too, provided plenty of opportunities for casual sexual encounters and Mike was very happy to take advantage.

Mike's affairs were mainly one-night stands – or even shorter liaisons. He did little if anything to conceal them and indeed seemed almost to get a kick from flaunting his behaviour. A consistent feature of almost every interview conducted as part of the research for this book was a reference to Mike and 'the girls'. Daphne Shadwell, his TV producer at ITV, is typical. She recalled him with great fondness as someone who 'could get away with murder' and yet was also 'such a dreadful womaniser'. She found his openness about it almost equally shocking. John Ammonds recalled 'the awful girls' who would hang around Mike at the television studios. Shadows star Bruce Welch was a raw teenager when he first met Mike and recalls his strongest memory of him being 'all the girls in his dressing room'.

Mike's obsession with sex reflected a seemingly insatiable sexual appetite. It was a constant and unchanging characteristic. One girlfriend recalled that Mike often needed sex two or three times every day. Sex, she said, seemed to act as a release for him from the nervous tensions that enveloped him.

Johnny Wiltshire observed Holliday's preoccupation when working closely with him in Blackpool in 1961. 'Mike would see a young couple standing at a bus stop,' Wiltshire recalled, 'and what would go through his mind was "Why are they there? Why aren't they at home having sex?"' Johnny also recalled a succession of females who passed through the house that he and Mike rented for the summer. 'There was one really lovely girl from Glasgow, a model, who Mike invited to stay for the week,' said Johnny. 'By the middle of the week, he was fed up with her and wanted a change. She didn't get the hint so Mike brought another woman home, twice her age, just to make the point.'

'Groupie' girls were just as much a phenomenon of the Fifties

64

pop scene as they were in the Swinging Sixties. Mike was a big star and found young girls flocking to his dressing room. His approach was direct and blunt. Johnny Wiltshire remembered Mike having a 'great chat-up line' when he needed it but John Ammonds recalled a more direct approach. He remembered a light-hearted conversation in which he had teased Mike that he 'must get a lot of refusals', only for Mike's to counter with a reply, the essence of which was 'yes, but I get a lot of fucks too'.

How Margie coped with this side of her husband's character isn't clear. She certainly knew what went on and indeed was later known to refer to Mike's big American car as a 'mobile bedroom'. According to some sources, she tried hard to get Mike to seek medical treatment but not surprisingly, it was to no avail. Few tomcats relish a trip to the vet. Margie was not the first celebrity wife to discover that her husband's sexual adventuring was something that she either had to put up with – or walk away from. Eventually, it got to the point where Margie was forced to take the latter option.

All of that was in the future. What was clear, even by the end of 1956, was that Michael Holliday was a creature with a complex molecular structure. He was 'Mr Relaxation' who was a nervous wreck; he was a star with a big future, and yet he talked of quitting; and he was the pleasant young man on TV whose dressing rooms antics would have shocked the nation.

The time bomb inside Michael Holliday was already ticking.

Chapter 8

6.5 Special

Mike started 1957 very much where he had left off at the end of 1956 – busy. It was a nice position to be in. His agent was turning people away, and with plenty of TV and radio on offer, he could stay away from the variety circuit that he found so stressful.

The first weeks of the New Year saw Mike maintaining his weekly spot on *The Spice Of Life*, a string of musical magazine appearances on radio, plus a month's cabaret at London's classy Dorchester Hotel. He also made a one-night return to Liverpool with the re-formed RAF Band, the Squadronnaires, and not surprisingly was given a hero's welcome in his home town.

It was three television bookings, however, that turned out to be more significant. Mike was becoming a firm favourite on TV on both channels and ITV were already beginning to wave a cheque book in Mike's direction. The BBC was horrified at the thought that Mike might sign an exclusive deal with ITV. They needed something that would enable them to hold onto the singer they rightly thought of as their own discovery.

The question was what. There was no obvious spot in the BBC evening schedule for a performer like Mike, although this is more a comment about the primitive nature of television scheduling than a reflection on Mike. Programmes were put together with little thought to continuity and audience retention. It wasn't quite a case of pulling a name out of a hat, but there were nights when the schedule looked exactly as if someone had. Even when Mike started his own regular series, he found himself amongst a schedule that included a documentary about the V1 flying bombs, a J.B. Priestley play and a feature on Stanley Matthews.

The programme schedulers found the beginning and the end of the evening's viewing the easiest bits to crack. Early evening had become the domain of news programmes such as *Tonight* whilst a slow, easy-on-the-ear programme seemed to be the obvious thing to bring down the curtain. Michael Holliday was a natural for that end slot and the BBC came up with the idea for a 15-minute programme built around him.

That first show, *A Musical Nightcap*, didn't feature Mike by name, but was nevertheless the prototype for the *Relax With Michael Holliday* series. It went out at 10.45 p.m. on Friday 18th January 1957. Like his first featured appearance on radio, the show was pre-recorded with no studio audience. In a show that was designed to send the viewers to sleep, all Mike needed to do was bring out the lazy, relaxed Mr Holliday for the formula to work. It did. Mike's songs were his favourite ballads and even if producer Eric Miller insisted on 'Gal With The Yaller Shoes', the gentle canter from the first radio show was slowed even further to a steady trot.

The pilot went well. Three months later, the BBC decided to try it again, this time under the banner of *Starlight*. The second show went out an hour earlier and was live. It also paired Mike for the first time with John Ammonds, who would play a major role in making Michael Holliday one of television's biggest stars.

Ammonds had joined the BBC during the war as a sound-effects trainee. By the early Fifties, he could see that television, not radio, was the medium of the future. When the BBC offered him the chance to move into television production, Ammonds jumped at it, even if it did mean relocating to Manchester and the BBC North Region.

The BBC training for TV producers took Ammonds back to London regularly. During one visit Tom Sloan, BBC Television's then Assistant Head of Light Entertainment tossed Ammonds the chance to produce *Starlight*. It was the start of a glittering television career. Ammonds went on to become one of the BBC's most successful producers. As well as Michael Holliday, Harry Worth, Val Doonican, Mike Yarwood and, most famously, Morecambe and Wise in their halcyon years in the 1970s, all benefited from the Ammonds touch.

John Ammonds looked back on his relationship with Mike with great fondness, but also enormous frustration. 'You would never have accused Mike of being a "professional",' he said, 'but if you tried to have a go at him, he just disarmed you by agreeing! "You see the trouble is, I'm not cut out for this, boss" he would say. "I should be back at sea." You just couldn't stay angry with him for long.'

Ammonds experience on the first *Starlight* programme set the tone for his relationship with Mike that would last until Holliday's death in 1963. 'It was just chaos,' said Ammonds. The show was set to go out live from the BBC's Riverside studios at 9.10 p.m. That meant the BBC could run a double-shift on studio usage and Ammonds found himself sharing a set that was seeing daytime use for the filming of a drama based on the story of Helen of Troy. 'Here we were doing this relaxed music show,' he recalled, 'from the ruins of ancient Greece! Harry Hayward conducted the music standing on the steps of Troy!'

The problems didn't end with the set. Mike arrived under-rehearsed, with neither the continuity dialogue nor the words to his songs in his mind. Holliday always struggled to remember lyrics. Even when he was singing the Crosby songs that he knew backwards, the rhyming scheme would often desert him once he was in front of the microphone. His solution was to scribble the words down on anything he could find, usually a bit of scrap paper or even his shirt cuffs.

That might have worked on radio, but it was no good for television. Mike's songs for *Starlight* were all relatively new for him and it was no great surprise when he suddenly departed from the composer's lyric in favour of his own. Ammonds was horrified. He resolved that for future shows, Mike would prepare his own cue cards, although Mike was no better at getting the right words onto the cards. As often as not, Holliday would scribble down the wrong words or would transpose the rhyming scheme. 'I always expected a writ for parody from one of the songwriters,' said Ammonds.

In John Ammonds's mind, *Starlight* had been a shambles. He feared that his spell as a producer might be over almost before it had begun. A consummate professional with an eye for detail, all he could think about was the errors that had littered the programme. To his great surprise, the reaction from Ammonds's colleagues back at the BBC was quite the reverse. 'People would stop me in the corridor and say, "Saw the show last night. Nice programme." I was amazed,' he said.

Ammonds, of course, had watched the show from the perspective of a television technician. He'd also seen it only from the floor of the studio. His colleagues, like every other viewer, had seen something different. Polish and precision were not the ingredients for a relaxed image, but the affable young man who ambled around the set not taking himself too seriously, clearly had that. Ammonds learned a big lesson in television production that night and realised that with a good producer alongside him, Michael Holliday had a big future in television. Nevertheless, when he returned to Manchester at the conclusion of his training, he had no thought that he might be that producer.

One other performance that stands out from the spring of 1957 underlined Mike's ability to dig himself into a hole and come up smelling of roses. In May, Mike appeared live at the BBC's *Festival Of Dance Music* at the Albert Hall. The show went out on the Light Programme. Mike's spot was a duet with fellow Liverpudlian Lita Roza. Roza had been Britain's first female chart-topper with 'How Much Is That Doggie In The Window?' in 1953, although was better known as one of a cadre of top-class vocalists in the famous Ted Heath swing band.

A young BBC announcer called David Jacobs compèred the show and made great play of the fact that Mike and Lita had never sung together before. Their song was the Cole Porter standard 'Let's Do It', one of the most famous of all 'catalogue songs'. Porter's lyric required a listing of the ways different creatures fell in love ('Birds do it, bees do it, even educated fleas do it'). There was only one line that stood repetition, the one that gave the song its title – 'Let's Do It, Let's Fall In Love'. Devoid of a crib-sheet, that was the only line that Mike knew.

Mike realised that he would never commit the full lyric to memory. Even though he would be on stage at the Albert Hall, he decided to fall back on his standard radio technique and scribbled the words down onto bits of paper. Mike stuffed his notes into the pocket of the jacket that he planned to wear for the show.

Being an Albert Hall concert, the show was a formal affair and it dawned on Mike at the last moment that he would need to wear a dinner suit. What he failed to do was remember to transfer his notes. It was only when David Jacobs had made the introductions that Mike realised he had a problem. He reached into his dinner jacket pocket for his notes and found nothing. His notes were still in his original jacket.

An archive copy of the broadcast reveals the extent of Mike's problem. An off-air voice is captured laughing at the convoluted rhyme that Mike comes up with in the third line of the song, and by the time orchestral break comes around, Mike is totally lost. Lita Roza was word perfect but even she caught the mood created by Mike's problem; 'even Michael Holliday tries to do it' she tossed in as an ad lib of her own.

The third significant television booking for Mike was quite different from the two-late night shows that had featured Mike. *6.5 Special* marked the BBC's entry into the pop music world.

Until 1957, television had observed a strict demarcation between children's and adults programmes. BBC even went as far as to take its programmes off the air between 6 and 7 p.m. The television-free hour was known as the 'Toddlers' Truce', but was about to end. Demand for TV space was growing all the time. The idea of taking programmes beyond midnight was still an

71

anathema, so the free early evening hour was an obvious target. What's more, the BBC was convinced that there was a new audience to be captured if it could come up with the right formula. That audience was the nation's teenage population. The new programme even took its name from television no-man's land. 'Its time to jive on the old *6.5*,' said host Pete Murray as *6.5 Special* opened its doors for the first time.

Few programmes can genuinely claim to be groundbreaking, but *6.5 Special* is one of them. 'We've got a hundred cats jumping here, some real cool characters to give us the gas, so just get on with it and have a ball,' said Murray.

And just in case the hip language went over the heads of any 'squares' who might be tuning in, fellow host (and producer) Jo Douglas offered a translation. 'What he means,' she said, 'is we've got some lively musicians and personalities mingling with us here, so just relax and catch the mood.'

The first *6.5 Special* hit the screens on 16th February 1957. Holliday headed the guest list along with Kenny Baker and his Jazzmen. It was a formula that served *6.5* well. Jazz, pop, skiffle, rock and even eccentric comedians such as Spike Milligan were all mixed together into an eclectic show that was new and different.

6.5's identity came as much from its production style as its content. The show was filmed in one of the usual BBC locations – Riverside studios – but the set was all new. What the BBC tried to do was create something that would have the feel of a youth club to it. What they came up with looked like the inside of a school gymnasium, or a church hall, or one of the dozens of similar rooms that acted as youth club venues up and down the country.

Having found a set that looked and felt like a youth club, the designers underlined the message by building the audience into the show. Youngsters in the studio rubbed shoulders with the performers. When a skiffle or rock group started to roll, everyone joined in. For the viewing population, *6.5 Special* was like watching a party taking place. It was a world away from the variety tradition of the BBC's usual shows. Viewed now, *6.5 Special* looks horribly dated, but only because of the way its new concepts have developed since. The interaction between the performers and the audience mapped out a line that led directly to *Top Of The Pops*, *Ready Steady Go* and all the pop music shows that have followed in their wake.

Michael Holliday was an unusual choice to head the guest list for such an innovative show. But he had a recent track record in the charts and even though his likeness to Crosby was also increasingly being commented on in the press, that too was no bad thing. A guest star who was a throwback to one of the icons of the previous generation might also give the new show a cross-generational appeal.

Whether Mike realised that *6.5* was such a significant booking is doubtful. Indeed, had he realised that he would be required to perform so close to – even amongst – his audience, he probably would have turned it down. Pete Murray later recalled that Mike never felt comfortable, even though he became something of a regular on the programme.

Mike's discomfort was all too apparent in his next appearance in August 1957. Mike was plugging a new single, 'Old Cape Cod'. The song was a slow ballad that required Mike to amble across an imaginary New England beach. As he weaved his way through the audience, hands stuffed firmly in his jacket pockets, Mike looked embarrassed to be crooning such a song for an audience that wanted to dance. His audience looked equally bemused.

The piece foreshadowed an appearance almost 20 years later by Bing Crosby on *Top Of The Pops*. In both instances, the on-camera teenage audience simply did not know what to do with a soft ballad on a show that was designed for dancing. It was only when Holliday picked up a hand-mike and moved into the livelier 'Love You Darlin'' that he came anywhere near the pulse of the show.

Holliday's regular appearances on television's main outlet for pop music were all the more incongruous because the year passed

73

without any further chart successes. Mike's hits in 1956 with 'Gal With The Yaller Shoes' and 'Hot Diggity' had been followed by another two-sided winner, before the hit stream temporarily dried up.

'Ten Thousand Miles' and 'The Runaway Train' were both songs with a railroad theme to them. The A side had Mike as a lonely rambler 'a-walking down the track, with tears in my eyes', searching for happiness and realising that it is 10,000 miles away – a long distance for a rambler – with the girl he left behind. When the song appeared a couple of years later on Bing Crosby's collection of 'authentic' cowboy songs, the title had become a more realistic '900 Miles'. Holliday's vocal on 'Ten Thousand Miles' demonstrates the confidence that he now felt in the recording studio. It opens with a soulful cry that 'Ten thousand miles is a long way from home' before picking up a strong tempo, supported by a guitar and percussion backing.

The B side was a more obvious train song, 'The Runaway Train', an American hillbilly song written by Carson Robison and Vernon Dalhart in the Twenties. Despite its B-side status, it proved to be one of the most durable of all of Mike's recordings and a regular request on BBC's *Children's Favourites* programmes, well past Mike's death. 'The Runaway Train' admittedly had a lot of Crosby in the vocal, although Mike's sense of rhythm and timing carries him through four light-hearted verses as the train crew struggle to control their runaway.

'Ten Thousand Miles' reached number 24 in the UK charts in October 1956 and was Mike's third consecutive chart single. EMI moved quickly to take up their option of Mike's services for a further year. Norrie Paramor was confident that the really big hit was just around the corner. It proved to be a false dawn.

Columbia released five singles during 1957 but not one made any impact on the charts. Mike's vocals were sound but much of the lack of success has to be put down to the choice of material. The first single sought to build on Mike's attachment to things yellow, or 'yaller' to use the American vernacular. 'Yaller Yaller Gold' was a Disney song from the film *Davy*

74

Crockett and The River Pirates. Mike found himself competing with Bing Crosby's son Gary for the chart honours, although the result was a resounding flop all round.

Next came two more covers. 'My House Is Your House (Mi Casa Su Casa)' was another Hoffman and Manning composition for Perry Como. David Hughes and a very young Matt Monro also recorded the title in the UK but surprisingly, no one managed a hit, not even Como. Mike's B side was a more direct attempt to reach out to a younger market and was a cover of Mickey (Baker) and Sylvia (Vanderpool)'s US chart entry 'Love Is Strange'. What now would be termed a soft-rock ballad didn't sit easily with Holliday's style. In particular, he struggled with the clipped delivery that was needed to match the lyric to the rhythm, as evidenced by the 24 takes that were needed before Paramor was satisfied. Then came 'Four Walls', a mainstream chart entry for country singer Jim Reeves in the USA, but neither Reeves's original nor Holliday's cover made any impact on the British charts.

The lack of chart success was a puzzle. Mike was coming up to his second anniversary as a solo singer and had certainly established himself as one of Britain's leading vocalists. His exposure to the record buyers through his radio and TV work was good. But why couldn't he find the big hit record? Almost in desperation, Paramor decided on a change of tack and pulled two sides from Mike's first long-player for the next single release.

LPs were still something of a novelty in Britain in 1957, although they had first appeared in the USA almost ten years before. Confusingly, they came in two sizes. The first American discs had retained the 10-inch format of the 78, a recognition that record shops had designed their racks on a 'one size fits all' basis. It was only when the 7-inch 45 rpm single broke the mould that the door opened for the 12-inch LP.

The 10-inch LP soon disappeared in the USA. Britain, however, was a year or two behind and Columbia decided to use the old 10-inch format for Mike's first LP release. Even though it was of the old size, it did at least accommodate ten tracks. Norrie Paramor booked Mike in for four sessions at Abbey Road in February and March 1957 for an album that was simply entitled *Hi!*

The album was a modest project and one that sought to capitalise on Holliday's emerging reputation as a balladeer rather than a pop singer. Norrie Paramor conducted a session band of between six and nine players, depending on the arrangement. The cover featured a right-face profile of Mike against a red background.

As the title implied, the album's *raison d'être* was simply the arrival of a 'new' singer. The ten songs ranged from the traditional 'Shenandoah' (widely described now as a sea shanty, although its story revolves around the Missouri River) to a recent Burl Ives novelty hit 'That's My Heart Strings'. In between, Paramor lined up Ivor Novello's 'We'll Gather Lilacs', the Kern/Mercer composition 'I'm Old Fashioned', and inevitably the odd title from the Crosby catalogue.

The single that Paramor pulled from the set paired Cole Porter's 'All Of You' with the less familiar 'It's The Good Things We Remember'. 'All Of You' was a nice album track but never a prospect for a hit single in its own right. After the triple flush of the previous year, it became the fourth straight Holliday single to be a resounding 'miss'.

One prescient critic also picked up on a worrying theme. '(Holliday's) resemblance to Bing Crosby is proving something of a handicap rather than an advantage since it always invites comparison,' he wrote.

Others had noticed it too. Babs and Teddie Beverley of the Beverley Sisters first worked with Mike in 1957. They saw Mike's obsession with Crosby as another contributing factor in his lack of self-worth. 'If you put yourself up against Bing Crosby, or Michelangelo or Jesus Christ, of course you are going to think you are lacking. Bing Crosby was a gigantic talent – Mike was putting himself up against the biggest talent in the world,' they said. 'If Mike had seen himself as competing with the likes of David Whitfield, it would have been different. But comparing himself to Bing all the time was bound to make him feel inadequate.'

Despite the lack of chart success, Mike was steadily carving out a niche as one of Britain's top singers. In June, he joined the cast of *Pleasureboat*, a television tour around Britain aboard a variety of sea and river pleasure cruisers, all fronted by comedian Kenneth Horne. Horne, too, was struck by the Crosby link and in a future edition of his *Beyond Our Ken* radio series, came up with a spoof movie called *The Michael Holliday Story* in which Bing Crosby took the role of Mike!

Mike made seven *Pleasureboat* trips that summer. One song that he featured regularly was 'Down By The River', written by Rodgers and Hart for Bing Crosby's 1935 film *Mississippi*. The song was a long-time favourite of Mike's and his increasing number of friends in Britain's Bing Crosby fan club encouraged him to record it. Plans were made to include it in Holliday's Abbey Road session on 20th August 1957 but a late start together with a high number of failed attempts at 'Old Cape Cod' meant that the song was dropped and never reappeared.

On radio, Mike followed up his first solo efforts from the previous year with two more series that gave him prime billing. The BBC broadcast four 15-minute shows entitled *The Michael Holliday Programme* in May and June, plus a new series of programmes called *Sentimental Journey*. It was Mike's most ambitious venture yet.

The show paired him with Edna Savage, a young vocalist who had made her breakthrough into show business around the same time as Mike. *Sentimental Journey* featured Mike and Edna in a series of musical travelogues around Britain and Europe. They played themselves, or at least two characters called Mike and Edna, but the programmes required the two of them to handle some modest dialogue. It wasn't *Gone With The Wind* but there was at least some semblance of a story line behind each show.

The first series of seven shows was such a success that the BBC immediately signed Mike and Edna for a further 12 shows between October and Christmas 1957. Plans were laid for a further series the following year and the music press carried reports of a possible switch to television.

77

The *Sentimental Journey* programmes were manna from heaven for Mike. He often talked about a desire to acquire some acting credentials, and this show at least required him to follow a story line, albeit a loose one. In musical terms, the shows gave him carte blanche to pick his songs. Each show featured five duets between the two stars, plus three or four solos from Mike. Holliday's Crosby repertoire was so broad that there was never any difficulty in finding some of Bing's songs that fitted into a particular week's script.

EMI captured four of the Holliday/Savage duets on an EP early in 1958. It was a disc that promised much more. Expecting the radio series to make the move to television, EMI had agreed to another 10-inch LP proposition and Mike and Edna were lined up to record ten duets in March 1958. In the end, only four of the masters were deemed suitable for release, reducing the LP concept down to an EP. The six unreleased duets disappeared.

In between radio recording sessions, Mike still found space for the occasional week's variety. In early August, he played a two-week engagement at the Finsbury Park Empire. Of all the theatres on the Moss Empire circuit, Finsbury Park was second only to the London Palladium in prestige. Built in 1910, the Empire was well past its peak by the time Mike first appeared there in 1956, but it continued to host high-ranking variety and pop performers until its closure in 1960.

Mike's visit in 1957 brought him into contact for the first time with Hal Monty. Monty was a vaudevillian comedian, a relic of variety's peak years in the Thirties and Forties. As television began closing the theatres, Monty began to see his future in artiste management and representation. Within a year of meeting Mike at Finsbury Park (where Monty was enough of a draw to warrant top-of-the-bill status) he had become Mike's personal manager. From then on he was a major influence on Holliday's life and career.

In September 1957, EMI issued Mike's recording of 'Old Cape Cod'. Hopes for a hit were higher than they had been for some time. The song had been big in the USA for Patti Page, but she seemed unlikely to repeat the success across the Atlantic. A slow, sentimental ballad, the song was well suited to Mike's style. He could even claim to have visited Cape Cod during days at sea.

Columbia pushed the record hard, and for once Mike was happy to sing it. All too often Mike was dismissive of the material that Paramor threw at him for the singles market, rubbishing it as trite and meaningless. 'Cape Cod' was different, perhaps because Crosby himself was already singing it on his radio show in the States. Yet despite a huge effort by EMI, it failed to break the losing streak.

Norrie Paramor was not unduly concerned at his lack of chart success. He believed that Mike was improving all the time and that the hits would come. Paramor had already persuaded EMI to tear up Mike's original year-by-year contract and replace it with a new deal that tied Mike to EMI until at least 1960, with options to extend into 1963. He also secured an increase in Holliday's royalties. All that Norrie Paramor needed to do was find the right song.

Mike's next session was due to take place at Abbey Road on 10th December 1957. Paramor had it in mind to record three titles, two for immediate release as a single and the third for stock. He had lots of new material to choose from but he still believed that the safest route was to find a song that had proved its worth in the USA.

One number in particular had caught his ear. Country singer Marty Robbins had achieved a modest hit with a new song that Paramor liked, even if he had never heard of the composers. With a tweak to the arrangement, this might be the one. He scribbled the title down on the session sheet and sent a copy of the Robbins recording off to Mike. The song was 'The Story Of My Life'.

79

Chapter 9

'The Story Of My Life'

Mention Abbey Road to any music buff and it immediately conjures up images of John, Paul, George and Ringo striding along the famous zebra crossing. Ever since the Fab Four set foot on that particular piece of St John's Wood tarmac, Abbey Road has been part of Beatles folklore.

Before then, the Abbey Road studios had enjoyed a long, if anonymous, career as the workhouse of EMI and HMV Records, although they always had a decent pedigree. HMV built the studios in 1932 when the recording industry was still in the first flush of youth. Situated in a smart London suburb, the studio's external façade had the look and feel of a wealthy stockbroker's home. The inside was rather different.

Abbey Road's designer would have got on well with the inventor of Dr Who's Tardis. The staid exterior gave no clue as to the cavernous studios that were on the inside. The main auditorium, Studio One, took pride of place. HMV built it with classical music in mind and it could easily accommodate a full symphony orchestra. When the studios were ready to see their first record cut, Sir Edward Elgar and the London Symphony Orchestra did the honours with a recording of Elgar's own composition, 'Land of Hope And Glory'.

Norrie Paramor's workshop, however, was the smaller Studio Two. Although nothing on the scale of Studio One, it was still 60 feet long and 38 feet wide. It may have been far less grand in appearance than its neighbour, but Studio Two very quickly established a reputation for providing top-class acoustics.

If necessary, the studio could easily accommodate a full orchestra. Indeed, the Glenn Miller Orchestra recorded there during the war, Miller's last sessions before his death over the English Channel. The smaller session bands who backed singers such as Mike, Alma Cogan and Ronnie Hilton felt just as much at home, and in the Fifties these were the bookings that dominated Studio Two's schedule.

For Holliday's session on 10th December 1957, Norrie Paramor had three songs lined up, one of which was the title song of a new film, *Rooney*. Mike was also scheduled to do two takes of the song for the film's opening and closing titles. J. Arthur Rank, the film company that was funding the afternoon session, wanted to capitalise on Holliday's involvement (even though he didn't appear in the film) by having the film's star, John Gregson, in the studio for some promotional pictures. Paramor knew that afternoon would be a stop-start affair. He decided to let the publicity process run its course and keep his three commercial titles for the evening.

Unlike his idol Bing Crosby, Holliday's recording sessions were usually evening affairs. Crosby insisted that his voice sounded best in the morning, but Mike was a nocturnal creature who liked to spend his mornings in bed. He was also notorious for turning up late, even when the session had a 7 p.m. start. Paramor never got to his bed in Hampstead before midnight but when it was an evening session with Mike it was always nearer 2 a.m. before his day was done.

Holliday and Paramor had settled on two titles to supplement the commercial version of 'Rooney'. The two titles were 'The Story Of My Life' and 'Keep Your Heart'. Paramor was pinning his hopes on the first of these for the hit single. He later told *New Musical Express* that he knew the song was right for Mike as soon as he heard it. Mike had been taken with Paramor's recommendation for 'The Story Of My Life', but in truth it was the other title that excited him more. The reason was simple. 'Keep Your Heart' was his own composition.

82

Mike had dabbled at song-writing since his days at sea. Most of the songs never got further than a home recording on Mike's tape machine although he had featured a song that he had a hand in writing at his previous session. 'Love Your Darlin'' became the B side to 'Old Cape Cod' and generally received a favourable response. Mike had used the song on *6.5 Special* a few days after the session. Mike's ability to remember words was no better even with his own songs, and the surviving film of the show captures Mike losing his way midway through the first chorus.

Mike used the name 'Milne' for his share of the composer credits on 'Love You Darlin'' and planned to do the same with 'Keep Your Heart', even though that song was all his own work. It was Norrie Paramor's suggestion that he use the name 'Holliday' on it. Paramor liked the song and his session sheets show that the decision to use the name 'Holliday' was taken there and then. Pat Boone later recorded the song too. Mike got almost as big a kick from having a name like Pat Boone record one of his songs as he did out of the success of his own recordings.

With Mike already there for the afternoon's film-related session, Paramor was able to get the evening under way on time. Mike Sammes led the vocal backing of eight male singers for 'Rooney', with three girls joining for the other two titles. Sammes himself provided the highly distinctive bass voice for the 'bom-boms' that punctuate 'The Story Of My Life'. Two electric and one bass guitar, plus session regulars Jock Cummins on drums and Joe Medell on bass, completed the musical support. The full cost of the session, excluding Mike's twopenny royalty, was £138.

Engineer Stuart Eltham approached the session just as any other. Ahead of the day, he completed his usual plan showing the layout of the instruments and voices around the studio and his allocation of microphones to capture them. With a limit of eight mikes available to him, positioning was critical.

Eltham also used an echo feature on most of Mike's recordings. His 'chamber' was a home-grown affair and relied on the use of a second tape head to capture the vocal, divert it and then replay into the main sound chamber with a one-second delay. Paramor liked the 'bigger' sound that resulted. The echo effect on 'The Story Of My Life' was particularly prominent, almost to the point of being a little too obvious.

Paramor made one other change for the evening session. So far, he had personally written the musical arrangements and conducted the sessions for each of Mike's recordings. This time he made a change. Paramor had two arrangers who he regarded as his regulars. One was Eric Jupp, whose only experience of working with Mike would turn out to be an abortive session on 'Starry Eyed' a couple of years later. The other was Ken Jones. He was best known for his work with Shirley Abicair and the Ralph Reader Gang Show, as well as being the arranger for the popular Mudlarks singing group. Paramor had asked Jones to come up with the arrangements for the last two titles on the session and it seemed natural that he should also conduct. Jones's fee was a healthy £30.

'Rooney' was wrapped up in seven takes and completed in the first hour of the session. 'Keep Your Heart' took ten takes before Paramor was happy, and it was into the third hour of the session before Mike got around to 'The Story Of My Life'. At first, he struggled with the fast pace of Jones's arrangement although by around the fourth or fifth take, Mike seemed comfortable with it. Paramor, however, wanted to experiment with the pace of the disc and Stuart Eltham had called 'Take 12' before Paramor was satisfied.

Ironically, the issued take was one on which Mike's diction was not up to its usual high standards. On the third and fourth lines of the song – 'I'll tell about the night we met / And how my heart can't forget' – Mike runs together 'And' and 'how', with the result that the letter 'h' on the word 'how' is clumsily dropped completely.

The perfectionist inside Mike was well aware of the disc's shortcomings. 'Just what was so different between "The Story Of My Life" and my other records, I will never know,' he told *Hit Parade* later in 1958. 'I am seldom happy with my recordings

84

and this one pleased me least of all. Just shows how wrong you can be.' Even in a private taped message to Stan White, a Bing Crosby collector who had become a close friend, Mike was self-deprecating. 'I didn't think I did much of a job on the vocal,' he said.

'The Story Of My Life' wasn't only a breakthrough for Michael Holliday. It was the first hit for two writers who would go on to become legends in the music business. Burt Bacharach had started writing music after leaving the US Army in 1952. He briefly worked as pianist for singer Vic Damone before he formed a partnership with lyricist Hal David. 'The Story Of My Life' was their first success and was followed almost immediately by 'Magic Moments' for Perry Como.

Marty Robbins's version of 'The Story Of My Life' reached number 15 in the American charts but was never a runner in the UK. It wasn't the first time that Robbins found himself entering the church as the bride and finishing up as the bridesmaid. In the USA, he had been the first singer to record hits such as 'Singin' The Blues' and 'Knee Deep In the Blues', only for Guy Mitchell to steal the honours on both songs. Robbins's next US hit was 'A White Sports Coat And A Pink Carnation', which the King Brothers and Terry Dene both scored with in the UK.

Robbins was destined to miss out again with 'The Story Of My Life'. The song became a much bigger hit in the UK than in the USA. Mike and three other British singers, Alma Cogan, Dave King and Gary Miller, all recorded versions at the same time. Amazingly, all four hit the charts.

Columbia released Mike's record as DB4058 in both 45 and 78 rpm formats. The record was in the shops in the first week of January 1958 and in the charts two weeks later. Gary Miller's version on Pye-Nixa entered at the same time, Miller at number 17 with Mike two places higher. A week later, Dave King's disc entered, followed in the last week of January by Alma Cogan.

Four separate versions of the same song in the charts at the same time was an unusual occurrence, although not unprecedented. 'Around The World' and 'The Ballad of Davy Crockett' were also songs that had sustained a quartet of hits just the year before, although in both cases the hits included the original American hit-maker. 'The Story Of My Life' was unusual in that the four hit versions were all home-grown.

Gary Miller's version of 'The Story Of My Life' eventually peaked at number 14. Dave King reached number 20, whilst Alma Cogan – many people's ante-post favourite – levelled out at number 25. By mid-February, Michael Holliday was sitting proudly in the number one spot, and from then on only one singer would ever be associated with that song.

It's easy to see why Michael Holliday won the race. Ken Jones's arrangement brought something that had been missing from Mike's earlier records. Of the four competing versions of 'The Story Of My Life', Holliday's is the one with the strongest rhythm and the fastest pace. Mike does his best to sound like Bing on the deeper notes, but the relatively high key for the song limits the Crosby connection. It is hard to imagine a Bing recording of 'The Story Of My Life', a reflection of the personal stamp that Mike put on it. For the first time since 'Gal With The Yaller Shoes', Columbia had a disc that had a real 'Mike Holliday' identity about it.

In contrast, Miller's version was slow and cumbersome. The lack of pace exposed the vocal more and highlighted Miller's overdramatic delivery. Alma Cogan's version was much nearer in overall sound to Mike's but her big hit-making days were behind her. Alma also suffered with a lyric that was overtly masculine. One key line in the song is 'I've got to take you for my wife' which Alma has to translate to 'You've got to take me for your wife'. The enforced change took away much of the momentum behind Hal David's lyric. Like Cogan, Dave King's hits were also in the past. 'The Story Of My Life' was his last chart entry, and within a couple of years he had given up singing in favour of his career as a comedian.

King's version takes too much from the Marty Robbins original. Stuart Eltham observed that one of the difficulties in covering an American hit was finding the balance between the original sound and adding a local identity. On 'The Story Of My Life', Holliday, Paramor and Jones pulled it off to perfection.

Mike's success exceeded everybody's expectations. The new single sold almost as many records as all of Mike's previous releases put together. From a first week's entry at number 15, the disc moved from number eight to number two, and then hit the top spot. The record it displaced was the mighty Elvis and 'Jailhouse Rock'.

Mike held the top spot for two weeks before Perry Como's 'Magic Moments' pushed him off. His stay at the top would have been longer but for the massive impact of Como's disc. 'Magic Moments' held the number one spot for an amazing eight weeks, but for four of them 'The Story Of My Life' was at number two. These two songs gave Bacharach and David a ten-week spell at the top of the British Hit Parade.

Mike's recording of 'The Story Of My Life' enjoyed six weeks in the Top Two and three months in the Top Twenty. Sales eventually reached 750,000, more than half of which were still the old-fashioned 78s. It gave Mike his first silver disc. More importantly, it changed his life like nothing had before.

Chapter 10

Relax With Michael Holliday

Michael Holliday could not have timed his ascent to the top of the charts better. In October 1957, his agent Richard Stone had continued his relentless pursuit of the BBC. The secret of a good agent is not only a doggedness of spirit, but also a happy knack of asking the right question at the right time. Stone's letter to Ronnie Waldman, dated 30th October 1957 was a case study in both qualities:

Dear Ronnie

MICHAEL HOLLIDAY

I am convinced that the time has come in the career of this artiste when the first television company to give him a relaxed production show will find themselves with one of the biggest television stars in the country.

It is worth pointing out that so far, he has never been given a television series other than isolated spots in regular programmes.

His radio series with Edna Savage, *Sentimental Journey*, is in the middle of its second run on BBC sound radio and you can hear it on Tuesday evenings on the Light Programme. It is half an hour of songs strung together by a story which Michael and Edna act themselves. This whole series, as listening figures prove, has been an immense success.

This may seem a trifle eulogistic from an agent, but I have

never been more convinced that the time is ripe for the final step forward in an artiste's career.

Yours sincerely

Richard Stone

Stone was guilty of gilding the lily slightly in his comment that Mike had never been featured other than 'in isolated spots on regular programmes'. The *A Musical Nightcap* and the *Starlight* programmes had already given Waldman and his number two, Tom Sloan, a feel of what Mike could do. Stone was pushing at an open door.

Waldman issued a contract for Mike to star in four programmes under the title *Relax With Michael Holliday*. It was a title that Mike disliked more and more as the years went by.

'I knew that title was a mistake,' he said in a letter tape to Stan White. 'I am definitely the most unrelaxed singer in the business.'

Waldman was keen to retain the partnership with John Ammonds, despite the latter's attachment to Manchester. It was a partnership that worked well. Waldman and Stone knew that Holliday could be an unpredictable individual and the fact that he seemed comfortable with the young producer was a big plus. Once Ammonds completed his producer training and headed back permanently to Manchester, the *Relax With Michael Holliday* programmes went with him. But for the first series, Ammonds returned to London to use the Riverside studios as the base for the programme.

Ammonds was keen to come up with a different angle for the shows and hit upon the idea of using Mike in a setting that would mimic his home. The first series of shows presented Mike in a make-believe flat, complete with settee, fireplace and even a veranda, illuminated by BBC moonlight. It worked a treat. Mike was always nervous and edgy on the set, but putting him in a home setting did everything possible to put him at ease. It

90

also meant that Ammonds had a choice of shots for Mike's songs, all of which were designed to contribute to the relaxed image.

The first *Relax With Michael Holliday* show went out on 10th January 1958. The slot was the end of schedule, 10.45 p.m. one, that had worked so well on Mike's first programme almost a year before. The timing of the show coincided exactly with the release of 'The Story Of My Life', although since the music publishers controlled the release date, it was more an act of good fortune than astute planning. When Mike's disc started its rapid climb up the charts, the BBC chiefs could hardly believe their luck.

The four-show series was due to end on 31st January, the week that 'The Story Of My Life' hit second place in the charts. Two more shows were hastily added to the series and plans laid for more shows in the spring. Mike closed out the last show of his first series with his new hit song. 'Since this series started, a song I recorded has jumped right up to number two on the Hit Parade,' said Mike in his introduction. 'Gee, imagine me up there with all those rock'n roll boys.'

In truth, Mike was in the middle of a very eclectic chart that demonstrates what a melting pot the late Fifties music scene had become. In Mike's second week at the top, the *New Musical Express* Top Ten was as follows:

1   'The Story Of My Life' – Michael Holliday
2   'Jailhouse Rock' – Elvis Presley
3   'Magic Moments' – Perry Como
4   'At The Hop' – Danny and The Juniors
5   'Oh Boy' – The Crickets
6   'All The Way' – Frank Sinatra
7= 'April Love' – Pat Boone
7= 'Love Me Forever' – Marion Ryan
7= 'Peggy Sue' – Buddy Holly
10 'You Are My Destiny' – Paul Anka

It was a chart of rare and unusual quality – three rock'n roll legends, two crooners whose careers dated back to the Thirties, and alongside Mike, Pat Boone and Marion Ryan seeking to occupy a shrinking middle ground.

With a number one record behind him, Mike was in demand like never before. 'Suddenly I'm wanted for practically every TV and radio show in existence,' Mike told one newspaper, with more than a little air of bewilderment. Short-term opportunities to promote the disc were almost ten a penny. Despite Mike's dislike of live appearances the variety circuit was still where most performers made their money. A week topping the bill could bring £400–£500 in income for a two shows a night, six-day stint. Stone moved quickly to secure a ten-week tour of the Moss Empires, with Mike topping the bill.

For Richard Stone, it was the culmination of two years' hard work. He was exactly the right man to help Mike exploit his success. The irony was that the Moss Empires tour contained the seeds of destruction for their relationship. Hal Monty took second billing on the tour. His influence on Holliday had been growing since their paths had first crossed at the Finsbury Park Empire. By the time the tour ended, Holliday had appointed Monty as his personal manager, a role that quickly began encroaching on Stone, who remained as Mike's agent.

Richard Stone continued in that role for another 12 months, but attributed Monty's influence to ending their relationship. 'From then on, Monty and I pulled in opposite directions,' he said in his autobiography. 'I was concerned with Michael's future, Hal was concerned with making a quick buck. Michael was not one to be put under pressure and Monty kept overbooking him behind my back. Finally Monty persuaded Michael that he didn't need me and took over all his business.'

The tour took Mike around the usual provincial theatres – Nottingham, Leicester, Newcastle, Brighton, Hanley and points beyond. It went well. 'MICHAEL HOLLIDAY IS A SELL-OUT' proclaimed *Melody Maker* in the last week of March. 'This is the best I have ever done,' Mike was quoted as saying 'and better still, it's the best money I have ever had.'

Stone was already laying down plans beyond the tour. The most lucrative bookings on the English variety circuit were the summer seasons in the top resorts. Brighton, Yarmouth, Weymouth and Scarborough were all big draws but the Mecca was Blackpool. With its three piers, the Tower, the Pleasure Beach and its tramway, it was Britain's premier holiday destination from the late 1890s until the Viva Espana days of the Sixties.

Stone secured Mike the next to top spot at the Blackpool Hippodrome in a show called *Light Up The Town*. Pianist Winifred Atwell topped the bill, with Joe Baker and Jack Douglas, and the Kaye Sisters also amongst the cast. Mike's spot came early in the second half of the show.

The ten-week variety tour finally ended in Bristol at the end of May. Mike had three weeks before the 12-week summer season in Blackpool was due to begin. Apart from a two-week skiing holiday, Mike had worked solidly since the start of the year. There were signs already that he was finding it hard to cope with the demands that success brought in its wake. The BBC had signed Mike for nine more *Relax* shows, but it was proving difficult to get Mike to find time to do them. Mike's letter to Tom Sloan at the BBC, dated 31st March 1958 reveals something of the way the pressure was already getting to him:

Dear Mr Sloan

I feel I must write to you and thank you personally for being so understanding. I have not been sleeping well now for the past year, and it has finally caught up with me. However, Mr John Ammonds has been to see me and we have fixed it so that I won't have a lot of worry and I think that after two weeks holiday, everything will be fine. I will get as many of them 'in the can' as possible and probably all nine. I do want these to be as good as the variety tour has proven to me just how popular the last series was.

I am glad that John Ammonds is doing the series, as he is a very nice chap and I know that he will help me a great deal and the way I feel at the moment, I will need a lot of help.

93

I am in Town next week and will ring you. Thanks for everything.

Yours sincerely

Michael

It was hardly the letter of someone who was enjoying stardom. A somewhat nonplussed Sloan replied that he was sure 'things would work out once you have had a good rest'. In the meantime, a solution to the problem of getting the next TV series 'in the can' presented itself. With John Ammonds now back in Manchester, Mike would do the shows whilst he was in Blackpool for the summer season.

Moving the shows to Manchester gave Ammonds the opportunity to introduce designer Ken Lawson to the production team. Lawson was a landscape artist and a talented painter. He had first moved into set design in London and had several West End productions to his name before moving with the BBC to Manchester. Lawson got on well with Mike, who found him easy to talk to. In future series when Ammonds struggled to shake Holliday from the depths of his depression, he turned to Lawson for help. 'See if you can talk him out of it, Ken' became a familiar plea.

The concept of the *Relax* shows taking place in Mike's 'flat' had worked well and there was no reason why the move to Manchester should herald any change. One curiosity of the BBC's Manchester set-up, though, was the studios themselves. Built in 1892 in the Rusholme district, just to the south-east of the city centre, the studios had spent most of their life as a Wesleyan chapel. Conversion took place in 1947 and the studios then housed a succession of Northern musical comedy films before being taken over by BBC Television, becoming the BBC Playhouse Theatre. As well as Mike's shows, they housed the Harry Worth programmes that John Ammonds produced, and in the Sixties became a first home for a television institution – *Top Of The Pops*.

Lawson was keen to add his flair to the concept that he

inherited for Mike's programmes. He came up with an intimate set that used one-half of the available studio space. A large stone fireplace was the focal point, in front of which was a double settee and a small dining table with a red and white checked kitchen tablecloth. A floor to ceiling bookcase adorned one side of the fireplace and on the far right of the studio, Lawson created a balcony. It was there that Mike usually wound up each show, with a homely message from a mythical 'Uncle Mike' and a wave of the hand.

One prop that Lawson had to give pride of place to was a Grundig tape recorder. Reel to reel tape recording had been invented in the Thirties and perfected in Germany during the war. Bing Crosby had pioneered its use in the broadcasting industry by becoming the first performer to use tape for the recording of radio broadcasts. Domestic tape recorders became popular in the Fifties and Mike had quickly become a tape recorder buff, preferring even to tape short message to friends rather than write letters.

He very quickly saw the opportunity to use the machine as part of his television act. Both Ammonds and Lawson's recollections are that the idea first came from Mike himself, and like many of Mike's ideas, was probably a lift from Crosby. The Old Groaner's 1934 film *Here Is My Heart* pre-dated tape recorders by 20 years, but one scene clearly is the source of Mike's routine.

Crosby's big song in the picture was a new composition, 'June in January', by Leo Robin and Ralph Ranger. As well as featuring the song early in the film, Crosby's writers also created a scene where Bing finds himself in a reflective moment. He opens up a gramophone and puts on his own recording of the song. Soon the scene turns into a plaintive duet with Bing tossing in the odd piece of conversation with his alter ego. Almost certainly the idea for Mike's duets with himself came from there.

The use of tape offered the opportunity to record a tailored duet, carefully constructed so that it sounded more natural than Crosby's routine with a standard commercial record. Holliday had first introduced it on the second show of the series from

95

Riverside. 'Come inside, there's something I want to show you,' he said looking directly into the camera. 'This is the age of gimmicks and I have been trying to think of one all week. I don't know how many of you own one of these things [a tape recorder] but they can be a lot of fun. I put my voice on it a little time ago and now I'm going to try and sing a duet with myself.' He added that if it didn't work, 'just send me a postcard and address it to Michael Holliday, care of the Dog House.'

Needless to say it worked to a T, although the song that Mike picked for the new routine was untypical. 'Just Between You and Me' was 1957 US hit for the Chordettes, but in time Mike found it was usually the older songs that lent themselves to the harmony the duet routine required.

Mike was feeling his way with the gimmick. In the next show, the tape recorder made another appearance and this time the song was an old favourite, 'Tiptoe Through The Tulips'. It was the song that Mike featured more than any other in the tape recorder routine, although in that first airing, Mike had actually overdubbed his voice three times onto the tape. When the show went out, he added his live voice to create a quartet. Next came an experiment with a virtual trio before Mike finally settled into a simple duet routine.

Doubtless the novelty of the tape recorder contributed a great deal to the popularity of the spot in the show and Mike soon found it was this routine that dominated the letters he received from viewers. Questions ranged from 'How do you do it?' to 'Whose is the other voice?', even though Mike had made it clear from the start that it was himself. As time went on, Mike started to throw the odd Crosbyism into the duet, perhaps even in his own mind playing out the fantasy of a duet with Bing.

There was no question that the routine was here to stay. By the time the summer series in Manchester came around, the voice on the tape had acquired a name and a personality. 'I wonder how the other fella is tonight?' Mike would ask as he ambled over to the tape machine, knocking gently on the casing. As if awakened from a slumber, the voice on the tape would stir, usually adding some caustic remark. 'What did you think of the show last week?' Mike would ask the character in the box. 'Well I thought I was very good' came the reply, 'couldn't make up my mind about you though.'

When Mike appeared on the Vera Lynn show on ITV a year or two later, the producers took the idea a stage further. As Mike settled down to a conversation with his other self, the voice of Vera Lynn suddenly turned up on the tape. Soon Vera and 'the other fella' were arguing over who would sing a duet with Mike:

Vera (on tape): Excuse me, but I was wondering if I could sing a duet with Mike?
Other Fella: Oh but I always sing the duets with him.
Vera: Well it is my show.
Other Fella: But it's my tape recorder.
Vera: Oh go on, just this once.
Other Fella: Well okay but are you sure you know the words?
Vera: I think so.
Other Fella: Good, because it's more than he does!

Mike then moved into 'Tiptoe Through The Tulips' joined by Vera on tape for the first part, and then in person. It was cleverly scripted and poked a little fun at all 'three' participants.

The duet routine seemed to encapsulate Mike's popularity on television. Technically primitive now, it was fresh and modern in the Fifties. The appeal though came from more than just the novelty value. Mike's treatment of 'The Other Fella' was similar to the way a ventriloquist treated his favourite dummy. The voice in the box took on a character of its own, with Mike seeming to believe it was real. When Mike wrapped up one of his last shows in 1963 with a long duet with the tape recorder, his *sotto voce* 'Goodbye old friend' as he moved away from the machine was, with hindsight, a poignant moment.

Mike finished the second series of shows by mid-September and they were broadcast almost immediately. Once again the

BBC dropped lucky with its timings. By the time the second series went out, Mike was yet again riding high in the charts.

Norrie Paramor had been around long enough to know that the best time to find a hit record was immediately on the tail of the last one. A new song by the prolific American songwriting team of Sid Tepper and Roy Bennett crossed his desk in January 1958 and Paramor earmarked it for Mike. Staying with the winning formula, Paramor again asked Ken Jones to come up with an arrangement and conduct the session.

Paramor had to go for a Saturday evening session to get the disc made quickly. 'In Love' was the only title scheduled, with Paramor planning to use the stock-piled 'Rooney' for the B-side. Paramor was famed for his ability to spot a winning sound whilst he was still in the studio, but occasionally he would change his mind when he heard the test pressing a day or two later. This was one of those occasions. His concerns with 'In Love' were more to do with the orchestrations than the vocal. Ken Jones's arrangement made use of electric rather than acoustic guitars and gave the song a 'tight' feel. It wasn't what Paramor was looking for. Four days later, he had Mike back at the studios for a repeat. Even then it was a protracted affair. With the studio clock showing half past midnight, Stuart Eltham's take count had reached 33 before Paramor was happy.

EMI Columbia pushed the follow-up disc as hard as they could. *New Musical Express* in the first week of March devoted its cover to a full-page ad for the disc, and the magazine's reviewer duly came up with the right words in his review. 'To an easy relaxed beat, Mike takes a casual vocal stroll. Could be another topper, safe to say it will end in the top five,' he said.

The result was a much more modest hit, reaching only number 26 in the charts in March 1958. 'In Love' very much hung on the coat tails of 'The Story Of My Life' that was still riding high in the same chart. It was the most overtly 'pop' song that Mike had recorded yet, which probably accounted for his difficulty in mastering it. The song explored just about every possible way to extend the words 'In' and 'Love' over several notes. It was exactly the kind of song that Mike hated. But it served its purpose of keeping Mike on the disc jockeys' turntables whilst the real follow-up to 'The Story Of My Life' was coming along right behind.

'Stairway Of Love' was another Tepper and Bennett composition, another Marty Robbins recording in the States and another UK competition between Mike and Alma Cogan. This time around, Marion Ryan and Terry Dene also joined the race, although Mike was the strong favourite.

Robbins's version flopped completely but Norrie Paramor was again convinced that with an arrangement that played down the country feel, the song would be a winner in the British market. Ken Jones had first crack at it but another late night at Abbey Road failed to give Paramor what he wanted. He insisted on a remake even though Mike by now was in the midst of a provincial variety tour. Paramor dug his heels in and demanded that Mike make the trip back to London. The only way to squeeze the replanned session into Mike's commitments was to schedule a Sunday session. So on 13th April, Mike made a 600-mile trip from Sunderland to Liverpool via St John's Wood for a rerun.

Paramor was vindicated. The second attempt produced another winner. Mike's vocal was clear and strong and his timing and feel for the lyric couldn't have been better. In the space of a few months, Paramor had found the Michael Holliday 'sound'. It was a journey akin to Glenn Miller's mythical odyssey in search of his famous Miller sound (or at least, that's what the writers of *The Glenn Miller Story* would have us believe). Out went the strings and elaboration of a year ago. Compared to 'The Story Of My Life' and 'Stairway Of Love', 'Old Cape Cod' sounded as though it had been recorded over a decade before rather than six months. Mike's singing had also gone up a gear. The three singles from early 1958 revealed a new confidence in his voice and a willingness to explore the things he could do with it. 'My House Is Your House' from a year before was melodic and tuneful, but now sounded boringly straight-laced.

'Stairway Of Love' immediately hit the mark. 'This could be another "Story Of My Life"' said *Melody Maker* and they were almost proved right. Whilst 'Stairway' didn't quite manage the top spot, Connie Francis's 'Who's Sorry Now' enjoying a six-week stint at the top, it catapulted Mike back into the top three and sustained a 15-week run in the charts. After a year of flops and failures, Mike had suddenly delivered two massive hits within the space of six months. *New Musical Express* ran a chart of charts for the first six months of the year with Mike in fourth place, the top-ranking British performer behind Elvis, Pat Boone and Perry Como. And even though Mike didn't repeat his chart successes during the latter part of the year, he was still at number nine in the *NME* Top 100 listing of best-sellers for the year, and the highest-placed British name.

The hit records were the last pieces in the jigsaw. By the time that the summer of 1958 was drawing to a close, Michael Holliday was firmly established as one of the biggest names in British showbusiness. Butlin's to Blackpool in less than three years. Mike seemed to have it all – records in the charts, his own TV and radio series, and as much variety work as he wanted. If ever there was a new star who looked set to stay at the top for many years to come, it was Michael Holliday.

But things are not always as they seem. Mike's foothold on the show business summit was much more precarious than it appeared at the time. He was by no means the only new star to appear in the last years of the Fifties decade, but his contemporaries were not his peers, either in age or in musical style. Adam Faith, Craig Douglas, Anthony Newley and above all, Cliff Richard were of a new generation when compared to Mike – ten to 15 years younger and musical descendants of Elvis, not Bing.

Compared to this band of newcomers, Mike was already an anachronism. He was turned 30 when his big break came his way and his true peers were Ronnie Hilton, Dickie Valentine and David Whitfield. By 1958, these singers were on the slide – at least in Hit Parade terms. They would each go on making records and earning money on the variety circuit and in pantomime for years to come, but none of them would see a record in the Top Ten ever again.

Yet Mike had something that these singers didn't have. His success on television stood him apart from this peer group, who somehow seemed to be a part of the 'radio days'. Anyone who was a child of television couldn't help but appear 'modern'. Now that the hit records had arrived, Mike was also a genuine pop star. There might have been an element of good fortune about the way 'The Story Of My Life' had landed in his lap, but even a blind squirrel occasionally finds an acorn. The question now was whether Mike had the physical and mental toughness to capitalise on his good fortune.

Chapter 11

Life Is A Circus

The first real doubts about Mike's ability to deal with life at the top came in the late summer of 1958. The Blackpool season had gone well, but it had been a busy time. Even by September, Mike had still not finished shuttling backwards and forwards between Blackpool and Manchester to fulfil his BBC TV commitments.

Meanwhile, things were not well at home. In early July, Margie had suddenly been taken ill and was rushed into hospital for major surgery. The nature of her illness was not disclosed, although Mike later said in a tape to Stan White that the doctors had told him that 'another couple of hours, and it could have been very serious indeed'. Margie's illness required a long convalescence, leaving Mike to spend the summer in Blackpool alone. It also meant that Mike had to add some long drives home in pre-motorway Britain to his already busy schedule.

Mike's own health also showed signs of cracking under the strain. He missed the final week of the summer season with what was described to the press as gastro-enteritis. How much of Mike's illness was stress-related isn't clear, although the cause was subsequently attributed to overwork rather than a mere tummy bug. As well as causing Mike to make an early exit from Blackpool, his illness also jeopardised two other important bookings that Richard Stone had lined up.

The closest Mike had come to the West End stage had been his regular outings at the Finsbury Park Empire. When Stone got the chance for Mike to do a fortnight's variety at the Prince Of Wales theatre, he jumped at it. Ironically, the Prince Of Wales was the theatre that would host Mike's memorial concert in 1964.

It was a good booking in a strong cast, with Mike sharing top billing with the American singing duo, the Kalin Twins. The complication was that it clashed with the schedule for another debut – in films. If Mike was to fulfil both commitments, he would need to be in two places at once – the Shepperton set by day and the West End stage by night.

Despite television's encroachment, films were still the primary visual medium of entertainment. Just as it had been a natural progression for Bing Crosby in the Thirties to go from radio crooner to screen heart-throb, the pop singers of the Fifties were still following the same path. Frankie Vaughan, Dennis Lotis and even the young Cliff Richard were quick to use the Top Ten as the launch pad for a film career, albeit with different degrees of success. It was a logical step for Mike, and after the success of 'The Story Of My Life', the entertainment press was full of stories about him going into films.

Mike was positive about the idea, even if he was worried about his looks. 'I'm the second ugliest fella in the world,' he told *Pop Parade*, 'only because there must be someone worse'.

Not everything that Mike said to the press was a true reflection of his real feelings and his copying of Bing Crosby didn't end merely with his singing. Crosby was famous for self-deprecation – 'just an average guy who could carry a tune' would suit as an epitaph he once said – and Mike slid easily into a similar vein. Nevertheless, he did have two worries about how he would come over on the big screen. One was to do with his long jaw. The other was his perennial hang-up with his height.

Nevertheless, he enjoyed being in front of a camera. Mike was developing a growing interest in photography, even to the point of adding some production to his home movies. One captured him with Michael junior in some Chaplinesque sequences shot in the privacy of their garden. Mike had also already tried his hand at something more than just singing. Richard Stone had secured earlier bookings in two radio plays. The first of these, *The Great Waltz*, had aired in 1957 although it was the second play, *Bigger Beggars*, that had more impact.

Caryl Brahms and Ned Sherrin were the writers of a play that looked at the influence of America on Britain's teenage population. It used some dialogue but its primary vehicle was song. A variety of American folk songs were adapted as the medium through which the story was told. Mike played the role of the teenage son of a café owner who hankers for a life at sea – an easy character for Mike to drop into. Even though Mike was by now 34 years of age, the anonymity of radio enabled him to deliver a convincing performance as a teenager.

Mike had top billing in the play, even though other actors had bigger parts. Sherrin recalled Holliday as 'singing beautifully' at the recording, even if being hit yet again by a severe bout of stage fright. At one stage in the recording, Mike actually went as far as locking himself in his dressing room. 'I always remember Caryl shouting "Mr Holliday, put on your trousers and come out",' said Sherrin.

Nevertheless, the reviews were good and the broadcast – in March 1958 – increased the speculation that Mike would soon make his big screen debut. If Stone's press interviews are to be believed, there was no shortage of film offers for Mike. Nevertheless, Stone was content to play a long game, waiting for the right property to come along. Some of the messages he put out were undoubtedly those of a canny agent building up a picture of Mike as spoilt for choice, but Stone was keen not to pitch Mike straight in at the deep end. He thought that a supporting role was the right place to start rather than look for top billing.

Eventually Mike signed for a part in a new Val Guest picture called *Clowns In Clover*. Guest had made his name as a writer before the war, handling the screenplays for Will Hay's *Oh Mr Porter* movies as well the big screen outings for the Crazy Gang. As a director, he was best known – and still is – for his classic British horror production, *Quatermass And The Pit*.

Guest wrote *Clowns In Clover* as the vehicle to bring the

Crazy Gang back to the cinema screens after an absence of almost 20 years. The Gang was one of the institutions of British show business, famed for bringing a Python-like zaniness to the Thirties stage. They were actually an amalgamation of four separate acts, three duos and a single. The duos were Nervo and Knox, Naughton and Gold and the most famous, Flanagan and Allen. 'Monsewer' Eddie Gray, an eccentric magician and fore-runner to Tommy Cooper, was the seventh member.

Bud Flanagan was the unofficial 'leader' of the Gang and when ill-health forced his partner, Chesney Allen, into semi-retirement, Flanagan brought the Gang back together as a sixsome. Even Allen was induced into making the odd cameo appearance. Despite all of them pushing 70, they had made a successful return to the West End. Guest's film ideas were intended to capitalise on that.

Prior to its release, *Clowns In Clover* became *Life Is A Circus*, taking its new title from one of the two songs that Guest wrote for the film. The screenplay revolved around the differing fortunes of two travelling circuses. The Gang were the lynchpins of Joe Winter's Circus, an old and decrepit organisation not unlike the Gang itself. Winter's Circus faced the threat of bankruptcy and its arch-rival, the Rickenbeck Circus, was poised to swallow them up.

Mike played the part of Carl Rickenbeck, the soft-hearted son of the film's 'baddy', Rickenbeck senior. Carl falls for Jo Winter's daughter, played by Shirley Eaton, and aids and abets the Crazy Gang's efforts to stave off closure. Guest wrote both the songs for Mike, the title song being shared with Flanagan and the Gang, plus 'For You', a love ballad for Mike's romancing of Shirley.

The scene where Mike sings 'For You' has Shirley and him meandering through a fairground arm in arm, vainly trying to win a prize on the stalls that the Gang have rigged to avoid having to hand out prizes. The scene brings out the influence of Bing on Mike like nothing before. Not only did he *sound* like Bing, but here too were Bing's mannerisms – the stiff gait,

106

the swinging left arm crooked at the elbow, and the feigned dance were all direct lifts from Crosby's song sequences in *Road To Morocco*. If Mike could have frozen one moment from his career to take along to a desert island, this surely would have been it.

If things had gone according to plan, the role of Carl Rickenbeck would have been a good one for Mike. The character was essentially the same clean-cut young man that Mike played on TV, and even if the role demanded a bit more energy, it wasn't unduly taxing. With support from the venerable old pros of the Crazy Gang, and Shirley Eaton to fall in love with, *Life Is A Circus* should have been the launch pad for a longer film career. As it was, it turned out to be Mike's only film.

Some of Mike's difficulties were down to illness. After missing the end of the Blackpool season, Mike also pulled out of the first week and then the second at the Prince Of Wales. Veteran comedians Jewell and Warriss stood in as last-minute replacements. Mike was also all set to ditch the film role too, until Guest and others persuaded him that his role could be trimmed and squeezed into eight days' work rather than the planned three weeks.

When Mike finally made it to the set at Shepperton Studios, he yet again found himself a prisoner of his emotions. 'It's more embarrassment than nerves,' he told *Pop Parade*. 'Fancy being embarrassed to hold Shirley Eaton! Believe me, I was. I felt such an idiot in front of all those technicians.'

Eaton herself recalled Mike as 'a terribly sweet man' but someone who was clearly short on confidence. 'He seemed to suffer terribly from low self-esteem,' she said.

Nevertheless, the filming seemed to go well. 'The producer seemed very pleased,' Mike told Stan White. 'I can't imagine why. I just played myself.'

Val Guest also endorsed that view. 'Mike has the hallmark of a real star in that he doesn't think he is any good,' he told the press. 'Generally this is a sign of real talent,' he added, although in Mike's case, it was probably more an indication of a lack of self-worth.

The film's release was delayed until May 1960. When it did finally appear, it came across as a run-of-the-mill, low-budget British comedy. Colour would have helped to bring the circus setting to life, but even at the cinema, black and white was still the norm, at least for Guest's budget. Mike's performance was adequate, although at times his attempt to 'act' is all too visible. The naturalness that was central to his TV image is missing. Overall, the film's story line is weak, and whilst the Crazy Gang's geriatric shenanigans with a Genie Of The Lamp (Lionel Jeffries) have their amusing moments, the film is quickly forgettable.

According to Mike, Val Guest wanted him to play the lead in another film the following year. Later correspondence, however, casts some doubt about Guest's enthusiasm. 'I know you always thought I should keep to music,' Mike said in a 1962 letter, 'but I honestly feel I would like to play a small dramatic part in a good film.'

Guest's reply was a gentle brush-off. 'I've tried like hell to find something dramatic for you but there just isn't anything,' he said.

Johnny Wiltshire recalled *Life Is A Circus* showing in Birmingham in May 1960. It was a week that he was supporting Mike at the Birmingham Hippodrome. Mike topped a bill that included Eric Morecambe and Ernie Wise, still looking for their big break. 'He dragged us all off to the cinema saying how good the film was,' said Johnny, 'but it was so bad he made us leave before the end.' One can only imagine the ribbing that he took from Eric and Ernie. It was the kind of thing that would have bounced off a tougher man, but Mike took anything of that nature very much to heart.

Mike's illness in September 1958 remains a mystery, but Richard Stone certainly gave the impression that there was more to it than a mere stomach bug. In a letter to the BBC dated 25th October 1958, he said that 'Mike will do nothing strenuous until the end of the year, then will come right back with a burst of radio and television'.

It was the clearest indication yet that Mike had been suffering from overwork, a view that Mike also endorsed in a private tape message. 'It's crazy to work yourself into that state,' he said. Three years later, however, it would happen again.

There were other signs that Mike was suffering from stress. Wynne Mason, a Crosby fan from Birmingham, thought she had obtained Mike's permission to create a fan club of sorts. She modelled the Michael Holliday Society on the British Crosby Society, the club in which Mike was proud to be an honorary member. Mrs Mason's initiative, with consequent press coverage, was well under way before word leaked out that Mike was having second thoughts.

Soon, the news of Mike's change of heart reached the press. Yet again it revived the stories that Mike was somehow anti-fan. It was left to his secretary, Joy Holdstock, to try and remedy the damage. 'I would imagine that he decided that the Society might in some way encroach upon that part of his life which he considers to be his personal property and quite probably this is the reason for his present attitude,' she wrote to Mrs Mason, offering to reimburse fully any costs incurred. The irony of it was that the enterprising Mrs Mason had already obtained Bing Crosby's agreement to accept honorary membership. It was something that probably hadn't lingered long on Bing's radar screen but it would certainly have given Mike a lift.

Mike's secretary put down his apparent aloofness to pressure of work. There is no doubt that 1958 was a busy year and Mike probably did overreach himself. He often described himself as 'lazy', a view that Margie encouraged in a press feature after his death. His schedule for 1958, however, was not that of a lazy man.

Mike's tally of live appearances in the eight months since 'The Story Of My Life' hit the charts came to an amazing 350 performances. The strain and effort involved for someone who didn't like live stage shows was enormous. Mike had found the time to record nine TV shows for the BBC, a 13-week series for Radio Luxembourg and fit in six more recording sessions at Abbey Road. Toss in the plethora of requests for charity appearances, store openings and bathing beauty contests that went with stardom, and it is little surprise that Mike was feeling the strain. 'You've no idea what it's like being a singer,' he told Stan White. 'Singing is the easy part, but all the letters, music, contracts are just endless.'

After *Life Is A Circus* was completed, Mike was again back on a provincial tour, playing one week cinema appearances in hotspots such as Doncaster, Taunton, Coventry, Worcester, Lincoln and Chesterfield. When that was over, he was off to Ireland for another week's worth of theatrical one-night stands for promoter Louis Rodgers. The promoter's teenage daughter, Cloda, made her debut on one of Mike's shows and later, as Clodagh Rodgers, was one of the top pop stars of the late Sixties.

By early December, the 'nothing strenuous period' that Richard Stone had referred to had shrunk to three weeks. Mike was glad of the chance to spend some time at home and although the year had been hard work, outwardly he seemed content. He used the time at home to catch up on correspondence, and a lengthy tape to Stan White was generally upbeat and full of plans for the future. Another TV series, a summer season in Scarborough and then another film was the agenda that Mike mapped out.

His immediate priorities, however, were about Margie. She was still not back to full health, and had a regular nurse on call whilst Mike was away. Once Mike was home, they had dispensed with the nurse, leaving Mike to describe his own role as 'head cook and bottle-washer', pronouncing 'cook' as 'cooook' in his natural Mersey style.

Mike and Margie also spent that month preparing for another house move. They both loved their home in Woodmansterne, Mike describing it as 'nice and homely' in a tape to Stan White, but it was equally clear that they had outgrown it. Mike talked of opening an office 'in town' but in the meantime, all the paraphernalia that went with stardom resided in the house. 'We're bursting at the seams,' said Mike.

A move up the property ladder was also a sensible one from a financial point of view. 1957 had been a good year, but it was nothing compared to the year that followed. Mike's earnings had soared on the back of the hit records and his gross income for the year to September 1958 reached £15,000, 300 per cent up on the year before. He and Margie could look for something rather more substantial than their small semi.

Neither Mike nor Margie wanted to move far, and in October 1958, they found what they wanted. The house was Dailson, a spacious, five-bedroom home on a private road in Addington, just south of Croydon. It was no more than a mile or two from Chipstead Way, but was a massive step up the property ladder. If Chipstead Way was solidly middle class, Dailson was genuinely a star's home.

Despite its size, Dailson was another semi-detached house although you would hardly have noticed. Built in 1920, as well as its five bedrooms it housed a large lounge, dining room and kitchen, and two massive basement rooms that Mike had earmarked for his growing interest in photography and his records. The private drive, Bishops Walk, straddled the Addington Hills and the property enjoyed two acres of grounds. There was an orchard and a paddock, all overlooking Addington golf course.

Dailson still stands today, albeit under a different name and commands a seven-figure market value. In 1958, Mike and Margie bought the house for £7,250. With little or no inflation on property prices in the Fifties, their selling price of the house in Chipstead Way was £2,800, almost identical to the sum they had paid for it two years before.

Mike used the sale proceeds to clear the mortgage on Chipstead Way. His intention was to pay cash for Dailson although in the end he changed his mind and took out a new loan. Despite Mike's increased earnings, his net income for the year in 1958 was 'only' around £5,000. It was ten times the national average, but a long way short of some of the figures that were bandied around in the press, and not enough yet for Mike to have built up any real capital. The new mortgage was £5,000.

Dailson offered Mike a refuge. 'It's a lumber being a big man,' he told *Picturegoer* in November. 'All I want is my private life to myself and that's something that you can't have with success.' Dailson would at least eliminate the fans who came up and peered through the window, whilst a carefully guarded ex-directory number would cut out the calls from the giggling telephonists. On 29th December 1958, the Hollidays moved into their dream house.

Chapter 12

'Welcome to California, Mr Holliday'

'It's the only ambition I have,' said Mike in a tape to Stan White early in 1959. Most show business stars in Mike's position would have been talking about another milestone en route to the top – a breakthrough into the United States, or perhaps closer to home, the ultimate TV spot – top of the bill on *Sunday Night At The London Palladium*. Mike's declared ambition was, however, something completely different. He was talking about meeting Bing Crosby.

It had almost happened once before, back when Mike was still Norman Milne. One of Mike's postings had been as a steward aboard the *Queen Mary*. On one transatlantic journey, Mike had heard a rumour that the first-class passenger list included Bing's name. Even though Mike was a tourist-class waiter, he was determined to discover if his idol was on board. He was, and Mike had three days to come up with a way of 'bumping into him' in the same accidental way that he would 'bump into' Eric Winstone at the Albert Hall.

Mike decided that his best chance was to find a ruse for entering the first-class dining room, but once he spotted the unmistakable figure of Bing, his tactical sense left him. Barging straight through the main door, his encounter was with the captain rather than the crooner. With no plausible excuse to explain his presence, Mike's initiative brought him a fine and a reprimand – and no meeting with Bing!

When Mike became Michael Holliday, however, a different

113

route presented itself for the fulfilment of Mike's ambition. One of the joys that fame brought Mike was that he attracted the attention of British Crosby fans – and in particular, a small group of enthusiasts in the British Crosby Society. Mike had been an avid collector of Crosby's recordings for as long as he could remember but his collection was nothing compared to those held by the leading UK collectors. He was simply amazed – and deeply envious – of the record and tape collections that people such as Bob Roberts, Frank Murphy, Fred Reynolds, Stan White and Johnny Joyce held. Radio shows, private recordings, unissued takes – there seemed to be no end to the treasures they possessed. 'I'm envious of you,' he once said to John Joyce, a Wolverhampton butcher. 'You've got a lovely wife and family, and all these Crosby records. What more could you want.'

Mike soon found himself on the inside of the circle of British Crosby collectors. The friendships that he built were easy to sustain because none of them were fans of his. As diehard Crosby fans for 25 years or more, none of them would have any truck with an alternative Bing, even if they did make him an honorary member of the British Crosby Society. The fact that they openly admitted to not being fans made Mike feel all the more at home. He knew that he could relax in their company, secure in the knowledge that if he arranged to visit them – which he did at every opportunity – it would be a private visit and not one where he would be engulfed by cousins and aunts, nieces and nephews and the neighbour's cat. Even then, Mike occasionally felt the need to check. 'Will there be anyone else there?' he asked Fred Reynolds, before accepting an invitation to tea during a week in Birmingham in 1962.

Collectors such as Joyce, Reynolds and Stan White saw a kindred spirit in Mike. They knew that his admiration of Bing was set in similar currency to their own. Its roots were a genuine enchantment with Bing's voice that in turn spawned an idolatry of anything and everything to do with Bing. Looked at from the outside, the hero-worship that such rabid fans exhibit may seem unnatural, but to those on the inside of the circle, the friendship

114

of like-minded individuals, blood brothers almost, is one of the additional pleasures that fanship brings. Michael Holliday may have been a big star with an uncanny ability to sound like Bing, but to the diehards of the Crosby fraternity, he was simply one of their own.

Bing Crosby was no stranger to singers who sounded like him. 'He sounds more like Bing than Bing himself!' had been a publicist's line since his emergence in the early Thirties. There had been a host of Bing Crosby soundalikes and imitators since then, but Crosby took an immediate interest in the latest heir to the title of 'Britain's Bing Crosby'.

Crosby was especially close to his group of British fans who formed the nucleus of the Crosby Society. He maintained a regular flow of letters and tapes with them, and made time to meet them on his occasional visits to Britain. It was through them that Bing first heard of Michael Holliday, and he was quick with his acknowledgement. 'With regard to Michael Holliday,' said Bing at the end of his message to the club in 1957, 'I did hear about him, in fact someone sent me a record of his. He sounds very good, they tell me he's a very personable young man and has a brilliant future. I certainly wish all the good things for him in show business.'

The news that Bing had one of his records left Mike feeling overwhelmed. Even when their friendship grew, he never plucked up the courage to hand over one of his discs to Bing. Nevertheless, the acknowledgement from Bing prompted Mike to set about fulfilling his ambition.

Crosby was not the easiest man to pin down. He managed the interface between the public and private sides to his life with an iron will, but once word came back through Crosby's office that Bing would be happy to meet Mike if his schedule permitted, Holliday set about making plans to travel to California in May 1959.

It was the first gap in another busy year. Mike had another TV series to record plus more variety work before heading off to Scarborough for a three-month summer season. After their bouts of ill-health the previous year, both he and Margie were keen to find time for a holiday, although the trip to the States, even then, wasn't purely vacational. Richard Stone and Hal Monty were both putting feelers out with American contacts, whilst Norrie Paramor had already persuaded his counterpart, Dave Dexter at Capitol Records, to issue two of Mike's singles. With interest starting to build, and talk of guest spots on the Perry Como and Ed Sullivan Shows, Holliday arranged to spend a few days in New York to discuss some openings before going on to California for the meeting with Bing.

Mike was no stranger to the USA from his days at sea, but it was Margie's first trip. They flew to New York but arrived in the midst of an early summer heatwave. Neither of them was comfortable in the heat and they decided to head straight for California the next day. From a career point of view, it was a curious move. Transatlantic travel was much less common and far more onerous then than now, and for Mike to pass up the opportunity of promoting himself in New York was a serious mistake. News of the new 'British Bing' and his 6,000-mile pilgrimage to meet his master had created interest in Michael Holliday that he should have capitalised on. The opportunity to launch his name in the USA never came around again.

Arriving in Los Angeles earlier than planned, Holliday made contact with Larry Crosby, Bing's elder brother who ran the crooner's Hollywood office. It was his first experience of entering the world of the private Bing. Larry was warm and welcoming. Yes, he was expected; yes, Bing was keen to meet him; but no, he couldn't tell him when Bing would be available as he still wasn't back from his holiday home in Mexico. No, they couldn't organise a time, it would depend on when Bing got back. Larry would 'ask Mr Crosby to call'. Meanwhile, Mike and Margie would just have to wait.

Holliday, like millions of others, mistook the genial, pipe-smoking Bing that appeared in the films, for the real thing. Whilst not displaying anything resembling the split in Holliday's personality, there were two sides to Bing Crosby too.

116

Outwardly, he had built the perfect public image – the happy-go-lucky character who puffed his pipe and breezed along with the breeze. He was, it seemed, just a regular guy – the type you would ideally have as a next-door neighbour, someone to chew the fat with over the garden fence. His persona appealed to all ages and both sexes. To the ladies, he was the romantic crooner. To the men, he was the all-American sportsman, the golfer, the fisherman, the baseball fan, and whilst he was a megastar, his stardom was based on his ordinariness. His ears stuck out such that he 'resembled a taxi cab with both doors open', he wore a hat to cover the baldness that had arrived in his twenties, and from his mid-thirties on he was fighting the same battle with a paunch that most men do. 'He taught America to relax,' said Tony Bennett, a summation of the Bing Crosby image.

But behind the stunning blue eyes, a different character resided. The private Bing Crosby was a much more complex person than his on-screen personality ever suggested. He was essentially an introvert who was sometimes reserved and distant and there were those who, incorrectly, perceived him as a cold man, insensitive to those around him and incapable of showing warmth and love. The iconoclasts who have gathered around the Crosby legend in the 25 years since his death have painted an even darker picture of a child-beating philanderer, a mean alcoholic who somehow managed to sustain a career of deceit for over 50 years.

In the years after his death, Crosby was an easy target for any writer seeking to make a fast buck. The image that had sustained him for over 50 years was one of American wholesomeness just waiting, it seemed, to be exposed as a fraud. It was not until Gary Giddins published the first part of his definitive biography in 2001 that a balanced picture began to emerge. Crosby was indeed a complex and complicated man. He was a product of a stern Catholic mother, a classical Jesuit education and a society that defined roles and behaviour in a different way from today. He was also a highly intelligent man who understood stardom's destructive qualities in a way that many others, Michael Holliday included, never came close to appreciating.

By the time Holliday met him, Crosby had been a star for 30 years. The experience had taught him that only he could impose any sense of balance into his life. It made him determined to carve out and protect a piece of his life that belonged to him and him alone.

Bing Crosby was no ogre, no mass-deceiver or purveyor of false gold. He was a uniquely talented singer and all-round entertainer. He was also a man totally in control of his life. *He* decided what he did and where he went. *He* decided who he called and who he saw. If Bing Crosby didn't want to see you, you didn't see him.

Michael Holliday found the waiting difficult. He and Margie spent the days 'relaxing' by the swimming pool at their hotel in Beverly Hills. For Margie, it was hardly a relaxing experience. Mike insisted on having a telephone hooked up to the poolside, just in case Bing called. The white enamel telephone was never more than a yard away. There were lots of calls – music publishers, A&R men, American stars such as Pat Boone and Guy Mitchell calling to say 'Hi'. Never one to miss a trip, Hal Monty was in New York (even if Mike wasn't) to help promote his new charge and was a regular caller. But no Bing.

Four days came and went, and by the Wednesday evening Mike was at a low point. Four days' anonymity was enough for the side of him that loved his stardom. He missed being known or being recognised around the hotel. He convinced himself that the whole idea of the trip had been misplaced. Who did he think he was? Why on earth would Bing Crosby ever call him? He'd had enough. 'Let's go home,' he said to Margie.

As ever, it was she who provided the stability. Margie persuaded her husband to give it a little longer. In the meantime, she suggested a night out at the famous Moulin Rouge nightclub, where Sammy Davis Jr was in cabaret. Returning to the hotel, Margie went to bed whilst Mike sat up until 3 a.m. With the call from Bing on his mind, his sleeping problems were back, and anyway he was fascinated by the fact that television in the USA ran through most of the night. Mike was glued to

118

the set in their room until the white dot disappeared from the screen.

At 9.00 a.m. the following morning, the telephone by Mike's side of the bed started to ring. Mike was fast asleep, but woke in time to pick up the receiver. The voice on the other end seemed at once familiar, yet distant.

'Hello, Mr Holliday, welcome to California.'

There was something about the voice that Mike knew well, so well, but he couldn't place it. Who was this? An agent? Another American performer?

Sleep was still numbing his brain and he could only mumble a polite 'Excuse me, but who am I talking to?' Within a second, he was wide awake.

'Oh, this is Bing Crosby!' came the reply.

Mike in his own words 'jumped about three feet in the air'. Bing explained that he was playing golf in Santa Barbara later that day, but if Mike and Margie would care to come to the course at around five in the afternoon, they could have a 'cup of tea', an English touch that Mike found highly amusing. 'We'll be there,' said Mike.

Later that day, Mike and Margie drove out to the Valley Golf Club to fulfil their lives' ambition. For almost the first time in his life, Mike arrived somewhere early and with every minute that passed, he grew more and more nervous. 'I just couldn't believe that inside the golf club, Bing Crosby was waiting to meet me,' he told Stan White when he returned home.

When the Hollidays finally plucked up the courage to drive into the club, they parked and walked out onto the terrace. Ahead of them lay an expanse of expensively manicured turf, glistening under the bright Californian sun. Bing was out there somewhere, they told each other, but where? They saw a figure they recognised – or so they thought, until the figure moved. 'I know Bing's walk,' said Mike, 'and that wasn't Bing.' Then they saw another figure in the distance, but no, that wasn't him either.

Then Margie turned around. A middle-aged man in a white flat cap and blue polo shirt was ambling towards them with a

119

gait that they had seen a thousand times on the cinema screen. Beneath the white golfing cap, a pipe jutted out, held jauntily at an angle. 'I think this is him,' said Margie. It was.

Crosby immediately acknowledged the English couple. 'Be with you in just a minute,' the famous voice boomed, as Crosby headed first to the locker room to wash up after his game. Within minutes, he was back, full of the famous Crosby charm and playing the perfect host.

Crosby was never comfortable with idolatry. Perry Como once recalled how, during a long TV duet with Crosby, he had found himself so lost in Bing's presence that he had stopped the medley and simply said 'You know, if it wasn't for him, I'd still be cutting hair [a reference to Como's early life as a barber].' After the taping was over, Crosby had chastised his disciple for his impromptu tribute.

'Don't ever do that again,' he said to Como, his voice carrying a tone that made it clear that to transgress would put a friendship at risk.

With his idol sat opposite him, Mike was transfixed. 'My mother always taught me not to stare,' Mike said later in his account of the meeting, 'but I just couldn't help it. I just stared straight at him.' Despite acting like a rabbit in the headlights, Mike professed to not feeling nervous. 'The only problem is that you don't believe you're really there, that you won't wake up and find it's all a dream,' he said later.

The sense of disbelief may have helped Mike to allow something of his natural personality to come through. Freed from the pressures of needing to be 'Michael Holliday', he was a highly likeable individual, a mischievous twinkle in his eye and a smile never far from his face. Most of Crosby's true personal friends resided away from the world of show business, with straightforward simplicity a common characteristic. The natural Mike was a good fit, and Crosby seemed to take a genuine liking to both him and Margie.

Seeing that Margie had a camera with her, Bing suggested that they take some pictures of the meeting, both still and home-movie. The surviving film shows a relaxed Mike, sitting alongside Bing in a pair of directors' chairs, sipping drinks. Mike looks comfortable and naturally relaxed, even if a beaming smile never leaves his face. Margie even persuaded Bing to ham it up with Mike and recreate the famous pat-a-cake routine that was a regular part of the Hope and Crosby *Road* pictures.

Crosby invited the couple to follow him back to his home in Holmby Hills, where they met his young wife Kathryn. The next day, they visited the Crosby office, where they were treated as if they were lifelong friends. Bing himself took time out to dig out some privately pressed LPs of unissued radio material, all of which were personally signed. For the Hollidays, the trip was simply a dream come true. 'Marge and I have loved him for so long,' he told Stan White. 'He is the master of everything ... The Great Croz.'

Even then, Mike didn't seem to realise just what a coup the visit had been. Whilst in Hollywood, Mike visited Capitol Records and met Dave Dexter, who was much impressed at Mike's souvenirs. 'How he did it, I have no idea,' he wrote to Paramor 'but he showed me photos with Bing Crosby. Crosby's own brothers and sons can't get Bing on the telephone, much less visit with him, so I suspect Holliday has a secret touch. I have known Bob Crosby [Bing's younger brother] for several years and he once told me that he went three or four years without ever seeing or hearing from Bing!'

When Mike returned to England, the press made much of his meeting with Bing. 'YOUNG GROANER MEETS OLD GROANER' was one headline, atop of Margie's photo of the two singers. From then on, Mike and Bing became regular correspondents and even if the flow of letters was greater from Croydon to California than in the opposite direction, Bing did at least reciprocate some of the attention that Mike foisted upon him.

The following year, Bing turned up in London en route from the Olympic Games in Rome. No sooner had Mike seen the picture of Bing and Kathryn in the *Daily Express* than he was on the phone to Bing's hotel. The telephonist was a Holliday fan, more in awe of Mike than Bing and was prepared to break the rules of 'no calls' and put Mike through to Bing's room. Mike had the phone hooked into his tape machine and recorded the conversation. When Bing recognises his voice with the words 'Hiya Michael, how are ya', Holliday is like a schoolboy who has just discovered that there really is a Santa Claus. 'Oh boy!!' is all he can say.

The call was brief, Crosby explaining that he was in London to make some recordings. Holliday was almost speechless. It had been one thing to meet his idol at the golf club in California, but the idea of seeing Bing at work was on a different plane altogether. Crosby had not performed in England since the war years and latterly, the famous crooner seemed to have settled for semi-retirement, focusing his attention on the second family that he and Kathryn were producing. Mike had asked him when they met in California whether he had plans to make some new recordings and received what seemed to be the standard, dismissive reply.

From the moment that he put the phone down, Mike had only one thought in his head. If Bing was making records, Michael Holliday was going to be there to see it. He called Patrick Doncaster, the record correspondent of the *Daily Mirror* who Holliday knew well. Within minutes, Doncaster was back on the phone. Crosby's session was taking place at the Decca studios at West Hampstead. 'But they might not let you in,' joked Doncaster, 'you work for the competition, you know.'

Mike had no intention of allowing commercial rivalry between Decca and EMI Columbia to get in the way of seeing Bing at work. Within an hour, he was sitting in the control booth, transfixed as Crosby went through the process of making a gramophone record, something he had first done 34 years ago, since when his global sales had reached a staggering 250 million.

Once the session was over, Crosby took time out for two radio interviews and then came into the booth. 'Is that old Holliday over there?' he said, seeing Mike in the corner of the room. Mike was thrilled to be recognised and the two of them chatted

122

for a few minutes. Crosby had by now reached the stage in his career where it was debatable whether he was a singer who golfed, or a golfer who sang, and sure enough, he had some golf lined up that afternoon. He was playing at Coombe Hill, he told Mike, so why didn't he and Margie come along.

Mike needed no second invitation, nor indeed did Margie. Later in the afternoon, Mike and Bing struck up a conversation with the impresario Val Parnell, the man behind TV's *Sunday Night At The London Palladium*. Crosby assumed, wrongly, that Parnell and Mike had not met, although by then Holliday had already made his debut on the Sunday night show.

'You should put him on the *Palladium*,' Bing said to Parnell, nodding in Mike's direction.

'No, no,' said Mike to Parnell, pointing to Bing, 'I want you to put *him* on the *Palladium*.'

'Me? Naw, I'm through,' was Crosby's self-deprecating reply.

Bing and Kathryn flew back to the USA a few days later. Few would have forecast that of the two stars who stood chatting at Coombe Hill that October afternoon, the then septuagenarian Crosby would be the one who would sell out the *Palladium* in the mid-1970s, not the young pretender. When Mike and Margie had returned from the USA in 1959, the only question seemed to be how brightly Michael Holliday's star would shine. The real question was how long.

Chapter 13

'I thought you were Michael Holliday'

Mike had picked up 1959 where he had left off 1958. After briefly playing his part in settling into Dailson – most of the domesticities associated with a new home were left to Margie – Mike was straight back into another heavy work schedule. Another television series, a long-playing record, and more live appearances were all lined up before the spring trip to the USA.

The BBC was delighted with the success of the 15-minute shows. Even though the last series had only ended three months ago, the Corporation wanted nine more shows. It was the same pattern as the previous year, but now the tape recorder routine took pride of place. 'Some people like it better than my solos,' said Mike. Norrie Paramor even piggybacked on the routine and had Mike double-track in the recording studio to create an EP called *Mike (And The Other Fella)*.

Mike once more recorded the shows at Dickenson Road in Manchester. He tried to cram as much as possible into his trips north. Some shows went out live, with Mike doing an early evening 'commercial' with his tape recorder. Mike then stayed on to record a second show the following day.

By now, the shows had developed into a predictable if comfortable pattern. The tape recorder routine had its own mini-portfolio of songs that were ideal duet material. Regular numbers included 'Back In The Old Routine', 'Bye Bye Blackbird' and two songs from the EP, 'Side By Side' and 'Winter Wonderland'. Mike even threw in the odd soft-shoe shuffle, although his dancing

125

deficiencies were also on a par with the notoriously flat-footed Bing Crosby.

Mike also built the tape recorder routine into his stage act. From then on, Mike hardly ever appeared without it. Taking the routine to the stage, however, was not without its own complications. When Mike sang his duets on television, his tape recorder was real, even though he used it as little more than a prop. The recording of Mike's other voice came through off-screen speakers, maintaining a constant sound balance with Mike's 'live' singing. In the theatre, Mike had to sing a genuine duet with the tape. To do that, he had to find ways of amplifying the voice on the tape as well as getting power to the machine.

Amplification was easy but the power supply usually involved running a cable to a back-stage plug. On one performance in Kettering, Mike was in mid-duet when Hal Monty inadvertently tripped over the wire and dislodged the plug. Seeing what he had done, Monty hastily reinserted the plug and restored the power. It meant that Mike's duet voice ground to a lugubrious halt before springing back to life.

Mike was furious. As soon as he finished the song, he leapt from his stool and dashed backstage. Identifying Monty as the culprit, Mike took a flying kick at his backside, calling him a 'stupid old bastard'. Even though none of this was visible to the theatre audience, the backstage commotion sounded like a slapstick comedy. The audience assumed, as audiences often do, that the diversion was all part of the act. When Mike and Monty heard the laughter, the mood changed. The 'accident' from then on formed part of the show.

The tape recorder duets took Mike into deeper waters with the BBC. Their policy of never mentioning or appearing to endorse any commercial product was strictly enforced. Even today, the BBC is still a non-commercial station, although its policy now is positively libertarian when compared to the discipline of the Fifties. Then, its neutrality bordered on neurosis.

Even a household name had to remain anonymous. In Mike's final series for the BBC in 1963, ventriloquist Denis Spicer was his guest. He and Holliday had worked together at Butlin's at Clacton. When Spicer mentioned that 'we haven't worked together since our days at ... er, the holiday camp,' Mike was horror-struck.

'I thought you were going to say the name!' he said.

'Nearly,' said Spicer, *sotto voce*.

Tape recorders in the late Fifties were the PlayStations of their day. All the leading electronic firms vied for a share of the market. Specialist companies such as Ferrograph and Revox made the top-notch machines, but in the consumer market, Grundig, Philips and Fidelity led the way. Mike soon saw the potential to link his routine to one of the manufacturers.

In January 1958, he approached Grundig, who quickly signed him as one of the 'Top Stars' they used to advertise their products. The first Grundig ads to feature Mike appeared in the autumn of that year, in time for Mike's second BBC series. The advertisements popped up in most of the music press, including *Radio Times*, and conveyed the impression that Mike used a Grundig machine in his BBC programmes.

When other manufacturers were quick to cry foul, the BBC, publicly at least, backed Mike, pointing out that more than one type of tape recorder had been used in the current series. The statement was true, but only just. Some people knew that Holliday had substituted his 'own' Grundig machine in place of a BBC Philips machine for the latter part of the series. The machine was Mike's own but only because Grundig had given it to him as part of the deal.

John Ammonds was aware of the sensitivity about advertising and approached the tape recorder shots with great care. When he panned in on the tape as part of his opening shot for one show, Holliday carefully positioned his hand over the Grundig name. But despite Ammonds's careful camera work, the BBC top brass was still uneasy. They were right to be concerned. Even Grundig seemed pleasantly surprised by the prominence that Mike was giving their machines. 'It's nice to know my efforts are appreciated,' said Mike in his reply to the company's letter of thanks.

Even without knowing the details of Mike's arrangement with Grundig, the Corporation nevertheless decided to make a stand and decided that for his next series, Mike would use another make of machine. The issue had the potential to become a major dispute between Mike and the BBC. The only reason that it didn't was that another more fundamental dispute got there first. It would be four years before the BBC had to decide whether to implement their restriction on the Grundig machines.

The rift between Mike and the BBC went back to the summer of 1958. After Mike's successes in the Hit Parade, Richard Stone had been quick to look for something bigger for Mike in the BBC's schedules. He floated the idea of giving Mike a half-hour show with guest artistes. The initial response was good. Eric Maschwitz, BBC Television's newly-appointed Head of Light Entertainment, said he was keen to explore the idea further for Mike's next series that was due early in 1959.

Stone, as ever, played a cautious game. 'Naturally the commercial boys are after Michael. I think you will agree that the BBC fee should now be a reasonably competitive one. He is, I consider, getting about one-quarter of the fee he could command for a similar series on commercial TV.'

Maschwitz was still keen to push the idea. 'I personally feel that he could carry this,' he said in an internal memorandum to Kenneth Adam, the Controller of Programmes in August 1958. Adam took several months to reply. When he did, it was clear that he didn't share Maschwitz's view. What's more, when the Controller tuned into the first two shows of Holliday's 1959 series, he didn't like what he saw.

A long internal memo contained a litany of complaints. Nothing was right – he criticised Ken Lawson's 'fussy' set, the generally over-elaborate production and Mike's own performance. Adam's comments were an amazing broadside against one of the BBC's top shows and left the production team feeling nonplussed.

It was as if Adam had some axe to grind with Mike. The set

128

was the same one that Ken Lawson had designed for the previous shows, including the balcony to which Adam took a particular dislike. 'I agree with you that it must be kept quiet, relaxed and easy, but I would have thought that all these adjectives applied,' B.W. Cave-Browne-Cave, the BBC's regional head, diplomatically replied.

Money was soon back on the agenda. Tom Sloan talked to Richard Stone in March 1959. He laid out the issue in an internal memorandum. 'It seems that Holliday is now part managed by Hal Monty who is, of course, very close to the Grades. There is intense pressure to get him on to the other channel. Stone insists that money is the all important thing and has suggested that an offer of something like £10,000 for 12 programmes is what Holliday and Monty have in mind.'

Sloan had suggested a roundtable to discuss Mike's 'career with us', but Stone said no, adding that 'all he [Holliday] was interested in was money'. The stand-off not only threatened Mike's career at the BBC but was also the clearest indication yet of the emerging conflict between Richard Stone and Hal Monty. Stone's approach was always long term, planting seeds and allowing them to nurture. Monty, in contrast, was wham, bam, thank you ma'am.

Kenneth Adam was never about to sanction £1,000 per show for Michael Holliday. In May 1959, he took a trip to Southend. 'I found Michael Holliday and Yana doing a one-night cinema stand,' he wrote to Eric Maschwitz. 'The house was not full and two policemen sent to deal with the teenagers had literally nothing to do. There were no crowds, no excitement. I saw Holliday taking an early morning walk next day. No one else recognised him. And this for a man they talk of asking us £1,000 a time for!'

Mike wasn't known for his early morning walks. The fact that no one else recognised him – one of the most familiar faces on television – begs the question as to whether Adam had the right man. It was academic. Eric Maschwitz could see that the die was cast.

Stone's proposal had been for an exclusive contract from 1st January 1960, with a guarantee of £10,000 over 12 months. Maschwitz used the upcoming telerecording of *Stars At Scarborough* as a play for time. Mike was down to act as star and compère for the show. The BBC, said Maschwitz, would like to judge how Holliday 'stands up' before committing to a more ambitious programme. Wait until after the Scarborough show was his advice to Stone who had little option but to agree. But by the time the Scarborough show had come and gone, so too had Richard Stone.

Stone later blamed his separation from Holliday on the growing influence of Hal Monty. With time to kill during the ten-week variety tour in 1958, Monty and Mike had become good friends. Monty was a generation older than Mike and the living embodiment of 'street-wise', a 'chancer' in the words of someone who knew him in his music-hall days. Mike's liking for him was more to do with his hatred of being alone than any deep-seated affection. Nevertheless, by the end of the tour, Hal Monty had taken on the role of Mike's personal manager. 'He just took over the job,' said Mike in a 1958 tape. 'He's a bit of a rough diamond but I've become very fond of him.'

The fondness wouldn't last. With no clear distinction between the role of Stone as agent and Monty as manager, Mike quickly found himself pulled in two different directions. Stone's influence on Mike was strong but distant. Monty, in contrast, was always there at Mike's shoulder, encouraging Mike to get it in cash and get it now. When Mike recorded a letter-tape to Stan White from his dressing room at the Sunderland Empire in 1958, Monty came into the room halfway through.

'Say hello to Stan,' said Mike.

''ello Stan,' said the gnarled voice in an accent that wouldn't be out of place in *EastEnders*. 'We're just counting out our "whack" but there's none for you.'

Mike's contemporaries paint a picture of Monty as a Fagin-like character, orchestrating Mike on a range of moneymaking errands, taking his cut and doing nicely for himself out of it.

'He wasn't what you would call a class act,' said one show business contemporary.

Mike might not have been an innocent young Oliver, but he was easy to influence. Others say that Monty was Mike's Svengali, something that Mike himself seemed to acknowledge in later years. 'I promised myself after my association with Hal Monty that I wouldn't be ordered around any more,' Mike said in 1962.

Richard Stone's autobiography implied that Monty had replaced him as Mike's sole representative, although the chronology of events casts doubt on Stone's interpretation. Stone was still actively handling Mike's bookings until the summer of 1959. By October, however, Mike was under contract to the Bernard Delfont Agency.

The move to Delfont was arguably a step up for Mike. The Stone and de Wolfe agency was well established, but the bulk of their clientele worked in the legitimate theatre. In contrast, the Delfont Agency had a broader range of stars on their books, including the Beverley Sisters, Winifred Atwell and Frankie Vaughan. Monty didn't displace Stone, but it is likely that it was Monty's influence that persuaded Mike to move across to the Delfont agency, where the managing director, Bernard Delfont, was Monty's former stage partner. Delfont was the brother of Lew and Leslie Grade, who largely controlled ITV. This was the link between Monty and the Grades that Tom Sloan had referred to.

A triumvirate comprising Delfont himself, Billy Marsh and Keith Devon managed the Delfont agency. Devon took on the responsibility for managing Mike. He found the relationship difficult from the start. His first letter to Mike in November 1959 set the tone. 'I have asked you two or three times over the telephone to come up to the office in order to plan together your future work,' he said. 'I must point out to you, Michael, that it is important that we have a meeting.'

Holliday's lack of commitment – he had apparently signed without even meeting his new agent – did not augur well for a close working relationship. It soon got worse. In December,

131

Devon wrote to Mike demanding that he work through him not round him. Mike had started the practice of sending new TV contracts straight to the TV company rather than back via Devon. When Holliday wrote to the BBC advising them of his change of agent, he specifically instructed them to send any payments direct to him rather than through the Delfont agency. 'I do not know the reason for your doing this,' Devon wrote.

The reason was Hal Monty. Since late 1958, Monty had been working to a 15 per cent entitlement of the gross earnings that he arranged for Mike (alongside the 10 per cent that Mike paid Stone). It was an expensive arrangement that on some bookings could cost Mike 25 per cent of the gross. Mike also began to suspect that he was actually paying more to Monty than he realised and by the summer of 1959, the relationship between the two was on the rocks.

Monty's routine was to ask for the gross contract sum – increasingly based on a percentage of the box office for live performances – paid to him in cash. Since he often negotiated a second bill spot for himself as a performer, he was usually on hand to deal direct with the theatre management and as Mike's manager, pick up both his own and Mike's dues. After his deducting his own commission, he paid the balance of Mike's fee over in cash.

It was an archetypal brown envelope routine. Despite requests from Mike, Monty rarely, if ever, produced accounts and Mike's growing suspicion was that there were side deals too that didn't pass through any books en route to Monty's pocket. The fuse blew during the summer season in Scarborough. Mike and Monty had a blazing row that ended with Mike firing the veteran comedian and agreeing to pay him a termination payment of £2,500.

It was a massive pay-off, indicative of Mike's lack of business nous. Margie witnessed the row and discouraged Mike from making any offer to Monty. 'Don't give it to him, he is taking advantage of you,' she had told Mike. Mike quickly realised that he had made a mistake. Within days, he had reconsidered and

132

proposed a different arrangement. Setting the termination payment aside, he proposed that Monty would act as his sole representative for a five-year period from 1st October 1959, taking 15 per cent of any earnings for which Monty was responsible.

Mike's volte-face was surprising and short-lived. The new agreement with Monty was the final coffin-nail in Mike's contract with Richard Stone but was itself over within a month. At the end of a week's variety in Leeds on 24th October 1959, Mike and Monty clashed again. Once more, there was a blazing row and again it was about money. Mike confronted Monty just as he was about to go on stage, demanding his salary for the week. Monty refused, saying he would pay Mike the following week. A slanging match ensued with Monty finally agreeing to stay until Mike's act was finished. 'We'll see if he can keep his word just once,' said Mike to Dave Cook, a friend who witnessed the argument.

When Mike left to go on stage, Monty took £100 from his briefcase – a lot less than Mike's normal contractual minimum for a week's variety – and gave it to Cook, saying 'Give him this' as he walked out.

It was the last straw for Mike. Somewhere in the row, Holliday had said to Monty 'you know we won't be meeting any more'. On returning home, he fired off a letter to Monty confirming their 'agreement' that Monty would terminate his position as Mike's manager. Monty, who had no such agreement in mind, took out an action against Mike for breach of contract.

Monty claimed an entitlement to 15 per cent of Mike's estimated earnings for the five-year period covered by the contract they had verbally struck only a few weeks before. Potentially, it was an enormous sum. The case hung over Mike's head for three years before it reached the courts. When it did, it brought with it the spectre of bankruptcy.

Meanwhile, the summer season in Scarborough had gone well. The resort was the pride of the Yorkshire seaside towns, the jewel in a coastal crown that also included Filey, Bridlington and Whitby. Whilst never in the same league as Blackpool,

Scarborough was the resort of choice for the Yorkshire mill towns whose families routinely headed to the coast in July and August each year. Scarborough's attractions included its two bays, its fleet of steamers, a cliff-top cable car railway, and a cricket ground that each year housed a week's cricket festival that brought the curtain down on the summer season.

Scarborough also supported three theatres, each of which housed a summer show. The Spa Theatre was the regular haunt of violinist Max Jaffa, with two other theatres, the Futurist and Floral Hall, staging a more populist summer season programme. Mike topped the bill at the Floral Hall, with *Heartbeat* star Bill Maynard, then a stand-up comic, plus impressionist Joan Turner – 'The Girl With A Thousand Voices' according to the programme. Richard Stone produced the show, whose title was *Let's Make A Night Of It.*

It was conventional summer season fare with the usual variety bill of dancers, jugglers and even a xylophonist thrown in. Mike was the fifteenth and last act to appear, singing seven or eight songs twice-nightly from mid-June to mid-September and pocketing £400 per week for the privilege. Most Sundays, he would drive over to Blackpool for a lucrative Sunday concert that would give him a further £250 fee. The rest of the time was his own, and he occupied himself with the usual array of personal appearances, beauty contests – and Scarborough's population of teenage girls.

One girl who met Mike that summer proved to be more than the usual one-night stand. Margaret Burrows was a stunningly attractive 16-year-old who was walking down Scarborough's main street one day when Mike drove by in his new American car. 'He looked at me and then turned round and came back,' said Margaret. 'I remember saying "I thought you were Michael Holliday" and him replying "I am Michael Holliday".'

The affair started immediately. Margaret spent most of the summer evenings with Mike in his dressing room at the Floral Hall, and on Sundays, travelled with him on his ride to Blackpool, at least as far as York, where she would catch the bus back home. After the end of the season the relationship continued sporadically, with Mike and Margaret meeting whenever his schedule brought him to the north of England. Despite the age difference, they continued to meet until she left to live abroad two years later.

Margaret's memories of Mike show the complex individual that he had become. 'I remember his cheeky grin and his laughing eyes when he was teasing me; the way he combed his hair; the way he had to pee every few minutes when he was nervous about going on stage. He was terrified of going on stage with his flies undone so he was always checking them. He was a bit of a nervous wreck, especially before a show.'

Margaret also recalls a fundamentally simple man, 'very clean-living' who smoked only occasionally, didn't drink much, didn't do drugs and didn't like parties or clubs. His only vice seemed to be the one that everyone inside show business knew about. 'He was a terrible womaniser,' said Margaret, 'with a liking for young girls, but he was very honest about it.'

'Honest' may not be the right word. Mike may have been very open about his sexual relationships but it was hardly honest. Just as Margaret was sure that Margie knew about her, she too found herself in the same position, if one step removed. 'He gave the stage doorman instructions to let me in at all times and twice when I arrived, he had a different girl there. He just introduced us and politely asked the other girl to leave. He had no guilt at all, he just thought it was completely normal.'

One can only imagine that it was Mike's guiltless innocence and beguiling charm that persuaded Margie, Margaret Burrows and others to forgive the perpetual betrayal. Margaret recalled Mike gossiping disapprovingly to her of the behaviour of another star who he knew was conducting a secret affair. 'I gave him a look and he started chuckling, realising he had no room to moralise.' Without the prompt, it seems the thought would not otherwise have occurred to him.

Despite Mike's wayward behaviour, Margie continued to play the role of devoted wife, at least in public. A feature prepared for *TV Times* in late 1959 built on the homely image of earlier pieces, but with the added dimension of the Hollidays' new-found affluence. The interview with Margie in Dailson's plushly carpeted lounge revealed the full extent of what making it to the big time really meant. The double garage housed Mike's American Ford Fairlane plus Margie's sports coupe. The fine furniture complemented the expensive stereo equipment whilst the 2-acre grounds were home to Mike's only true hobby – horses. Polly and later Shadow, the latter a Palomino filly, gave Mike an escape from the pressures that constantly enveloped him.

The year 1959 was every bit the one that Mike and Margie expected it to be. In money terms, it was the best ever. Mike's personal earnings topped £25,000, plus a further £7,000 via Michael Holliday Productions. Mike's business and personal expenses increased too, but he still earned net income of around £12,000. Holliday was now a rich man and his earnings took him into the group of one in a thousand in the UK whose income was 15 times the national average. It also took him into the category of surtax payers.

Surtax was Britain's mid-century supertax. Introduced in 1909, it was renamed 'surtax' in 1927, and lived on until 1972. It troubled less than a quarter of a million of the UK population in 1955, but for those caught by it, the impact was severe. Mike's taxable income for 1959 was £11,800, giving rise to income tax of £3,664 and surtax of £2,589. Mike's effective rate of tax was 53 per cent, prompting his accountant Bill Gudgin of Baker Todman to advise in simple terms that Mike needed to set aside 10 shillings of every pound earned.

Surtax brought an added complication in that it didn't fall payable until well after the date of assessment. The ability to defer part of the tax bill should have mitigated the overall impact. For Mike, it made it worse. Despite the ever-prudent accountant's advice, Mike saw no need to put money aside. Business was good and his star was high. This year's surtax could easily be paid from next year's earnings, and then next year he would do the same again. It was the show business way.

The approach was fine, providing earnings stayed at least constant from year to year. When Mike looked at the world at the end of 1959, there was nothing to suggest that the first year of the new Sixties decade would be any different from the last two years of the Fifties. Nothing, that is, except the 18 months that had gone by since his last hit record.

Chapter 14

'Starry Eyed'

Despite Mike's popularity on television, he was still first and foremost a singer, and a singer needed to sell records. The success of 'The Story Of My Life' and 'Stairway Of Love' had been the catalyst behind the great strides he made in 1958, and Norrie Paramor was keen to keep the run going.

Mike's first session after the success of 'Stairway Of Love' had been in June 1958. With Mike riding high, Paramor had no shortage of songs to pick from for his next single. Mike himself received a succession of music sheets in his postbag whilst Paramor found himself the target of an endless flow of song pluggers. All of them were convinced of the same thing. Their songs were 'just the thing for Mike'.

Despite the flurry of new material available to him, Paramor selected two oldies for the June session, plus one other new song. The new title was 'I'll Be Lovin' You Too', but the main focus at the session was on two aged ballads. 'I'll Always Be In Love With You' went all the way back to the 1920s when it had been a hit in the States for the collegiate sound of Fred Waring and his Pennsylvanians. The second oldie, 'Careless Hands', was a Crosby song from the late 1940s that Des O'Connor would revive again towards the end of the Sixties. It was a personal choice of Mike's and Paramor gave it a new arrangement and strong beat to bring it up to date.

Mike was in good voice at the session although the material was disappointing. Paramor was looking for something that wouldn't sound like a rehash of 'Stairway Of Love' but his decision to pick the old Fred Waring song as the A side for Mike's next single was a mistake. With the new song 'I'll Be Lovin' You Too' on the reverse, the critics were by no means convinced that he had made the right choice. Keith Fordyce in *New Musical Express* was diplomatic. 'Michael Holliday has a couple of good songs on Columbia although it's difficult to pick the stronger of the two,' he wrote. Over in *Melody Maker*, Laurie Henshaw even misread EMI's advance publicity and thought the B side was the main attraction. 'Michael Holliday delivers "I'll Be Lovin' You Too" with his usual engaging relaxation to a lilting rhythmical backing from the Mike Sammes Singers. This is another potential hit parader for the Holliday boy.'

'I'll Always Be In Love With You' was a pleasant recording and was the type of song that Mike could almost sing in his sleep. The Mike Sammes singers provided the choral backing that the number required, but it was the wrong song at the wrong time. 'I'll Be Lovin' You Too' was much closer in sound to the 'Stairway Of Love', perhaps too close, but nevertheless would have been more likely to carry on the run of Top Ten appearances.

Despite the error of judgement, Mike had a strong enough tailwind from the earlier hits to still push his Twenties ballad into the charts. 'I'll Always Be In Love With You' crept in at number 27 in July 1958. It was a fleeting visit that lasted just one week.

Mike's choice for his next single was another mistake. Having done well with two covers of Marty Robbins's hits, Norrie Paramor decided to try and make it three in a row. This time the song was a slow ballad, 'She Was Only Seventeen', that told a sentimental story of two teenagers who fell in love and proved all their critics wrong by making it last. Robbins's disc made no impact in the USA and Mike's UK cover went the same way.

Ironically, Mike's vocal performance on 'She Was Only Seventeen' was one of his best. It provides an excellent demonstration of what recording engineer Stuart Eltham meant when he talked about Mike's excellent diction. Mike also used the double-tracking recording technique to add his own backing vocal for the disc, another novelty feature, and a variant on his tape recorder routine.

The B side of the disc was a song called 'The Gay Vagabond'. Nowadays, a title like that would herald a story of a homosexual gypsy, rather than the happy-go-lucky rambler who was the real subject. It was never more than a B-side filler and the two songs came well short of what was required. 'She Was Only Seventeen' was Mike's first flop since 'Old Cape Cod'.

Strangely, the sales of 'She Was Only Seventeen' were actually a few thousand better than those of 'I'll Always Be In Love With You'. Both of them sold around the 40,000 mark. The sales were a reflection of just how popular Michael Holliday was in 1958, but were a long way short of the 120,000 that 'Stairway Of Love' had clocked up. Paramor was not unduly concerned. When *New Musical Express* came out with its overall chart for 1958, Mike was number nine and the highest-placed British singer. With the massive exposure Mike was now getting in the media, Paramor was convinced that the next big hit was not far away.

A sure sign that Norrie Paramor believed he had come up with a winner was when he hastily arranged a recording session with just one title on the slate. Mike's session on Sunday, 2nd November 1958 was one of these. The song that Paramor had found was 'My Heart Is An Open Book', with music by Lee Pockriss and words by 'The Story Of My Life' lyricist Hal David. It looked and sounded a sure-fire winner. The only competition was from a little-known American singer, Carl Dobkins Jr (who nevertheless took the song to number three in the US charts in January 1959) and the song suited Mike perfectly.

If ever there was a recording that carried Mike's signature – at least in the singles market – this was it. Ken Jones built his arrangement on three electric guitars, supported by bass and drums, with Jones himself playing piano on the session. The result was a wonderful record. Mike is in top vocal form, delivering a rendition that is relaxed and engaging. Yes, he sounds a lot like Bing, but the style is undeniably Michael Holliday. The record is one of the best defences against a charge that Holliday was nothing more than a Crosby copyist. Not surprisingly, 'My Heart Is An Open Book' is ever present in any Michael Holliday compilation.

Good records, however, don't always make the charts. 'Sing out of tune, Mike,' one of the backing singers shouted across to him during one session, 'you'll sell more records that way.' Despite the quality of the finished product, 'My Heart Is An Open Book' surprisingly joined the growing list of chart failures.

Underpromotion was probably the cause. Radio programmes at this time were still largely live or recorded shows, rather than DJs playing records, but in the 12 months from June 1958 Mike made only two appearances on BBC radio. One of them was a November edition of Brian Matthew's *Saturday Club*, when Mike took the opportunity to sing both of his last two singles, plus a cover of Connie Francis's chart-topper 'Who's Sorry Now'. That appearance apart, Mike didn't feature the song in any TV appearance in late 1958 and the music papers carried few, if any, ads for the disc. EMI's low-key approach was curious and in stark contrast to the heavy promotion earlier that year of Mike's other singles.

For Mike's first single of 1959, Paramor went back to the songwriting team of Sid Bennett and Roy Tepper, the duo who had written 'Stairway Of Love'. Their newest song was 'Palace Of Love', one word away from being the same song. It had all the ingredients that had worked so well just 12 months before, but perhaps it was too much of a clone. It bombed.

The reviewers were as puzzled as Mike. *Record Mail*'s review of 'Palace Of Love' was typical of the enthusiasm that greeted its release. 'This newest from Mike I rate *very* highly and I am sure he has a big hit on his hands here. It is extremely catchy and as you might expect, impeccably sung,' said the reviewer.

The sales of Mike's singles were suddenly in free-fall. The two discs from the middle of 1958 had each sold 40,000, but 'My Heart Is An Open Book' managed to sell only 30,000

142

records. 'Palace Of Love' was even worse. Sales barely topped 20,000.

Paramor left it until May 1959 before taking Mike back into the singles market. 'Moments Of Love' was a smooth ballad that Paramor had Mike squeeze into a Sunday session between variety weeks in Cheltenham and Glasgow. It was recorded at the Record Supervision Studios and was Mike's only session in the UK away from Abbey Road. Joe Meek, soon to become a Sixties legend as the man behind the Tornadoes' hit record of 'Telstar', was the recording engineer. Paramor's hopes for the song failed to materialise. In fact, the results were disastrous. Sales didn't even reach the 10,000 mark. It was Mike's worst return for two years. Amazingly, the next release was even worse. 'Life Is A Circus' and 'For You' were Mike's two songs from the *Life Is A Circus* film and were released as a single in August 1959. The timing was bizarre, as the film itself did not go on general release until May 1960. But even if the timing had been right, neither of the songs was right for the singles market. Sales were derisory.

Mike might have been losing the plot in the singles market, but he was still carving out a reputation as a top-quality vocalist. In January 1959, Mike had cut the first two of a dozen songs for his first 12-inch LP release. EMI provided a full 25-piece orchestra, that also backed the 'Life Is A Circus' single. The expense was wasted on the film songs but the two album tracks were gems.

The songs were 'Strange Music', from the 1944 musical *Song Of Norway* and 'The Folks Who Live On The Hill', a 1937 product of an occasional partnership between composer Jerome Kern and lyricist Oscar Hammerstein. Both were songs that Mike knew well, and indeed the Kern title was one of the rejected masters from Mike's *Sentimental Journey* sessions the previous year. Paramor's lush arrangement made full use of the 15-strong string section and Mike needed just four takes to produce a classic vocal rendition.

Norrie Paramor had ten more songs lined up for the rest of

the album and would normally have spread them over at least two further sessions. Mike's heavy TV and variety schedule, however, plus Paramor's own commitments with Cliff Richard and the Shadows meant that both sessions had to be crammed into a single day. That day was 26th March 1959. It was arguably the finest of Mike's recording career.

'Mike has always been at his happiest singing melodies of his own choice,' the album's sleeve note said. All 12 titles on the LP were his personal choice, although Paramor would have liked to see him branching out a little more. 'He has picked many songs here that were associated with Bing Crosby and hopes that the similarity is not marked,' he wrote in an internal EMI memo. Mike would go on to record three more 12-inch albums for Columbia, but *Mike*, the product of the March 1959 sessions, remained his favourite.

Recording ten titles in a single day would be a challenge for any singer. Mike was never a fast worker in the studio, unlike Bing Crosby who was known in the business as 'one-take Crosby' because of his in-and-out approach to sessions. Mike's recordings usually ran from seven to 17 takes, or even more. Some of that was down to nature of the material. The new songs that Paramor fed him for the singles market were never Mike's cup of tea. Surviving session tapes show how it usually took him several takes to shake off his natural, Forties-style approach to a song.

Mike was also as nervous in the studio as he was on stage. His spells at the microphone were punctuated with lengthy bouts of coughing and throat clearing, a process that often carried on into the first few bars of the song. The first three or four takes of a new song rarely got beyond the first eight bars. Even some of the issued takes had to be edited to eliminate any throat clearing from Mike as the orchestra started up.

The March session was different. Mike knew all the songs by heart and Paramor's arrangements, whilst fresh and modern, were sufficiently traditional for Mike to feel instantly at home. For the afternoon session, where five titles were slated, an eleven-piece orchestra provided the accompaniment with the emphasis again on a set of lush, strings-based arrangements. It says much for Stuart Eltham's technical wizardry that the 50 per cent reduction in the size of the orchestra from the two tracks recorded in January is barely noticeable.

Mike romped through the five songs in just over three hours. 'Did You Ever See A Dream Walking', a Crosby hit from 1933, took just one take. Irving Kahal and Sammy Fain's 'I'll Be Seeing You', an anthem of wartime parting, needed just two starts. Even Johnny Mercer and Hoagy Carmichael's 'Skylark' – a notoriously difficult song to sing – was despatched with just four takes. By the time the studio clock showed 5.15, Mike had all five of the afternoon's numbers wrapped up.

He was back in the studio at 7 p.m. for the evening session. Five more standards needed to be completed by 10 o'clock. For this batch of songs, Paramor was looking for an up-tempo, Dixieland treatment. This time, Paramor was conducting an eight-piece band, with rhythm section plus trumpet, trombone and tenor sax/clarinet.

The five numbers included Irving Berlin's ballad 'Be Careful It's My Heart', written for Crosby's 1942 picture *Holiday Inn*. The song had been expected to be the big hit from the film until Berlin unveiled 'White Christmas' in the same movie. Crosby's rendition had been as a slow ballad, but Paramor's treatment and Mike's vocal demonstrated that even the tenderest ballad could be made to swing.

The other four songs fitted naturally to the faster pace. 'In The Good Old Summertime' had the three brass members of the eight-strong band working overtime, with Eltham's echo prominent. Mike's vocal, completed in just three takes, is a wonderful example of rhythm singing. And for once, the apprentice outshone his master. Crosby had recorded the song in 1951 and would do so again in his final session in 1977, but neither of his versions competes with Holliday's.

The final song on the evening session was yet another oldie. Dorothy Fields and Jimmy McHugh wrote 'I Can't Give You Anything But Love' in 1928, but even 75 years on, the song shows no sign of falling out of favour. Mike's treatment owes a lot to Crosby's 'Now You Has Jazz', his classic duet with Louis Armstrong from the 1956 movie, *High Society*. Mike uses Field's rarely heard verse – 'Gee but its tough to be broke kid / its not a joke kid, it's a curse' – to mimic the way Crosby opened 'Jazz' ('Dear gentlefolk of Newport, or maybe I should say hats and cats'). Holliday then allows the melody to build, taking the first chorus with just guitar and percussion support before the brass is let loose during the first orchestral break. Over the break, Mike talks Paramor through the members of the band ('This is Henry, who's playing the liquorice stick – always wanted to play one of them when I was a boy') in a manner identical to Crosby's trawl around the members of Armstrong's All-Stars. And just as Crosby ended his piece with 'And that's jazz', Mike signs off in the same manner, throwing in 'And that's love' as the orchestra ends its final release.

The album appeared in the shops in September 1959. Mike was featured in a strong colour cover, sitting in a park enjoying the 1959 summer – one of the best of the post-war decade. The album's title was simply *Mike*, although up until the point of release, the working title had been *Takin' It Easy*. That original title even survived long enough for the first batch of discs to be pressed with *Takin' It Easy* on the label. Why the change was made isn't clear. It may simply have been nothing more than Mike's resistance to anything that added to the 'Mr Relaxation' tag that was already weighing heavily on his shoulders.

With Mike still riding the crest of his successes in 1958, the critics found *Mike* an easy album to praise. 'As each new release comes along, you find an extra maturity about his work,' said *Record Mail*, whilst *Melody Maker*'s reviewer offered the view that 'his rendering of "The Folks Who Live On The Hill" alone makes the record worth buying'.

Sales were good. Britain's LP market was still a fledgling in 1959, with 78s (still), 45s and EPs dominating the sales figures. The 12-inch version of *Mike* sold 5,000 copies, a more than acceptable return. It was sufficient, too, to prompt EMI to release

146

the album on three separate EP records. One oddity was that although EMI possessed a stereo master of the album, these were used only for the EPs. In later years, EMI lost sight of the fact that they had recorded the album in stereo. Two re-releases, on the Encore label in 1965 and Memoir in 1988, were both taken from the original mono LP master.

With the LP in the shops, Norrie Paramor turned his attention to getting Mike back into the singles charts. It was not unlike the situation they had faced at the end of 1957. No one doubted the quality of Mike's vocals, and what's more, he now had a hit-making track record. All it needed was the right song.

When Mike returned to London in November 1959, his stress levels were high. A series of one-nighters in Ireland had been cut short by what the press described as a throat ailment. As with Mike's illness in 1958, the press release may have been a screen for something different. Although Mike was rushed back to London for a Harley Street appointment in the first week of October, the 'throat ailment' seems not to have impaired his ability to sing. A commitment to record a television show for ITV on 6th October was honoured, and the following Sunday Mike made his debut on television's most prestigious show – *Sunday Night At The London Palladium*.

Val Parnell's hour of live TV variety had become the flagship of ITV's weekend schedule. The show first went on the air in 1955, but only took off when Bruce Forsyth replaced Tommy Trinder as the host and compere in 1958. Forsyth made his reputation in the show's audience-participation game slot, *Beat The Clock*, a spot that subsequently spawned *The Generation Game*, again with Forsyth. Whilst *Beat The Clock* offered ten minutes of riotous fun, the rest of the hour offered the best of traditional variety. It was a prestigious booking for any performer.

Mike took second spot to American singer Lena Horne on the show that went out on 11th October 1959. His had been a late booking and something that he felt had been foisted upon him. 'It all came in rather a hurry and I didn't have anything ready,' he told Stan White. 'Marge thinks I picked the wrong songs.'

147

No tape survives, but Mike seems to have failed to pick up the pace of the show. 'He was little boy lost on the Palladium stage,' one critic said.

After the Palladium, Mike went into two weeks' variety in Manchester and Leeds, taking the opportunity of a spell in the north to continue his summer liaison with Margaret Burrows. The week at the Leeds Empire culminated in the split with Hal Monty, and Mike was still reeling from the stress of that when Norrie Paramor rang him and asked him to look over some possible singles.

Mike's first reaction to the songs that Paramor had in mind was that none of them were suitable. A day later, the arranger was back on the phone. He had another song that had just come in which he wanted Mike to take a look at. Its title was 'Starry Eyed'.

The song was the latest from the pen of American lyricist Earl Shuman, to a melody by Mort Garson. Shuman and Garson would produce 'Theme For A Dream' in 1961, a song that Paramor chose to direct towards Cliff Richard rather than to Mike. Mike could tell that Paramor was enthusiastic about 'Starry Eyed' and they immediately booked a slot in Abbey Road. This time, Paramor gave the task of coming up with an arrangement for the song to Eric Jupp. Like Ken Jones, Jupp was a regular EMI session man and also handled the arrangements for Cyril Stapleton's BBC Show Band.

Paramor's selection of Ken Jones to handle the arrangement for 'The Story Of My Life' in December 1957 had been a masterstroke. Jupp's appointment, he hoped, would have a similar revitalising effect. This time however, the move backfired.

Holliday had misgivings from the start. No one questioned Jupp's musical pedigree, but his style was more elaborate and ornate than Holliday was used to. When he turned up at Abbey Road for an evening session on 30th October 1959, Mike found that the various suggestions he had made about the scoring of 'Starry Eyed' had been ignored. Jupp's arrangement put a premium on strings, and Holliday found six violinists in the studio, plus an eight-strong vocal group led by Mike Sammes.

148

'The Man Who Would Be Bing' - Norman Milne in Crosby-like pose
Photo courtesy Michael Milne

Mike sings at an outdoor concert at Butlin's, 1954, as Eric Winstone (right) conducts
Photo courtesy Michael Milne

Recording in the 'garden shed', Abbey Road Studio 2, December 1957. Mike recorded 'The Story Of My Life' at this session

Photo © EMI Records

THE CRAZY GANG · BUD FLANAGAN · NERVO AND KNOX · NAUGHTON AND GOLD

with "Monsewer" Eddie Gray

"LIFE IS A CIRCUS" u

also starring SHIRLEY EATON and MICHAEL HOLLIDAY   LIONEL JEFFRIES   ERIC POHLMAN   JOSEPH TOMELTY

Produced by M. Smedley Aston.   Written and Directed by Val Guest.   Guest Star CHESNEY ALLEN   British Lion Films

On the set of *Life Is A Circus*, with Shirley Eaton, September 1958

With Margie in the grounds of *Dailson*, 1959

Photo courtesy Michael Milne

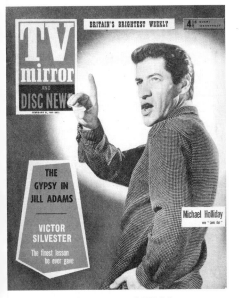

Featured on the cover of *TV Mirror*,
February 1959

Margie with Bing, California, May 1959
Photo courtesy Michael Milne

Mike parks his Ford Fairlane, Floral Hall, Scarborough, 1959

Mike recounts his wartime service alongside featured star Russ Conway (right) on BBC's *This Is Your Life*, December 1959, with host Eamonn Andrews (left)

Mike and his faithful tape recorder, 1960
Photo © EMI Records

Mike and Bing - 'The Great Croz' -
London, October 1960
Photo courtesy Michael Milne

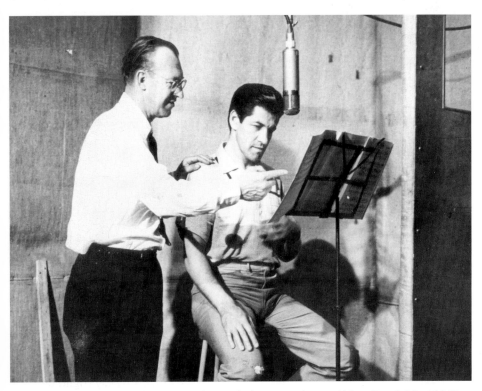

Norrie Paramor gives Mike some pointers during a session at Abbey Road, May 1960
Photo © EMI Records

Mike and Margie face the press after Mike's release from hospital, October 1961

Running through the script for BBC Light Programme's *The Bob Hope Show*, November 1961 with (L to R) Jerry Desmonde, Jeannie Carson, Peter Sellers and Bob Hope

Mike appears at an
EMI/Radio Luxembourg
promotion, September
1962 as Margie and Mike
junior look on

Photo © EMI Records

Mike on the set of *Holliday At Home*, January 1963

Photo courtesy Kenneth Lawson

Fellow crooner, Dickie Valentine (right) guests on *Holliday At Home*, January 1963

The final hours - with Freddie Mills (right), 29 October 1963

The biggest problem with the arrangement came at the start of the record. The song itself was typical Fifties – simple, non-offensive lyrics around a boy-girl love theme, an uncomplicated rhythm in the background, and a simple and easy to remember melody. Jupp's arrangement had the rhythm couched in a 'bell' effect, with Sammes's group of four girls and four boys providing the 'bong-bong-bong' bell theme. The arrangement required the singers to start the record off in a very high key. It was apparent from the first take that they would struggle. Of the 13 takes that were recorded that night, nine of them collapsed inside the first eight bars as the singers struggled with the key for their opening.

Paramor, who produced the session, pronounced himself satisfied with take 13 and moved onto the two other scheduled numbers, 'I Have Waited' and 'The Steady Game'. Mike had misgivings and called Paramor the next day to express them. When Paramor heard the test pressing of the session later that day, he was of the same view. The final take of 'Starry Eyed' was easy on the ear, but lacked a commercial edge. Mike's vocal was as ever, tuneful and melodic, but it was essentially what Mike himself called a 'lope-a-long' performance – pleasant and relaxed, but not commercial.

Mike was back in the studio a week later for a new arrangement, this time written by Paramor who also conducted the session. Eric Jupp never worked with Mike again. Paramor's treatment required only bass, drums and two electric guitars. The singing group was in evidence again, but less prominent than in the first session. Paramor's treatment also took the song along at a faster pace, requiring Mike to deliver a crisp, clipped vocal – not his usual style by any means.

The result was spectacular. 'Starry Eyed' was released in December 1959 and entered the first chart of the Sixties at number 28. Within two weeks, it was at number five, and on 30th January 1960, it gave Mike his second number one hit. He was only the thirteenth performer since the charts began in 1952 to take a second record to the top spot.

There could be no better way to start the new decade. The hitmaker was back. The Sixties, it seemed, would hold no terrors for Michael Holliday.

Chapter 15

Be My Guest

The overtures that Hal Monty and the Delfont Agency had put out to the ITV companies had started to bear fruit in the autumn of 1959. Even before then, Mike had been no stranger to ITV, but from the end of 1959 he became a regular part of the line-up.

His first featured programme was unusual to say the least. ITV sought to bring the thrills and spills of the circus ring to the small screen with a new show called *Hippodrome*. Mike was recruited as master of ceremonies, if not quite ringmaster, and to sing a couple of songs. It was a show with a Continental flavour, with all of the acts bar Mike drawn from touring circuses around Europe. Mike was usually the only British face in the cast. Jugglers, clowns, trapeze artistes and trampolinists made their way to the Wood Green Empire where a made-for-television circus ring was set up.

Mike was uneasy. 'I wasn't sure it was right for me,' he said in a taped letter, 'singing in a circus.' Norrie Paramor's involvement as musical director helped put Mike at ease and the producer's willingness to let him sing songs from the *Mike* album rather than promote his singles was another plus. And with a fee of £300 per show, the money was good.

Mike recorded nine *Hippodrome* shows for Associated-Rediffusion (ARTV) between September 1959 and March 1961. The shows went down well, so much so that ARTV offered Mike a 26-show contract. Mike said no. He had never really

151

come to terms with the idea of performing in a circus ring. 'I feel if I do too many I will eventually lose my identity and become the fella who sings with the circus,' said Mike in a letter to ARTV in November 1960.

Mike's other ITV appearances were more conventional. They included a guest spot on *Those Beverley Sisters* in January 1960, regular appearances alongside Sheila Buxton in a Western-oriented programme called *Buckaroo*, and a *Saturday Spectacular* of his own in March.

Mike's tape recorder made the trip with him across from the BBC, as did the hang-up about his height. The show with the Beverley Sisters was carefully staged so that he was never seen standing alongside the three sisters. Mike sang 'Starry Eyed' (as he did on just about every appearance in the early months of 1960) sitting on some stairs whilst the Bevs sat across the set from him. For the finale, Mike joined the sisters and comedienne Irene Handl for a spoof of the Avons' hit 'Seven Little Girls Sitting In The Back Seat'. Mike took the role of the driver in a vintage car prop, with the producer making a clever use of mirrors to double up the images of the Bevs to create the seven girls. The production worked well, and again avoided Mike having to stand alongside the taller trio.

Saturday Spectacular, however, was more of a challenge. It ran for a full hour with Mike topping the bill, even though it was fellow singer Glen Mason who acted as master of ceremonies. Mike appeared in camera alongside all the guests who included comedienne Libby Morris and the comedy double act of Mike and Bernie Winters (a poor-man's Morecambe and Wise). There was no way of avoiding a height comparison, no matter where the cameras were placed. The only solution was for Mike to wear a pair of outrageous 'lifts' in his shoes that almost turned them into miniature stilts. Shoes apart, the rest of the show was classic Michael Holliday. His first appearance in the show found him in a hammock, and whilst he donned a tuxedo for 'Skylark' and 'Starry Eyed', the familiar sweater was back for a very relaxed tape recorder duet.

152

The press made much of Mike's move to ITV, so much so that critics thought he had severed all links with the BBC. One tabloid TV critic, James Green commented that he had been surprised to come across Mike – 'the one-time blue-eyed boy of the BBC' – recording a programme in the Beeb's Manchester studios. Mike had in fact not signed any exclusive deal with ITV. The show that Green was referring to was the product of the debate about the half-hour shows that Richard Stone had started over 12 months before.

Despite the misgivings of the BBC hierarchy, John Ammonds was convinced that Holliday had a lot more to give – and wanted to try and keep his talent at the BBC. Ammonds was close to Tom Sloan and worked hard to persuade him to allow Mike to do a half-hour pilot. The show retained the same set from Mike's 15-minute shows, and indeed took the idea of Mike's flat into the title as *Holliday At Home*. Sheila Buxton and Dave King were signed up as guests, together with four girl dancers and the Northern Dance Orchestra. Rehearsals and taping was set for the first week of December 1959.

The choice of Dave King as the main guest was an interesting one and quite a coup for John Ammonds. King was also known to be contracted to ITV, but he and Mike were near neighbours in Addington. King was one of the few friends that Mike had on the inside of show business. By 1960, he was metamorphosing from singer to comedian, but for a few years in the mid-Fifties he had been a rival to Mike for the title of 'Britain's Bing Crosby'. His biggest hit record had been a number five placing in 1956 with 'Memories Are Made Of This', and he had been one of the also-rans in the race to the top with 'The Story Of My Life'.

King's singing days were behind him but the combination of two Crosby soundalikes was too good an opportunity to miss. Writer Ronnie Taylor came up with a routine for the show that played on their similarity to Bing as well as Mike's recent meeting with his idol:

Mike (to King):	He's [Bing] a great fan of yours, you know, although I must warn you. He has noticed it.
King:	Noticed it? Noticed what?
Mike:	You know, the bit about your voice sounding just like his.
King (exasperated):	My voice! My voice! Are you trying to tell me that I sing like Bing Crosby?
Mike:	Well that's what Bing says.
King:	He didn't happen to mention in passing that your voice is a dead pinch, did he?
Mike:	He didn't say that at all.
King:	Well he must be the only bloke who hasn't.

To prove to each other that they sounded nothing like Bing, Mike and Dave took turns at Crosby's 1932 hit song 'Please':

Dave:	There, does that sound anything like Crosby?
Mike:	Well, no...
Dave:	Go on then, you have a go.
Mike: (after singing)	Now be quite honest, truthful. Do I sound like Crosby?
Dave:	No. But I tell you something though.
Mike:	What's that?
Dave:	Its uncanny the way Crosby sounds like us!

Despite the subject matter, Mike was a long way short of being word perfect with the dialogue and even managed to mix up the words to the few bars of 'Please'. The errors went beyond the duet with King. Mike had arrived for the show's rehearsal and taping seriously under-prepared. John Ammonds was furious.
In January 1960, he wrote a long letter to Mike. Ammonds

154

had studied the tape of the show and had serious doubts as to whether it could even be broadcast. His letter pulled no punches:

> You must know how hard I worked myself to do all that I could to make it go well. I came down from Manchester to make sure that Dave King would definitely take part and tried to arrange things so that you had as little as possible to worry about. To put it bluntly, you did not bother to work on the script at all. Autocue is all very well, but not to stare at all the time! Why couldn't you have tried to learn *some* of the script?

Ammonds acknowledged that Mike had again been unwell during the rehearsals but he clearly felt badly let down:

> It was a bit late to realise the night before we went on that miming and doing a routine you didn't know was a difficult job.

Ammonds continued in similar vein to Keith Devon, Mike's new agent, who had enquired how the recording had gone. 'The show could have been a really first class programme,' he said, 'but I'll give you three guesses why it wasn't,' before laying the same litany of under-preparation that he had given to Mike. 'All of this will come as no great surprise to you,' he added. 'You know the difficulties with this artiste as well as I do.'

Devon perhaps hadn't appreciated the difficulties associated with Mike, although he was learning fast. Mike remained anxious to use Devon purely as a bookings agent, as distinct from the manager/agent role that Richard Stone had filled in the pre-Monty days. But after the spell with Monty, it was a case of once bitten, twice shy. With the help of a new personal secretary, plus Margie, he was intent on managing himself.

With a court case hanging over him, Mike could make few public statements about the fallout with Hal Monty. 'I had a personal manager for 18 months or so, but it didn't work out,' was his standard line to the press. He went on to espouse the virtues of self-management – no agent, no 10 per cent, he said

155

in several interviews, despite still being contracted to the Delfont Agency.

Whilst few would deny that the break with Monty was a move for the better, it was equally clear to those who knew Mike well that he needed a guiding hand. Babs and Teddie Beverley said later that the thing Mike lacked was self-discipline. He desperately needed a good manager. Guitarist Johnny Wiltshire started working closely with Mike in 1959 and observed the same thing. Mike not only needed someone to organise him, he said, but he also needed companionship and reassurance. The friendship with Wiltshire provided some of that, although as the Beverleys pointed out, Mike needed it all the time. They recalled a week's variety together where each evening ended with a long session to rebuild Mike's confidence and self-esteem.

The truth was that Mike had none of the qualities he needed if he was to manage his own affairs. He had no real business sense, was disorganised and inattentive to detail, and also highly sensitive. Wiltshire with his band, the Trebletones, toured widely with Holliday during 1959–61 and as Wiltshire took on the role of friend and confidant, he had sympathy for Keith Devon's ongoing struggle to build any kind of business relationship with Mike. 'Will you please sort him out!' was a regular plea from Devon to the guitarist.

'Mike was a highly sensitive person,' said Wiltshire. 'He even hated being on stage on his own.' That sensitivity gave rise to its own stock of unusual incidents. Wiltshire was back-stage one night when Mike suddenly appeared in the wings, having completed only the first song of his act. 'I didn't like the way the bass player in the pit was looking at me,' he said.

On another occasion, Wiltshire recalled Mike handing over the arrangements for his songs to an orchestra leader. 'These are in a bit of a state,' said the bandleader dismissively. Mike took the music back and without a word to anyone, went home.

In June 1960, Mike's disorganisation and lack of preparation landed him in the middle of the biggest public row yet with the BBC. Keith Devon had booked him to appear on Joan Regan's

Be My Guest programme. The show had recently moved to a prime-time spot. Devon regarded it as a prestigious booking.

Foreshadowing the Vera Lynn tape recorder duet later in the year, Mike had come up with the idea of a routine that involved both the tape and Regan. It was an intricate routine and needed plenty of rehearsal. But when the final band call came for the show, Mike was nowhere to be seen. After waiting for a couple of hours, producer John Street decided to make alternative arrangements and called in Dennis Lotis as a last-minute replacement for Mike.

The BBC issued a press release that made headlines. 'MIKE HOLLIDAY IS SACKED FROM TONIGHT'S SHOW', said the papers. Holliday was devastated. A tougher individual would have brushed it off but for someone with Mike's lack of self-belief, being 'sacked' by the BBC was massive. He was immediately on the phone to Tom Sloan, interrupting a meeting and insisting that he be put through. He followed up the call with a long letter, recounting in detail how he had misunderstood the location of the studio for the show. Mike had gone to the Television Centre, and then Lime Grove rather than the Riverside studios. Mike's concern was the insinuation that he had been late, or indeed just hadn't bothered to turn up. 'There are two commissionaires at TV Centre who will remember me asking [where the show was],' he wrote to Sloan.

The timing couldn't have been worse. Only a month or two before, Mike had heard from ARTV that they had decided against offering him an exclusive contract. 'It is difficult to forecast on a long-term basis what our requirements would be,' wrote their Head of Light Entertainment, Alan Morris. The words had the vagueness of an archetypal rejection letter.

With ARTV having turned him down (albeit surprisingly), Mike concluded that it had been a mistake to break away from the BBC. With John Ammonds's criticisms of his performance in the half-hour show still ringing in his ear, he had written to Tom Sloan only two weeks before the *Be My Guest* debacle, asking for an appointment to discuss another series of 15-minute

157

shows. 'I didn't really want to do half an hour but allowed myself to be talked into it,' he said. 'I'm much happier in the more intimate fifteen-minute shows which seem to have a great deal of appeal to the public.'

Sloan had been due to see him but the *Be My Guest* affair cooled his response. 'I can only advise you in your best interests that you do not get yourself into a similar situation in the future,' he said in reply to Mike's explanation for his non-appearance. 'I hope that it will be possible to see you in our programmes from time to time,' he added. It was hardly the commitment that Mike was seeking. Other than a guest spot on a Dickie Valentine show in September 1960, it would be two years before the familiar face of Michael Holliday was seen again on BBC television.

Joan Regan remembered the 'sacking' incident but still recalled Mike with great affection. 'He was a lovely fella,' she said, 'but a bit "dizzy".' 'Dizzy' is a polite expression for someone who by now was building a reputation for being highly unreliable.

Maurice Burman of *Melody Maker* took the opportunity of the *Be My Guest* episode to lay some charges in front of Mike. 'I don't do that sort of thing deliberately and I don't like putting other people out,' said Mike. At the same time, Mike admitted to turning up late for 'big TV shows' to avoid hanging around whilst other acts rehearsed their numbers.

Burman also rattled the skeleton of an interview that he had arranged with Mike three months previously, when Mike hadn't turned up. 'My wife was taken into hospital and I've been meaning to phone you ever since,' was Mike's reply. It was classic Holliday – genuinely sorry, full of remorse and offering enough charm to get himself off the hook.

Norrie Paramor said after Mike's death that it was almost worth putting up with Mike's lateness just to hear his outrageous excuses. Johnny Pearson, who worked with Mike on both television and radio, recalled one session when Mike arrived late, looking very distraught. He got little sympathy from the producer. 'What's the excuse this time?' he asked. 'Sorry boss,' said Mike 'but my horse died.'

The response brought howls of laughter from the band at the most excessive excuse yet, but the sad part of it, said Pearson, was that it was true. 'Mike really loved his horses and one of them had died in his arms. He was in tears.'

Mike's love of horses reflected his enthusiasm for Western films. The role of a singing cowboy, riding the range with just a horse for a friend, was close to Mike's definition of Paradise. The closest that he came to it was as a 20-inch puppet called Tex Tucker.

Tex Tucker was the sheriff in *Four Feather Falls*, a make-believe Western town that provided the title for a new piece of children's television. The show was one of the first products from a new company, AP Films Ltd. *Four Feather Falls* was the latest step on the route to stardom for one of the company's founders, Gerry Anderson. His later creations of *Supercar*, *Stingray*, and ultimately *Thunderbirds* would establish him as a legend.

Puppets were popular in the Fifties. *Muffin The Mule* and *Pinky and Perky* are now part of Fifties folklore but Anderson was taking the art to a higher plane. *Four Feather Falls* featured over a dozen different characters and each episode was meticulously choreographed. The series also introduced a new approach to voice synchronisation. For the first time, the lip movement of the puppets was triggered by impulses from the recordings of the character's voices rather than by someone pulling strings. Whilst still indelibly wooden, the new technique marked a major step forward in realistic animation.

Each *Four Feather Falls* episode took days to film, and production of the series ran through most of 1959. The first show went out on 25th February 1960. The story-lines all revolved around the wholesome character of the sheriff. Tucker had been granted four pieces of Indian magic as a reward for saving the life of the daughter of local Indian Chief, Kalamakooya. The magic gave the power of speech to Tex's two deputies, horse Rocky and dog Dusty, as well as enabling Tex to fire his guns automatically by simply raising his hands.

Granada TV commissioned 39 episodes of *Four Feather Falls*.

159

Actors such as Nicholas Parsons and Kenneth Connor provided the speaking voices for the characters, with Parsons providing the non-singing voice of Tex. But when the puppet sheriff wasn't tracking down the show's regular cast of bandits and baddies, he was riding the range as a singing cowboy. That was where Mike came in. His role was to make Tex Tucker into a Roy Rogers character. Mike needed just an afternoon to record the six songs that were woven into the episodes, but nevertheless, he took the most prominent billing when the credits rolled at the end of each programme. EMI leapt onto the bandwagon too, and had Mike reprise the titles in the studio for a six-track EP.

Mike's increasing involvement in TV and radio commercials around this time was another growing part of his portfolio. His regular series on Radio Luxembourg all had commercial sponsors and the associated adverts were highly lucrative. Johnny Wiltshire recalled going along with Mike to record one jingle with a fee of 1,000 guineas for an afternoon's work. 'Mike couldn't believe it,' said Wiltshire.

One of Mike's best known jingles was 'Make The Day', an advertisement for Cadbury's Milk Tray chocolates. Cadbury's had sponsored Mike's earlier programmes on the 208 Station and in February 1960, they were behind a new series of 26 programmes scheduled on Mondays and Fridays over 13 weeks.

Lucky Numbers asked listeners to write in with the song title that they considered their lucky number. Winners had their songs performed by Mike and entered a draw for a holiday in Luxembourg. The series exposed Mike to a range of different songs, not unlike the material that he had performed in the Winstone days. His *Lucky Numbers* songs included several Lonnie Donegan hits, Cliff Richard's 'A Voice In The Wilderness' and Max Bygraves's 'Tulips From Amsterdam'. Ronnie Aldrich and the Squadronnaires, a throwback band from the Second World War, provided the backing. Under duress from Norrie Paramor, Aldrich also managed to weave Mike's newest singles into the *Lucky Numbers* repertoire.

Mike's best-known TV commercial, however, was for Shell petrol. The company's highly durable slogan was 'You Can Be

Sure Of Shell' and early in 1961, Mike recorded a series of television commercials that featured 'The Shell Song'. The success of the ads led to Mike being asked to record a full two and a half minute version of the song for a disc that was given away at Shell petrol stations.

In November 1961, the ad took an unusual twist when Shell seized on Bing Crosby's presence in the UK and enlisted him to record another version of the song. 'We had to pay out a fair amount of money to get him but it's a great shot in the arm for the advertising film business,' a Shell spokesman said. Shell went out of their way to make it known that this time the voice was Bing himself, but the similarity of voice cast doubt as to whether other versions of the ad were Mike or Bing. Shell were quick to see the commercial potential. 'We have provided the public with a talking point – is it Bing or is it Holliday? That's good to have people talking about our product,' they said.

Mike reached the summer of 1960 still at the pinnacle of British show business. He had been there for just three years but it felt like he had been around much longer. 'He didn't come across as a pop star,' said Johnny Pearson. 'His appeal was more like a pal, someone who was nice to have around.' It was no surprise. Mike, whether deliberately or not, had taken more than just Crosby's voice as a role model. The affable, easy-going image that Bing Crosby marketed had been highly successful. It was no surprise that large chunks of that rubbed off on Mike, and the results were the same.

The questions for Mike in the summer of 1960 should have been about where to go next. He was an established star on both radio and TV and one of the few performers to have hit the top of the Hit Parade more than once. And much as he hated live appearances, he was in constant demand for personal appearances. More films perhaps, an assault on the US market, or maybe the British Empire territories of Australia and the Far East. All of them offered possibilities.

But those close to Mike were beginning to sense that something wasn't right. In the same month as the mix-up over *Be My Guest*, Mike was three hours late for a concert in Crewe and failed to appear at all for a similar engagement in Bangor. His lateness for appointments was also routine but was becoming tiresome. Increasingly, the business was starting to see Michael Holliday as 'difficult'.

Others noticed Mike retreating more into himself. 'His stardom seemed to lay heavily on his shoulders,' said Russ Conway in a BBC interview in 1993. 'It was as if he wanted the acknowledgement of his ability without having to go out there and show it,' said Conway. 'I watched him as he was leaving my flat one night and thought "there goes a troubled lad", but I didn't know what the trouble was. I didn't feel it was my business to ask.'

A year later, producer Ernest Maxin worked with Mike in summer season in Blackpool and observed the same thing. 'I knew there was something on his mind,' said Maxin, 'but the worst thing, knowing him, would be to say "What's worrying you?".'

Not everyone saw it. Margaret Burrows, the girl that Mike had met in Scarborough the previous year, continued to see him through 1960. She recalled no real change in his demeanour. 'I saw him several times during 1960 and spoke to him often on the phone,' she said, 'and he was always his usual, cheerful self. I never saw him depressed, even though he sometimes got annoyed if things went wrong.'

The most alarming change of all, however, was Mike's attitude to work. He had always been quick to point to his lack of ambition and how he didn't see show business as 'a real job'. It was a good public line, one that helped build the image of 'casual ol' Mike'. Until 1960, however, that public line had masked an individual who had undoubtedly worked his socks off to get to the top of the tree. But once there, his attitude changed. In the summer of 1960, he started turning work down – beginning with a lucrative summer season booking.

162

Chapter 16

The Last Good Year

It looked like 1960 was destined to be another big year. 'Starry Eyed' had progressed to the top of the charts at almost the identical time to 'The Story Of My Life' in 1958. It meant that Mike could look forward to another year when the work would come chasing him. His ITV appearances gave him good television exposure through the winter months, whilst the BBC finally screened the contentious half-hour show on 5th April 1960. John Ammonds's editing had eliminated many of the glitches and the reviews were good. Critics welcomed Mike back like an old friend and generally applauded the step up in the level of ambition in the show.

Meanwhile, Norrie Paramor set about finding the follow-up to 'Starry Eyed'. Another song from lyricist Earl Shuman caught his eye. 'Dream Talk' had much the same musical structure as 'Starry Eyed', but with a melody that was sufficiently different to avoid it sounding like the same record. With the usual boy-meets-girl lyric, it was a natural follow-up. The recording date was set for 10th March 1960.

Paramor's choice of song prompted a diplomatic incident with EMI. Wally Ridley, Paramor's counterpart at Columbia's sister label HMV, had arranged for Alma Cogan to record the same song a week earlier. Two years previously, Mike and Alma had competed for the honours on 'The Story Of My Life' and 'Stairway Of Love' and no one seemed bothered. Since then, things had changed. EMI's policy was that their contracted singers would not now compete with each other.

The dilemma facing EMI was whether to go with Holliday or Cogan. Alma's hit-making days were fading away although she was still one of EMI's biggest names. But Mike was just coming off a number one spot. By the time the mix-up came to light, Alma was already in the studio. Ridley had not followed the policy of advising his fellow A&R men that Cogan would record the song, and it was too late to pull the plug.

EMI prevailed upon Mike and Paramor to leave 'Dream Talk' to Alma, which they agreed to do, only for the company to have a last-minute change of heart. With the consent of the publisher, EMI agreed to both recordings going ahead and Mike went into Abbey Road on 10th March as planned.

With an agreed release date of 1st April, Paramor needed the session to go well. It didn't. The outcome was the same as Mike's first attempt at 'Starry Eyed'. Once again, it was the arrangement – this time his own – that left Paramor dissatisfied. The pace was too gentle, allowing Mike to lapse into his natural style of crooning. Paramor was looking for the crisper vocal that had made 'Starry Eyed' a winner. A week later, Mike was back in the studio. This time Paramor wrote the arrangement around a tighter, electric guitar backing.

The results were disappointing for both Mike and Alma. 'Dream Talk' is in the history books only because it was the first Michael Holliday single to be released only as a 45 rpm single and not on 78. Sales just tipped the 25,000 mark. It was enough for the record to tiptoe into the now extended Hit Parade at number 39, but no more. Some listings incorrectly attribute the success to the record's B side, 'Skylark'. With no singles stockpiled, Paramor had been forced to lift the Hoagy Carmichael song from the *Mike* album as a B-side filler.

Alma Cogan's version – which sounded very much like the arrangement that Paramor had rejected – suffered a similar fate. If EMI had stuck to its policy of only putting one version out, one or other – and more likely Mike – might have registered a Top Twenty spot. As it was, Norrie Paramor was left looking for something else to build on the momentum from 'Starry Eyed'.

Mike meanwhile headed off to a West End function to receive his silver disc to mark sales of 250,000 for 'Starry Eyed'.

Paramor had two projects in mind for Mike's next session and booked Mike into Abbey Road for a full week in June 1960. One day was set aside for another single with three sessions lined up for a second 12-inch album. Mike was let out on the fifth day to record *Be My Guest* with Joan Regan, but of course, never made it.

Paramor had found an unusual song as the next A-side release. 'Little Boy Lost' was based on the true story of an Australian boy who had miraculously survived three days alone in the Australian outback. The song's writers transplanted the story from Australia to the American West. The song, with a distinct cowboy feel to it, would not have been out of place in an episode of *Four Feather Falls*. Paramor again found an arrangement that showcased a prominent electric guitar. Mike's voice was well to the fore, exploiting the song's low notes as only he could.

'Little Boy Lost' also nudged its way into the Top Fifty, but only just. Its one-week appearance at number 50 in September 1960 was scant reward for another good record with what seemed a good commercial sound. The record buying public clearly didn't agree. Like 'Dream Talk', 'Little Boy Lost' has its place in the history books for all the wrong reasons. Its modest chart success was Michael Holliday's final appearance in a British pop chart.

Any self-respecting bookmaker would have laid long odds against such an outcome. The Sixties music revolution still hadn't extended beyond the doors of the Cavern Club in Liverpool, and with solo vocalists such as Frankie Vaughan and Perry Como still churning out hits, it seemed only a matter of time before Michael Holliday came up with his next one.

With hindsight, neither Mike nor Norrie Paramor appreciated how significant LPs would become for singers in the Holliday mould. The *Mike* album from 1959 had sold well, but albums were still seen as the icing on the cake. Within a few years, Mike's brand of singers would have all but deserted the singles market. By the end of the decade, even the Beatles were recording

165

albums and pulling tracks from them for a single release.

Even though LPs were not seen as the main fare, EMI was keen to follow up the success of *Mike*. Paramor and Mike had drawn up a long list of titles for that first full album, three times as many as could ever have been accommodated. Picking another twelve from the same list was a simple task.

The LP was recorded over three sessions. The first two saw Mike lay down seven ballads, backed by a 19-piece orchestra with a heavy strings bias. The remaining five titles were recorded at the final session on 3rd June. For these, Mike had an eight-piece band with a strong Dixieland sound. As with *Mike*, the album underwent a last-minute change of title from *Mike Sings And Swings* to *Holliday Mixture*. This time the change was made in time for the new title to appear on the label, although Mike was dissatisfied with the sound. He felt that the pressing put too much emphasis on the bass with the result that his vocals lost clarity, and insisted that the album was re-pressed. It was, but not before 1,000 copies had been released. Mike was still unhappy with the second version, believing this time the engineers had over-compensated.

Despite the technical problems, the finished product was every bit as good as the *Mike* album. All the songs were standards and inevitably, 11 of the 12 had strong associations with Crosby. Even the odd man out (Al Jolson's 'Swanee') had appeared on a recent Crosby LP. Mike again demonstrated an ability to bring something new to Crosby's songs, prompting one reviewer to comment that 'anything Bing can do, Mike can do better – or so it seems'. Mike's vocals on tracks such as 'Just A Prayer Away' and 'I Promise You' are almost faultless – perfect examples of breath control, diction and the reading of a lyric.

The up-tempo songs on *Holliday Mixture* added to Mike's reputation as a rhythm singer. They included the Irving Berlin standard 'Alexander's Ragtime Band' and one song that had special significance for Mike. 'Margie', a song from 1920, first appeared on disc in a recording by the Original Dixieland Jazz Band. Bing Crosby revived the song on radio in the late Fifties and one line in particular caught Mike's ear. The original lyric said, 'I have bought a home and ring and everything' to which Bing added 'a TV and everything' into the line. Mike had first heard Bing's version on a tape from Stan White. 'TV and everything,' chuckled Mike in his taped reply, 'like that!' Mike duly replicated the line in his album track but went on to personalise it even more. When he and Margie added a dog to their growing coterie of animals at Dailson, Mike changed the line on a BBC broadcast to 'I have a bought a home and a ring, a poodle and everything'.

Mike's schedule after his week of recording would normally have seen him taking a summer show on a short provincial run-in ready for the start of the season. This year, however, his summer was clear. Keith Devon had tried hard to persuade him to take a summer booking. It was still the most lucrative part of the entertainment calendar and almost unthinkable for a major star to turn his back on it.

Knowing that Mike had spent the last two summers in Blackpool and Scarborough – both 500-mile round trips from home – Devon had been sensitive to Mike's desire to be closer to home. He had come up with offers for shows in Yarmouth and then Brighton. The latter seemed ideal – it was one of the primary resorts for holidaymakers from the Home Counties and no more than 60 miles from Mike's home. Still Mike said no. Devon came back with a proposal for Weymouth, but again met the same response.

Devon's frustration continued to grow. 'It's a pity that you declined to go to Weymouth,' he wrote, 'as I do feel that you would have had a most happy season there.' Mike's one concession was a three-night spell at Weymouth over the Whitsuntide holiday weekend, introducing covers of 'Why' and 'Travellin' Light' into his act for the first time. 'Michael Holliday, the so relaxed singer with the so relaxed voice, makes it all seem so easy,' said one local review.

Devon arranged another early summer booking in Torquay. That eventually disappeared when the local theatre management got fed up with waiting for Mike to sign the contract. Whilst

Devon looked around for other bookings to fill the summer void, Mike himself made arrangements with impresario Louis Rodgers for a two-week Irish tour. It was low-key to say the least. At a time when Mike could have been heading the cast at a top summer season resort, he was playing a series of one-nighters in small ballrooms in County Cork.

It was the same story when Devon came up with more variety dates. Mike turned down a week's variety in his home town of Liverpool, telling Devon that 'I do not wish to do any variety for a while and will let you know when'.

When the agent next turned his attention to the pantomime season, again he found Holliday hard to please. 'I did have one or two first-class suggestions for you to play pantomime this season, but you told me you were not interested,' he wrote to Mike in May 1960.

By August, Mike had changed his mind again. He agreed to a four-week appearance in *Mother Goose*, two weeks in Gloucester, followed by a fortnight in the Yorkshire mill town of Dewsbury. They were hardly top-line venues but both the money (£325 per week) and the format (a self-standing 20-minute guest appearance) were the critical things and both were good.

It is a moot point whether Mike's attitude was based on a need to protect himself from the pressures that live performing put him under, or whether he was developing a death wish about his career. Press interviews that he gave at the time contain evidence of both. He told Gordon Tucker for a piece called *ShowTime* that he was comfortably off, didn't like touring, and thought that variety was 'dying fast'. When he added, however, that he 'hadn't overlooked the possibility that some day people won't want to hear me sing any more', it suggested that he was beginning to talk himself out of the business. Talk of plans to buy a farm in Sussex or Ireland added to that impression.

Nevertheless, Tucker's article painted a picture of a man who seemed to be in control; honest enough to admit that what he did wasn't hard work; willing to admit that he had money in the bank without sounding like a braggart; and realistic enough to see that his success might not last forever. But beneath the surface, the picture was less clear-cut.

Mike's behaviour was now becoming increasingly erratic. In July 1960, he served notice on the Delfont Agency. It came without warning, although the signs had been there almost from the start that Mike wanted away. His notice letter had gone to Delfont himself, who intervened personally to persuade him to carry on. Yet again the working relationship was redefined, a compromise that just confused everyone even more.

Holliday himself compounded it. In August 1960, he scribbled a handwritten note to the BBC that was addressed to no one in particular. 'Dear Sir,' said the letter, 'This is to inform you that I am not solely represented by any agent and any future bookings should be referred to me directly.' It was a misleading letter in the light of the decision to stay with Delfont, although its style held a bigger clue to Mike's state of mind. He was a big star and well known at the highest levels in the BBC, yet his letter had more in keeping with his hopeful punt for an audition in 1955.

Mike's confidence in his financial standing was also misplaced. Baker Todman, the accountants he had appointed in 1958, had taken time to get Mike's financial affairs under control. Part of the problem had been the inadequacy of Mike's record-keeping. The business customs of late 1950s Britain compounded the problem. This was still a cash society, with most of Mike's live appearances being 'cash on the night' affairs. It was only when Keith Devon brought in a 'percentage take' arrangement that cheques started to appear. Even then, many of Mike's one-nighters were still done on a part cash basis. As late as October 1959, the accountants were still telling Mike that that 'no records have been kept of your income, no details are available of the amounts paid into your bank account and no details are available of cash expenditure'.

By the middle of 1960, however, things were coming under control. Mike dealt with his outstanding tax liability of £1,250 from 1958 promptly, and the correspondence from his accountants indicates a degree of order for the first time. Mike's accounts for 1959 were also nearing completion, and revealed handsome earnings. It was no surprise to find Mike telling *Photoplay* that 'I'm earning enough money to keep me and the tax man happy. What's the point in killing myself to try and make more?'

Despite responding diligently to his accountant's requests, Mike was still making no provision for the tax liabilities that came with his increased earnings. At the same time, his outgoings were increasing. The cars, the horses, the luxurious fittings in Dailson all ate into Mike's earnings, as too did his generosity. He made sure that his mother in Liverpool was well supported and was equally generous towards his girlfriends. Margaret Burrows recalled Mike on more than one occasion handing over a wad of notes that equated almost to her annual salary to 'go and do some shopping'. When she failed to spend the money in the two hours or so that Mike was otherwise engaged, she was, he said, 'the only woman who has ever given me money back'.

None of that would have been a concern had Mike's earnings continued at their 1959 level, but they didn't. The royalties from 'Starry Eyed' were good, but not enough to compensate for no summer season, no BBC TV series and limited radio income. When Baker Todman drew up Mike's 1960 accounts, his gross earnings were down from £32,000 to £14,000. Net income assessable for tax fell from £12,000 to £5,000. It was still good money by ordinary standards, but in comparative terms, Mike was back to where he had been two years before. Money would soon join the list of things that kept him awake at night.

The autumn of 1960 was dominated by Bing Crosby's visit to Britain and the time that Mike spent in his company. Two weeks ahead of his second meeting with Bing, however, Mike had started a new series of radio programmes for the BBC. It would turn out to be the most durable and happiest engagement of his career.

Holliday With Strings was a play on the title of David Rose's famous piece 'Holiday For Strings', written in 1943. The show

170

paired Mike with pianist and arranger Johnny Pearson, later to become musical director for *Top Of The Pops* and composer and arranger of the music in TV's *All Creatures Great And Small*. It was a 30-minute show for the Light Programme, broadcast in the prime-time mid-evening slot.

John Browell, a BBC staff producer, handled the shows. Browell had been responsible for producing Eric Winstone's broadcasts from Butlin's at Clacton and remembered Mike from those days. Although he hadn't seen Mike since, they soon established a happy working relationship for the *Holliday With Strings* shows.

The pattern of the show couldn't have suited Mike more. They were recorded at the BBC's Paris studios in Lower Regent Street, with a three-hour rehearsal and run-through of the material. The show itself was done in a single live take rather than an edit of songs and dialogue. Mike featured six or seven songs in each show, with Johnny Pearson and the orchestra also taking a handful of solo spots. The linking dialogue was minimal, and in essence all that Mike needed to do was turn up and sing. Browell realised that Mike felt at home. 'He was a singer, not an entertainer' was Browell's perceptive observation in 1991.

Johnny Pearson, speaking in a BBC radio feature in 1993, remembered the shows very fondly. Mike was, he said, an assured performer. 'He was a very good listener and picked things up very quickly. You only needed to run through something once with him.' Even then, Mike's problem with lyrics still surfaced. 'Gee John, almost missed the boat on that one,' was a familiar line.

Mike featured a broad range of songs on *Holliday With Strings*. They included tracks from his albums, the latest singles, covers of hits by Matt Monro and Ronnie Carroll, plus the odd gem from Mike's Crosby songbook that he never got round to recording. The success of the shows went beyond anyone's expectations. The first series of 13 shows was immediately extended to another 13 and then 13 more. It meant Mike had an unbroken run of 39 weeks from October 1960 through to June 1961. The show returned again in April 1962 for a further 17 weeks.

171

With a weekly schedule for *Holliday With Strings* plus *Lucky Numbers* and ITV's *Hippodrome*, Mike was at home for most of the autumn of 1960. He and Margie still presented a picture of domestic harmony, although that was briefly disturbed in November when Michael junior fell from the roof of the portico that adjoined Dailson and suffered a fractured skull.

For a day or two, his condition was critical. Mike and Margie mounted a round-the-clock vigil by his hospital bed before being told that he was out of danger, freeing Mike to honour a charity commitment in Manchester.

Outwardly, Mike and Margie's marriage still seemed strong. The letter tapes to Stan White continued to paint a picture of happy domesticity, whilst Johnny Wiltshire recalled Mike's genuine love and affection for Margie. Wiltshire and his wife spent Christmas Day with the Hollidays and he was left in no doubt about Mike's feelings for Margie. 'He thought the world of her,' he said.

But still the procession of girls into his dressing room went on. Margie travelled with him only infrequently, and with Michael junior heading off to boarding school, suddenly she had time on her hands. The pretty, homely wife of the late 1950s now began to take on the look of a show business wife. Her hair was dyed and expensively coiffeured, the jewellery became more apparent, and her clothes reflected the wealth that they now enjoyed (as indeed did Mike's). They were beginning to drift apart. 1960 would be the last good year.

Chapter 17

'That Freddie Mills Business'

Mike had seen out 1960 with a busy month in ITV's studios. Early in the month, he recorded a guest spot on *Vera Lynn's Saturday Spectacular*. The show was in effect a Christmas special and Mike topped the bill in a strong cast that also included comedian Freddie Frinton, who performed his famous 'drunken toff' routine. Aside from the tape recorder duet with Vera, Mike had three solos.

The first was his new record, recorded just the week before. 'Catch Me A Kiss' was indeed catchy, if corny, and Mike's decision to feature it was the source of another minor row within EMI. Mike should have sung 'Stay In Love' which was the designated A side of his new single, although the disc was another of those where the distinction between the A and B sides was far from clear. 'Stay In Love' was a pleasant ballad but not chart material. *Melody Maker*'s review echoed the view. ' "Catch Me a Kiss",' it said, 'was a lively number with a spark of originality. Definitely the better side.'

The stronger commercial appeal of the B side was probably the reason why Mike chose to sing it on the show (although in fact, he mimed to the record). The marketing chiefs were soon on Norrie Paramor's tail. 'Michael agreed to support us 100 per cent on this record,' they said, 'but we were somewhat disappointed on Saturday evening when he sang the B side. We really must all work on one side.'

True to form, Mike had turned up late for recording of the

TV show and again was under-rehearsed. Appearing in a tuxedo, he went in front of the cameras with one part of his bow tie tucked under the collar, as intended, but with the other half waving freely on top of his shirt. The roving mike that he wore around his neck dangled like an ill-fitting hangman's noose.

By now, there was also a noticeable change in his physical appearance. The fresh, youthful face of two years ago had disappeared. Always lean, now he looked drawn and tired. His eyes seemed to have lost their sparkle and his eyelids hung heavy and hooded.

His soft-shoe shuffle in the middle of 'Catch Me A Kiss' was amateurish to say the least, whilst his patter between his first and second songs came across as confused. His attempted joke at Vera's expense came across as an unpleasant dig, implying that by the time he got to rehearsal, 'Vera Lynn had taken all the best songs'. The reality, of course, was that the host's songs and his own were entirely separate.

Mike's other two songs were 'The Folks Who Live On The Hill', and 'I've Got My Love To Keep Me Warm'. He made mistakes with the words on both, transposing some lines on 'Folks' whilst coming up with a strange set of homegrown lyrics for 'I've Got My Love To Keep Me Warm'. A core line in the song is 'What do I care how much it may storm / I've got my love to keep me warm'. Mike's first attempt came out as 'What do I care if rainbows don't call', followed next time around by 'What do I care if he don't cut his hair'. It was an attempted joke at the expense of bandleader Jack Parnell, but was lost on everyone else in the studio.

On Christmas Eve, Mike was one of the stars in ITV's *A Christmas Card From The Stars*. From there, he headed to Gloucester for the pantomime that Keith Devon had booked. *Mother Goose* opened on Boxing Day and ran for a two-week season, followed by another two weeks in Dewsbury. The pantomime and a few nights' cabaret in Manchester were Mike's only live appearances until the summer of 1961. The rest of his work was entirely studio based. *Holliday With Strings* and his

174

Luxembourg programmes continued their weekly runs, whilst in February he finally began his own series for ITV.

The 12 shows that Mike did for Associated-Rediffusion were a long way from the grand plans that Richard Stone had trailed in trying to hold the BBC to ransom. Mike handled his own negotiations with ARTV, freezing Keith Devon out yet again. 'I would certainly like to do some intimate programmes such as I did for the BBC a while back,' Mike said in a November 1960 letter. This was Mike returning to his comfort zone. Who could blame him? The criticisms that John Ammonds had made of his efforts in the BBC half-hour show were the kind that Mike took very much to heart.

Mike's offer to ARTV was something of a sop as he again turned down a 26-week offer on *Hippodrome*. This time, however, ARTV's Head of Light Entertainment Alan Morris took up the idea. He teamed Mike with producer Daphne Shadwell for 12 shows that aired at 7.15 p.m. each Friday from March to May. It was a good slot. Friday was a popular evening and Mike's show came just before the highly popular *Emergency Ward 10*. *Mike On Holliday* also featured Johnny Pearson, Mike's arranger from his current BBC radio series.

Nevertheless, the shows were low-budget, low-profile affairs. Mike's fee was only around £200 per show. The set, too, was simple and conventional. ARTV's budget did not run to the re-creation of Mike's TV 'flat', and with several designers taking turns what emerged was a conventional TV music set. Ken Lawson, Mike's set designer at the BBC, recalled the shows as possessing none of the individuality of the BBC programmes.

Daphne Shadwell's experiences with Mike were much like John Ammonds's. He was, she said, much smaller than she expected, always late, and always seemed to have a different girl with him. Mike didn't seem interested in socialising after the shows, she said, but nevertheless she developed a fondness for him (although the relationship was strictly professional).

The frustrations were also there. 'The series seems to be going well and everyone agrees that your pleasing personality has really

175

come across,' she said in a letter to Mike in May 1961, as the pre-recorded series was coming to its end. Mike by then had left for the summer in Blackpool. 'I wonder if there is anyone there to shout at you and make sure you're there on time!' she added. 'Don't forget to *work hard* and *pull your socks up!*'

Mike had some recording to do before heading off to Blackpool. The continuing drop in the sales of his singles was becoming an increasing concern for Norrie Paramor. 'Stay In Love' had flopped, the confusion over the A side not helping its prospects. Sales at just 10,000 copies were a disaster.

Mike's next single, in February 1961, did no better. The song, 'The Miracle Of Monday Morning', was published by Paramor's brother. *Melody Maker* said it was 'simple and tuneful, but whether it is a strong enough combination to collect the big dividends remains to be seen'. It was a polite way of forecasting a flop.

In May, Paramor thought he had finally found the song that would take Mike back into the charts. The writers were Sid Tepper and Roy Bennett, the partnership that had produced 'Stairway Of Love'. 'Dream Boy Dream' was the only title scheduled for Mike's Abbey Road session on 15th May 1961. Paramor was looking for a different treatment from Mike. More than any song he had done before, 'Dream Boy Dream' demanded a tight, clipped vocal. It was almost a song for a non-singer – a Rex Harrison in *My Fair Lady* or a Glynis Johns on 'Send In The Clowns'. To his delight, Paramor managed to get the sound that he wanted without recourse to a second session.

EMI released the record immediately; the reviews were encouraging. *Record Mirror* said 'You'll be surprised when you hear this – it's a new style for Michael and the disc is half over before you realise who it is. A good number very effectively put over. This might put Mr H. back into the top 20 after far too long an absence.' Mike, however, remained to be convinced. 'There seem to have a lot of mixed opinions about "Dream Boy Dream",' he said in a letter to Paramor, 'so we'll just have to wait and see and hope for the best.'

Wishing and hoping was all to no avail. With sales of just 5,000, 'Dream Boy Dream's' sales were calamitous. Mike was further away from chart success than he had ever been.

It is tempting to put the blame on Mike's lack of success in the charts on the Sixties revolution in pop music. The effects of that, however, were not seen in the charts until 1963. The 1961 charts had the same eclectic feel to them as the charts from the last years of the Fifties. If Frank Sinatra could find the Top Twenty with a recording of 'Ol' Macdonald Had A Farm', there was no inherent reason why Michael Holliday should not be there too.

Much of the blame rested on Mike's own shoulders. His unwillingness to make personal appearances, together with his distanced relationship from his agent Keith Devon, was beginning to tell. Just like his ARTV series, Mike was happy in his comfort zone. *Holliday With Strings* was full of the Crosby numbers that he loved, with little thought to promoting the singles that he held in such disdain. With no live appearances and no TV or radio spots on pop music shows, the absence of a record in the charts was no great surprise.

Much has been made of Mike's slavish attachment to Crosby. Was he wrong to follow Bing's wake so closely? Many of the people who Mike trusted urged him to break away from the dependence on Crosby's songs. Others, however, were happy for Mike to continue down the Crosby line. Despite suggestions to the contrary, Norrie Paramor seems to have been one of them. When a Blackpool collaboration with organist Reginald Dixon was proposed, Paramor wrote to Mike with 'a special request from yours truly' to include Crosby's 1936 hit 'Pennies From Heaven'. What's more, the 'tribute' album to Bing that Paramor had first proposed in 1958 was again back on the agenda.

Before that, however, Mike put another 12-inch LP together with a jazz combo led by veteran trombonist George Chisholm. *Happy Holliday* was an overt Dixieland album, supported by an all-star group that Chisholm assembled for the sessions. Chisholm had a long career in British dance bands behind him, although

177

at the time of his recordings with Mike he was best known for his slapstick comedy spots on TV's *Black And White Minstrels Show*.

Happy Holliday was a pleasant album and whilst Mike was clearly at home with the material, it lacked the variety that Paramor had brought to his two previous 12-inch LPs. Part of the difficulty was the band that Chisholm assembled for the sessions. Whilst thoroughbred in its jazz pedigree, its raucous tone didn't accommodate Mike's vocals as well as it might have. A month before the session with Chisholm, Mike had recorded four tracks for the BBC Overseas *Star Show* with the legendary Ted Heath band. Heath's ability to swing whilst still leaving the vocalist prominent was a quality that the *Happy Holliday* album lacked.

There was never any likelihood of Mike turning his back on the Crosby songbook. When he heard that Bing would be back in London in the late summer of 1961 to film *Road To Hong Kong* with Bob Hope, Mike couldn't resist the temptation to make contact.

'Sorry I bothered you too much whilst you were in London,' he wrote to Bing in April 1961, referring to the way he had gatecrashed the recording session the previous year, 'but I was so excited. I used to wake up in the morning and say "Gee, I wonder what's he's doing now and if he'll ring me".' Even 40 years on, the letter's fannish sentiments are adolescent in the least. 'One thing you'll be glad to hear is that you won't have me bothering you when you arrive because I'll be doing Summer Season in Blackpool,' he added. 'But don't be surprised if I give you a ring.'

Mike's Blackpool commitment started almost as soon as he had recorded his last ARTV show. As ever, Blackpool was supporting its usual array of summer shows and Mike was part of the top-ranked Bernard Delfont production at the North Pier Pavilion. Delfont's *Showtime* was in its fifth Blackpool season. Such was the pulling power of the resort that holidaymakers would often queue after the show to book the same seats for the same week the following year.

178

Showtime boasted a 'six-star cast' that included Des O'Connor, pop duo the Allisons, ventriloquist Terry Hall with Lenny the Lion, and comedian Stan Stennett. Mike was top of the bill again, although his solo spot in the show came at the end of the first half of the programme rather than in the customary final spot. Instead, all six stars brought the curtain down with a 'Minstrel Medley'.

With the Delfont company producing the show, Mike had little alternative but to allow Keith Devon to handle the booking. He insisted, however, that Devon book Johnny Wiltshire and the Trebletones into the show, even paying £20 from his own take to supplement their weekly salary. But with his own contract topping £400 per week, plus several Sunday concerts to top that up, it was a lucrative engagement.

When Mike packed his bags and headed for an unusually early May start to the season in Blackpool, it was the start of a five-month period away from home. He and Wiltshire rented a house for the summer. Whilst on the surface he seemed happy with the booking, underneath there were more signs that something was wrong. What few people knew was that he had been under the regular eye of a local doctor in Croydon since April. He was beginning to suffer from the depression that would eventually kill him.

His behaviour had become increasingly contradictory and unpredictable, never more so than in his attitude to work. Early in 1961, Mike received an approach from an Indian promoter for a lengthy series of concerts throughout India and Ceylon. It seemed to contain all the things that Mike disliked – live appearances, a long time away from home, and few of the home comforts of Dailson. Mike nevertheless responded enthusiastically to the approach, and entered into direct negotiations for a tour that would begin as soon as the Blackpool season was over.

Mike's willingness to commit to the season in Blackpool and then the tour may have also been an indication that severe cracks were now appearing in his marriage. His increasing depression and unpredictability, plus the continuing reliance on tablets for sleep, inevitably put the relationship with Margie under great strain. His phone calls to Margie during the summer of 1961 revealed a deep unhappiness. And for the first time, there was the suggestion from Mike that life wasn't worth living.

Mike's unfaithfulness only added to the strains in the marriage. His open pursuit of so many young girls would in itself have become a *cause célèbre*, although since Mike's death other rumours have developed to the effect that Michael Holliday, at least towards the end of his life, became gay or at least, bisexual. The source of such rumours is inevitably hard to trace and invariably based on second or third-hand accounts. The trail usually leads however to what has come to be known as 'that Freddie Mills business'.

Mills died in mysterious circumstances in 1965, 18 months after Mike's death. The ex-boxer was found dead in his car outside the nightclub where Mike had spent his last night, a rifle wedged between his legs in an apparent suicide. Speculation about Mills's death and whether he had in fact been murdered has grown almost from the night that his body was found. One story that began appearing in the tabloids in the 1970s was that Mills and Holliday had been homosexual lovers. Endless spins on the story have positioned their 'affair' as part of a complex underworld plot of homosexual rivalry and unpaid protection monies.

Such stories are always high on hype and low on evidence. Mills's family has always refuted any suggestion that the ex-boxer was gay; nevertheless, the rumour mill continued to build the story to the point that many people now regard it as 'fact'.

The truth of the matter is that Holliday and Mills had met when the ex-boxer joined the cast of *6.5 Special* in 1957. They got on well and became friends, but not particularly close ones. There is no evidence from any of Mike's friends that he and Mills saw each other on a regular basis. Mills himself said at the inquest into Mike's death that Mike had visited Mills's club that night for the first time, a fact confirmed by Basil le Marquand,

Mike's minder during the last weeks of his life. Nevertheless, the 'gay' tag has stuck.

If there had been a gay or bisexual side to Michael Holliday, then Johnny Wiltshire would surely have seen evidence of it. The house they rented for the summer of 1961 was a small property in the Bispham district of Blackpool. 'I just couldn't believe the stories that came out after Mike died,' said Wiltshire. 'He had so many girlfriends, it just wasn't true.' In four months under the same roof, Wiltshire saw nothing to suggest that Mike had an interest in anything other than girls.

Others who knew Mike say the same thing. Interviewed in 1990 for a programme about the death of Freddie Mills, disc jockey Pete Murray was forthright in his dismissal of a relationship between Holliday and Mills, or indeed any suggestion that Mike may have been gay. 'Michael Holliday was the number one crumpet man of all time,' he said. Daphne Shadwell, Mike's 1961 TV producer, recalled her astonishment at some of the outrageous stories that she said Johnny Pearson told her about Mike and the girls, stories that more than bore out Margie's view about the American car being a bedroom on wheels.

Margaret Burrows is equally aghast at how the suggestion of a gay side to Mike has stuck. 'I came to know him pretty well and could recognise the glint in his eye,' she said. 'I was with him at lots of parties where there were young boys and girls. He never showed any interest in the boys, he was always too busy ogling the girls.' Burrows also recalled Mike's amusement when a shortage of hotel rooms caused a 'straight' musician to have to share with another who was known to be gay. His reaction, she says, was hardly that of a latent homosexual.

Curiously, Mike's constant pursuit of young girls, openly and publicly, may have contributed to the rumours about a gay side to his sexual proclivities. Many in show business seemed to find Mike's behaviour so outrageous that it became an embarrassment, even by the standards of an industry not known for its moral purity. Whilst some people are now prepared to talk about Mike's antics, others, even 40 years on, are reluctant to do so. 'You

181

know about...' is as much they will say. Such an open line could, and has been, taken to imply a reference to homosexuality.

It is, of course, impossible to say that Mike never experimented. His sexual drive was high and his search for variety constant. Nevertheless, there is little, if any, evidence to suggest that a latent homosexuality lay at the root of the depression that engulfed him or that it contributed to his death.

If sexual confusion was not a contributory factor in Mike's emerging depressive state, financial worries were. In May 1961, Baker Todman wrote to Mike advising him that the Revenue had now agreed his tax assessment for 1959. It had been the year when Mike's earnings had soared beyond the £30,000 mark and the income tax due was £3,664. One-half was due immediately and the other on 1st July. Mike also owed £490 in surtax in respect of his 1958 earnings, giving a tax debt of over £4,000. The amount was high but not beyond Mike's means. With Mike away, Margie settled the debt on 19th August 1961.

Two weeks later, Baker Todman were in touch again to say that the surtax for 1959 had now been agreed and that the amount due was a further £2,589. Mike had six months before this debt would become due, but as of then, it was a debt that he couldn't meet. That said, there was hardly the need for panic. Mike's summer season would generate gross income of over £10,000. Nevertheless, debts – at least of this scale – were something that Mike had never known. The news only fuelled his depression.

The mounting tax problems debts brought a sense of belt-tightening to the Holliday home for the first time in a number of years. Several 'on account' purchases were returned unopened and Mike's long-time Crosby friend John Joyce was surprised to receive a letter from Mike's secretary returning some films that Mike had requested. Mike had asked Joyce to send him copies of some early Crosby movies. Joyce has sent the films to Blackpool as requested, where Mike had intended to borrow, or if need be, buy a projector to show them. 'As Mr Holliday has far too much cinema equipment at home, his business manager

182

has advised him against buying a projector just to show a few films during his Blackpool season,' his secretary said.

Not everything about the summer was downcast. Johnny Wiltshire recalled a broadly happy time in the house that he and Mike shared. Neither of them could cook and their staple diet in the house was corned beef and chips. They supplemented that with lots of steaks – Mike's favourite meal – in The Lancastrian after the show or at Mike's mother's house in Liverpool. ' "Come'ed bollocks" was his standard phrase,' said Wiltshire, ' "let's shoot down to Liverpool".' And whilst Wiltshire observed a melancholia that sometimes overcame him on their trips to Mike's hometown, he had no inkling of what was to come.

On Sunday 24th September, Mike had no Sunday concert and decided to drive home to Dailson. He had seen little of Margie during the summer. Johnny Wiltshire recalled her spending a few days in Blackpool but not much more. Mike's schedule meant that any trips he made home necessitated a 500-mile round trip over Sunday and Monday. In pre-motorway Britain, it was an arduous drive.

On Monday 25th September, Mike was admitted to Warlingham Park Hospital in Surrey. The hospital, now closed, specialised in psychiatric illnesses. What happened between Sunday evening and Monday morning was never revealed and news of Mike's 'breakdown' took a further 48 hours to come into the open. Finally, on Thursday 28th September, the papers carried the story that Mike had entered hospital suffering from 'nervous trouble'. Margie was quoted as saying that 'Michael has been overdoing things and has to take sedatives at night so that he can relax for his public.'

A day later, Mike left hospital and returned to Dailson. He and Margie held a photo call for the national press. They posed both inside and outside their home, the inside shots capturing Mike on a sofa with Margie – looking more glamorous than ever – at his side. 'THE RELAXED MR HOLLIDAY STRIPS OFF THE MASK' said the headline. 'Most people would assume I am the last person to suffer from nerves,' said Mike, 'but they don't understand the tension I have to endure.'

Mike's description of his symptoms was classically that of someone suffering from depression. 'This all started on Sunday night,' he said. 'I'd driven down from Blackpool and suddenly I began to tremble and feel a terrible urge to cry. On Monday, I felt even worse and the doctor slapped me straight into hospital.'

Michael Holliday's 'nervous breakdown' was news enough, although the truth about what happened that Sunday evening was more startling. It emerged only at the inquest into Mike's death two years later. Mike's hospitalisation in 1961 had come about because he had taken an overdose of sleeping tablets. 'He took them because he was depressed,' said Margie.

Whether the overdose had been accidental or deliberate, no one knew. Nor, indeed, was it clear whether Margie had been there when he took the tablets. When Mike died in 1963, he and Margie were separated although it was not the first time they had parted. 'Mike had come home once or twice and found that Margie had gone,' said Basil le Marquand, Mike's minder during the last months of his life. That night in September 1961 may have been one such instance. The overdose was more likely a cry for help, a plea to Margie, than a genuine suicide attempt.

Mike told the press that he would take three weeks off work. 'From now on, I'll take things much easier', he said. 'I have to go to India and then do pantomime in Torquay, but it's ridiculous to work yourself into the state I was in.' Margie held his hand and gazed lovingly at him while the press men snapped their pictures. Once more, the Hollidays presented themselves to the outside world as the idyllic couple, square pegs in the round hole of show business. Mike's illness, they said, had made them see the world differently. Things would get better from now on.

They didn't.

Chapter 18

Men in Suits

Mike's convalescence lasted less than three weeks. 'I suppose you will have heard that I wasn't too well a while ago, but I have just returned from a short holiday in Ireland and am feeling pretty good now,' he said in a letter to Bing Crosby in early November 1961. The 'holiday' was actually a series of one-nighters in local ballrooms. Much as Mike might have wanted to take things easier, the fact was that he needed the money.

Louis Rodgers, who Mike knew well and, more importantly, seemed to trust, was the man behind the Irish tour. Even that relationship started to go sour. When Mike returned to Dailson in early November, Rodgers's cheque for Mike's share of the Irish take was £350 less than he expected. The dispute rumbled on for six months before Mike, desperate for some work in the summer of 1962, decided to put it behind him. 'I think I've only got two chances of getting my money from you and that's a "dog's chance" and "no chance",' he said in a letter to the Irishman. 'Maybe we can make it up if we do some summer work together.'

Shortly before he left for Ireland, Mike had heard that the planned tour of India and Ceylon was also in doubt. The problem, said the promoters, was new rules governing work permits for Mike, Wiltshire and the Trebletones. 'This is entirely due to a change of policy by the Indian Government,' they told Mike.

The cancellation of the tour at such short notice was a major blow. Mike had no particular desire to spend several weeks in

India but the money on offer had looked too good to turn down – over £250 per show. It would easily have been Mike's most profitable engagement ever, and at a time when he desperately needed it.

Mike filled the gap left by the aborted tour with a week's variety in Chester and a series of cabaret performances in London and Birmingham. The Chester week was a disaster. Mike's return, based on a percentage of the week's takings, was only £132. 'I'm sorry it was such a bad week,' the booking agent said.

With the tax debt hanging over him, it is not difficult to see why Mike believed that he was facing a financial crisis. Mike's problem, however, was more one of cash flow. He needed cash to meet his immediate debts but his underlying earnings were still good. His accounts for the year to September 1961 showed gross earnings of almost £20,000. Even after deducting his outgoings, his net figure was still £9,700.

Bolstered by the lucrative season in Blackpool, the figures represented a small improvement on Mike's 1960 earnings, and judged against average earnings it was a handsome living. Nevertheless, the air of financial stringency remained. Mike's illness had left Johnny Wiltshire alone in the rented house in Blackpool for the last week of the season. When he came to leave, he found the lettings agent on the doorstep claiming rights to some of his and Mike's belongings. The rent, the agent said, was unpaid, something that Mike's ever-loyal personal secretary vehemently disputed.

Mike's money problems also forced him to make changes to some of his other plans. Talk of buying a farm was put on hold, as were his plans to begin breeding horses. Earlier in the year, he had bought his first palomino, Shadow, believing her to be in foal. It turned out to be a false pregnancy although the horse herself became a favourite of Mike's. He did find the money to buy a silver saddle and bridle for her and the hours he spent riding Shadow across the Surrey hills were amongst the most genuinely relaxed and contented of his life.

He had no choice, however, but to abandon his plans to

186

purchase a second palomino. Instead, he found himself needing to sell Polly, the black horse that he had owned since 1959. The deal brought more strife. A prospective buyer accused him of gazumping the sale and accepting another offer that was £25 higher. 'Doubtless you wouldn't want me to tell everyone that you needed the £25 so badly,' the affronted buyer told him.

One highlight of an otherwise unhappy autumn was Mike's guest appearance with Bob Hope on a BBC radio special, scheduled for Christmas Day broadcast. Mike appeared in a sketch where Hope, with the aid of Peter Sellers, was tracking the heir to an English country estate. When Sellers announces that their search has been successful, he asks the mystery personality to introduce himself by using his 'inimitable voice'.

The voice that sings a few bars of 'Where The Blue of The Night' (Bing Crosby's theme song) is all too familiar, with its easy style and deep, rich tone. Bob Hope's response too, is predictable. 'No! Not Bing Crosby. No! It's not fair,' he screams. When Michael Holliday is revealed as the owner of the voice, Hope's response is typical – 'Michael, I can remember when Dad used to be able to sing almost as well as that,' leaving Mike to take centre stage with yet another Crosby song.

A few weeks later, Mike missed an even better opportunity to stand in for Bing. Decca Records decided to release a single of Crosby's main song from *Road To Hong Kong*. The scene in the film ended with Bing in an amorous clinch with Joan Collins, causing him to omit the last word of the song. With Bing back in the USA, someone else was needed to add the word 'love' to make 'Let's Not Be Sensible' a complete take. Mike was desperate to be given the chance to add one word to a record by his idol but his EMI contract was a blockage. Mike Sammes, the 'bom-bom' singer on 'The Story Of My Life', got the job instead. 'I would have given anything to do it,' Mike told friends.

After the Bob Hope show, Mike's pantomime season in Torquay started on Boxing Day 1961. It ran for four weeks through until the end of January. Like the summer season, it was another Delfont production. Mike topped the cast that included Tommy

Fields, brother of Gracie, an up and coming young comedian called Ted Rogers, plus Johnny Wiltshire and the Trebletones.

Wiltshire remembered the panto well. The five of them spent the month in a lodging house, one that Mike had unearthed from one of his first variety tours. 'He could have stayed in a nice hotel and left the rest of us to the digs,' said Wiltshire, 'but he would never have done that. It would have looked like he thought he was the star.' Mike took along his projector and some films. Some of them – at least whilst the landlady was about – were the home movies of the visit to Bing or Mike and his horses. 'As soon as she was gone, he would start showing blue movies,' laughed Wiltshire.

Wiltshire again saw little evidence of any personal or domestic turmoil in Mike during those four weeks, although other evidence suggests that it was there. Margaret Burrows had last seen Mike towards the end of 1960 before leaving for a spell abroad. When she returned briefly to England in January 1962, Scarborough entertainments manager, Dave Cook, made a beeline for her. Cook had become a close friend of Holliday's from the 1959 summer season. 'Where the hell have you been?' he asked. 'Mike's been looking everywhere for you.' Without more ado, Cook marched the newly engaged eighteen-year-old to the nearest telephone box where she found herself talking to Mike.

'He asked me to marry him,' she said, 'even though he was already married. He told me that his marriage was over.'

Mike implored her to come to Torquay. She refused. Her time with Mike in Scarborough had been genuinely good fun and she had developed an equally genuine fondness for him. But she had seen enough to know that an emotional involvement would only bring the same heartache that she knew Margie must have been suffering. And she had met someone else. She never spoke to him again.

January 1962 brought more bad news. On the 10th, Holliday's solicitors Rubinstein, Nash & Co wrote to him to tell him that the case that Hal Monty had brought in 1959 had finally been set down for trial. The court date was still six months away, but the serious business of preparing proofs of evidence needed to begin now.

Mike had always been reluctant to see the case come to court. His antipathy towards Monty was real enough and he firmly believed that the veteran comedian had persistently short-changed him. 'I am waiting for a court case to come up by Mr Hal Monty,' he said in a letter to his old boss, Eric Winstone, in March 1961. 'Believe it or not, he is suing *me*.'

Nevertheless, Mike was uncomfortable with going to court. In his heart of hearts, he was hoping that the whole thing would just go away. Rubinsteins tried hard to persuade Mike in 1960 to put forward third-party evidence to suggest that Monty had previously lied under oath. Mike refused. 'I don't want to dig up dirt that does not concern me,' he said in his reply. 'If the case does reach the court, I shall just hope that "me learned judge" will see fair play.'

Mike's response was evidence of both his naivety and his inherent sense of fair play. His stardom brought wealth and worry, but those who knew him from his early days maintain that his character never changed. He remained an essentially simple person, who retained the values that his mother had instilled in him – pay your debts, sort out your own problems and stay well clear of men in suits. Putting himself in the hands of solicitors and judges never sat easily. As the case developed, Rubinsteins joined the list of advisors who had discovered how difficult and frustrating Mike could be.

Mike returned from Torquay at the end of January 1962. He had a week's work ahead of him rehearsing and recording for what turned out to be his final album. The LP was the long-awaited tribute album to Bing that had been on the cards since 1958. With support from Norrie Paramor and the Mike Sammes Singers, Holliday recorded 14 tracks for *To Bing – From Mike* in the first week of February. The album cover showed Mike and Bing together in the California sunshine, whilst Derek Johnson's sleeve notes played up their personal friendship with more than a little poetic licence. Its suggestion that Bing and

Mike had become golfing partners was a little beyond the pale. (Margaret Burrows recalled that she and Mike had attempted to play golf in Scarborough once. She had turned up in a pair of high heels whilst Mike was equally ill-equipped. He got bored after 20 minutes, she said.)

Whatever the off-stage pressures that he was facing, they had no effect on his ability to convey the familiar relaxed style. Paramor repeated the variety that he had used on the two albums in 1959 and 1960, surrounding Mike with lush strings for several of the tracks and a small jazz group for others. Although this was the only album that was an overt tribute to Bing, in truth any of Mike's albums could have had the same title. (Although in Mike's defence, Crosby recorded almost 2,000 songs in his career. Putting together an album of songs that he *hadn't* recorded would have been no mean feat.)

Mike was in good voice on all three sessions for the album although, perhaps influenced by its title, seemed to make a more overt attempt at copying Bing than usual. Whilst most reviewers made the obvious comments about the similarity in voices, one reviewer went deeper. 'Mike's voice is more in the back of his throat than Bing's,' said John Mitchell in *Record Roundabout*. 'When he goes from loud to soft, he lacks Bing's controlled smoothness. Rhythmically, he hasn't the same flow,' he added.

Mike was back in Abbey Road a few weeks later to cut his first single since the 'Dream Boy Dream' débacle in May 1961. Paramor selected two new songs for the session. A country and western number, 'I Don't Want You To See Me Cry', was marked out as the A side. The result, yet again, was a pleasant disc but not a hit. *Melody Maker*'s view was that it was 'too monotonous to make the charts'.

Also in March 1962, Mike recorded the first show of a second series of *Holliday With Strings*. Producer John Browell repeated the highly successful formula from the first series, and Mike looked forward to renewing his acquaintance with Johnny Pearson. The 17-show series gave Mike everything he needed bar one

190

thing – money. The BBC's standard fee for a radio appearance was a parsimonious £47 per show.

If Mike thought that his work would enable him to take his mind away from the clouds hanging over him, he was mistaken. Margie's mother had been ill for some time, but despite treatment from a top Harley Street consultant, her condition worsened and she died in March. As well as dealing with the bereavement, Mike and Margie were also under constant badgering from Rubinsteins to strengthen their evidence in the Hal Monty case. Mike's vagueness worried his lawyers. If Mike failed to come up with detailed evidence to counter Monty's claims, he would lose. The stakes were high. Monty's claim was for 15 per cent of Mike's estimated total earnings from 1959 to 1964. If Mike lost, he could be facing damages of £20,000 plus costs. Even without knowing the extent of Mike's tax debts, the lawyers knew that losing the case would bankrupt him.

At the end of March, the tax spectre raised its head again. Mike needed to find £1,500 as the first instalment for his 1961/62 liability. Demonstrating that his earnings were likely to be lower, Bill Gudgin of Baker Todman negotiated the payment down to £750, which Mike paid promptly. Two weeks later, they were in touch again to say that they now had the 1959 surtax demand. The amount was still £2,589, the same as when they had first alerted Mike to it in September 1961. Did Mike want them to try and get the revenue to accept instalments? The answer was obvious.

Quite where all the money had gone is hard to say, but there is no question that Mike's finances in 1962 were in a parlous state. Shortly after the letters from Baker Todman, Mike's bankers alerted him to the fact that his current account had moved into overdraft. He had other accounts with the bank that were still in surplus, and as a good Liverpudlian, had never believed in putting all his money in the bank anyway. But Mike was a big star and had found credit easy to come by. Everything from his butcher's bills to the food for his horses was on account. It was a difficult tap to turn off.

191

The accountants were successful in persuading the Inland Revenue to accept instalments against the surtax demand at £300 per month, but with an upfront payment of £750. They were clearly concerned that Mike was now sailing very close to the wind. 'The Special Commissioners do not like accepting instalments for surtax and will not admit that they do in fact accept [them],' they told Mike. They also continued to press Mike to put money aside from his gross income to meet future liabilities.

Still the demands kept on coming, leaving Mike feeling like Mickey Mouse's Sorcerer's Apprentice in *Fantasia*. It was not part of his psyche to be comfortable with debts, but above all else he hated to be pressurised. His response to his accountant was characteristic: 'Please deal with Margie,' he said in a phone call when the accountant rang to tell him that the tax on *Michael Holliday Productions* for 1960/61 was £1,152.

By June 1962, Baker Todman's assessment was that the set-aside from income needed to be 50 per cent if Mike was to escape from his debts, let alone fund future tax demands. Mike agreed. 'We should get Margie to automatically send me a cheque for 50 per cent of all sums banked,' Bill Gudgin, the accountant who handled Mike's work, told him. 'As you know she has only to lift the phone, tell me what she is banking and I will tell her the amount to put on the cheque to send to me.'

Mike's workload whilst all this was going on was light. Apart from the weekly radio shows, he made only one TV appearance on ITV's *Thank Your Lucky Stars*. A *TV Times* picture showed him riding Shadow across the land at the rear of Dailson, whilst in an accompanying interview, he still talked of going into farming. For the foreseeable future, it was no more than a pipe dream.

Meanwhile, the denouement with Hal Monty was imminent, with the case set down for a June hearing. Mike's next move astonished everyone. With the court case due any day and the tax position reaching crisis point, he and Margie left London for a three-week holiday in Italy. The timing was itself bizarre, compounded by the extensive press coverage of the Hollidays

192

at Heathrow Airport. The press captured them in the departure lounge, with a further set of pictures showing them walking arm in arm across the tarmac to the plane.

The holiday did little to persuade the tax commissioners to look sympathetically on the pleas for special terms to pay off his debts. Mike's solicitors were equally taken aback that he should absent himself at such a critical time. They sought an arrangement with Monty's solicitors to have the case deferred for a further month, but wrote a lengthy letter to Mike, care of the Grand Hotel, Venice, asking that he clear up a raft of inconsistencies in his proof of evidence.

Mike told his solicitors that he had taken Margie on holiday because she had been unwell. There was no question that the previous nine months had been highly stressful – Mike's breakdown and overdose, the death of Margie's mother and the tax and court issues – although whether Margie's 'illness' was any more than this isn't clear. Certainly the images of Margie at the airport – smartly dressed, with jewellery flowing – did not give any indication of a period of convalescence.

The three-week break may have been an attempt – possibly a final one – to heal the breaches in their marriage. Moreover, when he left the UK, Mike thought that he had reached a settlement with Monty. Before he left for Rome on Tuesday 12th June, Mike had called Rubinsteins to tell them that he had been in direct contact with Monty and had agreed a settlement.

Mike had made the approach to Monty, who was in India. Monty reported the conversation to his solicitors, saying that Mike had said that he wanted to go to Italy without the case hanging over him and that he (Holliday) would settle the case on his return. Monty refused, apparently telling Mike that 'he had put me in the promise land [sic] too many times'. The conversation went on. Monty said that Mike had told him that he had only £4,500 in the bank 'and a few thousand in cash' and that to pay Monty off in full would bankrupt him. No mention was made of the tax debt, and indeed given the difficulties Mike was having in coming up with much less than these sums to satisfy his accountant, he was probably overstating his financial position, a strange negotiating tack. In the end, said Monty, they had agreed that Mike would pay him £1,000 now, another £1,000 before the end of the year, and that Mike would also take Monty back as his manager for a 12-month period.

Given the way that Mike had consistently decried Monty ever since the break-up, the final piece in the agreement was simply staggering. Nevertheless, the deal gave Mike the peace of mind that he sought. He immediately wrote a cheque for £1,000 and delivered it to Monty's secretary. He left for Rome believing that the case was behind him.

By the time Mike arrived in Venice, the deal was in pieces. Rubinsteins had contacted Monty's solicitors and found that their respective clients had given differing accounts of the settlement terms. The critical piece was the re-engagement of Monty. Mike claimed that he had agreed to pay Monty 10 per cent of those earnings over the 12 months 'for which Monty was responsible'. His intentions were clear. He would treat Monty the same way that he had treated Keith Devon, making his own bookings and in so doing, limiting the commission. Monty's claim was that Mike had agreed to pay him 10 per cent of 'all earnings'.

A letter from Rubinsteins awaited Mike when he and Margie arrived in Venice. It told him that the two sets of solicitors had failed to agree on what it was that their clients had agreed on. Their advice was clear and stark – either accept the terms as set out by Monty or come straight back home within the next week and fight the case.

Chapter 19

'Love to Marge'

There was no doubt that Mike wanted to settle. His response was not a balanced judgement based on an analysis of his chances of winning, which everybody seemed to think were good. It was simply that he couldn't face the idea of a courtroom confrontation. And as ever, he found it impossible to trust his advisors. His first response to Rubinsteins' letter was to try to lay it all back at their door. He had lost faith in the firm, he told them and that was why he had decided to settle.

One of the firm's partners, Michael Rubinstein, produced a lengthy and vigorous defence of his firm's support to Mike. Their view was that Mike had a winnable case and there was no reason to throw in the towel now. But if Mike's instructions were that they should settle, then they would do so, but he still needed Mike to be there – or at least be accessible. 'Without your instructions, I cannot negotiate on terms, so the case will go on. Even if it is settled at the door of the court, you will undoubtedly find yourself liable for substantially greater costs than would be payable at present.'

The case, meanwhile, had been set down for hearing on 10th July. Once more, Rubinstein implored Mike to return to England. The response came the next day. 'WISH TO PROCEED WITH CASE BUT AM CONTRACTED TO WORK WEEK JULY 9TH. PREPARED TO RETURN SOON IF NECESSARY. PLEASE ADVICE [sic]. HOLLIDAY.'

Mike's inability to see that he needed to put the court ahead of a week's variety in Clacton wasn't exactly what Rubinsteins were looking for, but his willingness to return was at least a start. Preparation for the hearing went on, and as it did Michael Rubinstein's personal confidence in the outcome seemed to grow.

But Mike was never going to court. On the morning of 9th July, he met Monty and agreed a settlement. He would pay his former manager £1,000 plus all costs arising from the court action. It was a better deal than the one they had agreed in June but the sting was still in the tail. Monty would take on the role of Mike's personal manager for 12 months. His pay would be 10 per cent of Mike's earnings, regardless of whether he had booked them or not. This time, to make sure the deal stuck, Mike typed out the terms himself. Both Monty and Holliday signed the agreement. One single piece of paper, riddled with typing errors, ended the dispute between them.

Mike's solicitors had little option but to accept what Mike had done, but couldn't resist pointing out the flaws in his action. The agreement placed no limit on Monty's costs; it made no mention of the counter-claim Mike had against Monty from 1958–59, nor did it tie down a variety of other loose ends. They asked Mike to attend a conference with his Counsel but he refused, citing a worry about adding to his legal costs.

Mike's worry about his costs caused alarm bells to ring at Rubinsteins. Their next letter to Mike asked for £250 against their costs 'at once'. 'I feel sure that you will see to it that your obligations to those who have tried to help you are met before you start making payments to Hal Monty,' they said.

Mike retained the firm to handle the negotiations with Monty on his costs, which they successfully reduced from £762 to £456. Despite the lower figure, Mike was still struggling to make the payments, both to Monty and to his own advisors. All of his available funds were going to the taxman.

Rubinsteins' pursuit of their debt was good-natured, in contrast to the approach of Monty's solicitors who persistently threatened further court action. In March 1963, Mike still owed a balance of £196 to the firm as well as Monty's costs. Mike wrote to Rubinsteins offering to cover the balance in two instalments. The firm graciously accepted the proposal. 'We were very amused by your letter,' they said. 'Needless to say this firm had, of course, no intention of "seeing you at your front door".'

The settlement meant that Hal Monty was back playing a major role in Mike's life and his career. It was clear to everyone that Mike needed a personal manager, and even Mike himself seemed to have got the message. That hadn't stopped Mike from sacking the one man who had been keen to play the role. In April 1962, he wrote to Keith Devon effectively ending their arrangement on the grounds that Mike felt that what he really needed was a personal manager. 'I do this without any malice,' he said to Devon, 'it's just that I don't think you have sufficient time to devote to my interests.'

Devon was incredulous. 'The fact that you have turned down a considerable number of engagements for reasons best known to yourself does not alter in any way the great amount of work that has been offered to you. As you well remember, you recently turned down a 15-week summer season at Weymouth at £300 per week.'

'Thank you for your letter,' said Mike in his reply, 'and in spite of the lecture, I still love you. It seems I heard all that before.'

Despite Holliday's reputation for being a difficult client, there was no shortage of offers from willing managers and agents. The bandleader Eric Winstone, Mike's former boss from Butlin's, had offered his services in 1961 but Mike was reluctant. His previous experience with Hal Monty had he said, left him 'a little bit wary'. Mike also came close to an agreement with John Heyman of Publicity and Allied Interests. It was enough for Heyman to badge himself as 'Manager to Michael Holliday'. It was a step further than Mike wanted to go and for a time, there were signs of another dispute. Mike cancelled the arrangement in October 1962.

Re-enter Hal Monty. The vaudevillian is a much-maligned character in the Michael Holliday story. Everyone who knew Mike is clear that what he needed was a good manager; they are just as clear that Monty was not the man for the job.

Monty's side of the story is uncaptured. Nevertheless, it would be foolish to believe that his experiences with Mike were any different from those of others who sought to offer advice and guidance. Stan White echoed Mike's description of Monty as a 'rough diamond' but said he was someone who knew the showbiz scene inside out. 'His main problem,' said White, 'was that Mike had employed him to manage things, but most of the time Mike ignored his advice.'

Monty's approach in 1962 was to put the past behind him and carry on where they had left off in 1959. His greatest asset was that he knew where to find work, providing he could persuade Mike to take it. Mike's decision to turn his back on a summer season in 1962 was symptomatic of what was becoming a self-fulfilling prophecy. He was again beginning to talk about quitting show business and returning to the sea or buying a farm. It was almost as if Mike was carrying his hero-worship of Bing Crosby to absurd lengths.

Crosby was in his second marriage and raising a young family. He was rapidly losing interest in work. But Crosby was turning 60 and a millionaire more times over than he could count. It was one thing for him to say he was winding down. For Mike, 37 and heavily in debt, it made no sense. But still he talked himself down. 'I can't hit the high notes any more,' an off-line microphone captured him saying to Norrie Paramor at one session around this time.

Monty filled the vacant summer with three weeks of variety in Nottingham, Bristol and Liverpool plus a series of one-nighters in the emerging club scene in Birmingham and Manchester. Mike's reappearance on the provincial variety scene went down well. 'His return to the stage after 18 months of TV and radio activity gave Bristol theatregoers one of the most polished, professional "pop" acts for many a moon,' said one review of the Bristol show. The money at £200 wasn't brilliant but Mike was in no position to be choosy.

Nevertheless, Mike was no happier on the stage than he had ever been. 'I'm a darned sight better than I was last year, but even so, I don't care for these variety tours,' he told the press in Liverpool. 'They upset me. I'm seriously thinking of doing no more and sticking to radio and television. I'm 38 – never mind about the publicity man saying I'm 33. If I can't start to relax now, I'll never get down to doing it.'

It was also in that summer that John Ammonds made a welcome return into Mike's life. Despite his ongoing radio work, Mike had not appeared on BBC television for over two years. Ammonds now offered him the chance to appear in two editions of *The Saturday Show*. The programme was a summer variety show, filmed in Blackpool. Ammonds as producer also had responsibility for casting, and saw the opportunity to bring Mike back to BBC Television.

Mike no longer commanded top billing, taking second spot to Jimmy James and Tommy Cooper respectively, but came across well. Both shows featured the tape recorder routine prominently, something that the press picked out as the high spot in an otherwise mundane programme. Mike's self-doubt meant that he saw it differently. A week after the recording, he wrote to Ammonds apologising for dashing off straight after the show. 'I felt rather low as I thought I didn't do a good show,' he said. 'I was so close to the front row of the audience that I felt a little embarrassed.'

The letter concluded with Mike saying that he was enclosing 'that thing I promised you in the past for your patience'. 'That thing' was a large amount of cash. Ammonds was nonplussed.

'I had the shock of my life,' he said when he opened the envelope and found £200 enclosed. With strict BBC rules forbidding acceptance of such large sums, Ammonds had no option but to decline the gift. 'I would be quite happy for you to get me a nice Dunhill pipe,' he said.

That Mike should give away £200 cash when surrounded by far greater debts is inexplicable. Did he have money hidden away that was not disclosed to his accountants? Perhaps so, but why in that case did he allow his tax debts to mount and the pressure to grow? There is no answer. Some say that Mike had other debts and was in fear of his life. But debts to whom and for

199

what? As with the Freddie Mills stories, there is no evidence, not even second-hand, to substantiate such rumours.

A conversation with Ammonds during the recording of the shows had once more turned to the idea of a half-hour series, first mooted in 1959. 'I can tell you that there is a *possibility* of a half-hour series in January,' Ammonds said in a letter to Mike in October 1962. 'Nothing definite yet but I'm pushing it naturally. Tom Sloan was delighted with your performance in the Blackpool shows.' Ammonds added an inadvertent backhanded compliment. 'For all your faults, I love working with you,' he said.

Hal Monty meanwhile was looking further afield for work opportunities. Mike's UK career might be in danger of stalling, although he knew that another BBC series could give it a massive lift. In the meantime, Monty took himself off to South Africa, India, Japan and Australia, reporting back enthusiastically on the interest in Mike. Closer to home, he also turned up bookings on Dutch TV and theatre opportunities in Germany (which Mike turned down) before finally persuading Mike to accept a six-week cabaret engagement in South Africa for November and December 1962. The booking required Mike to do three weeks in Johannesburg and then a further three weeks in Cape Town and Durban. It was, said Monty, 'easy work' with just one show per night with a supporting cast that left Mike needing to do no more than pick up a microphone and sing.

Monty's influence extended beyond the professional side of Mike's career. Whilst on the one hand exhorting Mike to bring Margie to South Africa – 'it would make a wonderful holiday for her and will help to get you really together again' – he seemed equally happy to encourage Mike's philanderings. 'What's the crumpet like?' he scribbled as a PS to a letter in September, enquiring about Mike's current engagement in Birmingham. 'Very nice here,' he added.

Monty's letters continued in similar vein, anticipating with relish a trip to Japan and its geisha girls. 'You ain't seen nothing yet,' he scribbled on a card once he arrived. And when Monty wrote to Mike with details of the flat he had booked for Mike's summer season in Jersey, it was, he said, near a dance hall so that Mike would be 'well accommodated'.

Monty sent his letters quite openly to Mike at Dailson and indeed mostly ended them with a 'love to Marge' message. That, plus the fact that Margie handled much of Mike's post whilst he was away in South Africa, gives lie to any suggestion that this was a time of another separation. It was simply an outrageous example of the double standards that seemed to sit so easily with Mike.

Meanwhile, the tax problem refused to go away. It was a massive worry for Mike. When his accountant pressed him for money to meet the monthly instalments on the surtax debt, he wrote a response that seemed to come from the heart:

> Can you tell the taxman that it isn't a matter of my not having made prior provision for my Income Tax liabilities. Over the past two years I have been robbed, cheated and generally taken advantage of by every villain in show business and outside, and it will take some time to pay my debts. I will send them all when I can. I'll be sending you £100 as this month's instalment. £300 is too much for me.

Mike's response reflected his mental state. His treatment for depression had continued through the year and he was beginning to show signs of paranoia.

The facts were that he *had* failed to make any provision for his tax liabilities. And whilst he genuinely believed he had been 'robbed and cheated' (an apparent reference to Monty), it ignored the fact that he had convinced Rubinsteins that he had a winnable case. The decision to make a settlement had been Mike's alone.

There were other signs, too, that he believed the world was against him. When he began work on his BBC series in January 1963, one day he arrived late at the airport and missed his flight to Manchester. He called John Ammonds to tell him, explaining that he thought fate had decreed that he should miss the plane

201

because he 'wasn't intended to come to Manchester today'. Ammonds response was short and to the point – get the next plane or I'll sue you!

Baker Todman knew that they would never persuade the surtax commissioners to accept a lower monthly figure than the previously agreed £300. It was a case of Mike just trying to get through it. 'If you can only struggle through to the end of January, all this should be behind you,' his accountant told him. With an eye to the future, the firm also got Mike's approval to wind up Michael Holliday Productions, a move that would reduce Mike's future tax burden and remove some of the complexity from his affairs.

The accountants nursed Mike through the autumn. Most of his income from his variety weeks and club appearances went towards the tax debts, with Baker Todman exercising considerable skill in allocating the cash between the surtax Special Commissioners, who operated separately from the branch of the Revenue who were chasing Mike for his regular income tax. Not surprisingly, the accountants occasionally let their frustration show. When Mike was reluctant to sign up to any firm instalment plan, they wrote to him in no uncertain terms. 'We have to give the Collector some idea even if it is only a percentage of your earnings. As we have suggested from time to time before, we cannot do anything without your cooperation.' It was the line that all of Mike's advisors eventually found themselves saying.

In December 1962, the accountants provided Mike with a summary of where he stood. The good news was that his arrears from previous years were down to £1,000. Mike had one more instalment of £300 to make on the surtax to remove that particular monkey from his back. The bad news was that the tax on his company from 1961 would fall due on 1st January 1963. That increased the debt by £1,509, taking the total beyond £2,500 once again.

At least the accountants could see a light at the end of the tunnel, albeit in a way that only accountants can. 'As far as I can remember, you have had a fairly poor year to September

1962,' Bill Gudgin wrote. The 'poor year' had been the main reason why Mike was in such trouble, although it did at least offer the crumb of comfort that the tax demand from that year would be low. That meant, said Gudgin, that if Mike could come up with a way of way clearing £2,000 or so of the current debt, he would be in the clear.

It was easier said than done. With Mike struggling to meet instalments of even £300 per month, coming up with £2,000 seemed a big 'if'. But the money in South Africa had been good and there was more good news waiting when Mike got back from home. Whilst he had been away, Hal Monty had finalised the deal with the BBC for six half-hour shows. Filming of the series would begin immediately in the New Year. The fee for the series was £2,000. Monty had also booked Mike in a summer season in Jersey at £300 per week for ten shows per week and had cabled Mike in South Africa to say that he had options in New Zealand to follow the summer on the Channel Island. And still there was Australia, Japan and the Far East, geisha girls an' all.

Britain went into January 1963 with the country paralysed by an Arctic winter. But for Michael Holliday, things were looking up. 1963 was looking like a new beginning.

Chapter 20

Holliday At Home

The BBC scheduled Mike's new series for a prime-time Friday night spot between 7.30 and 8 p.m. Mike recorded the first show on 2nd January 1963 for broadcast three weeks later. It was the return of the prodigal son. *Radio Times* ran a 'welcome back' feature. 'That easy-going ex-seadog is back on TV tonight,' it said, adding that the new series would catch the singer in many moods, 'sometimes contrasting with the relaxed approach that has made him so popular in previous appearances'.

The picture that accompanied the piece showed Mike with one of the new props that designer Ken Lawson came up with for the show. The piece was a black Scandinavian rocking chair that Lawson bought in a Manchester store for £3. For the new series, Mike's tape recorder duets would be done from the rocking chair. It took the relaxed image to a new plane. After Mike's death, the chair became an indelible part of the image of his BBC successor – Val Doonican.

With a generous budget that John Ammonds had been able to secure, Ken Lawson approached the new series with glee. The series' title was *Holliday At Home*, the same as for the pilot show back in 1960. There was no need or question of moving away from the idea of Mike in his TV flat. This time however, the set was all new.

Holliday At Home was the first series to use the entire studio space in Dickenson Road, although as a former chapel, its T-shape brought limitations. The former transept provided the bar of the 'T' and Lawson used that as a home base for the set and made it the focal point of Mike's new home. He constructed an elaborate stone fireplace, complete with a real fire, plus a water cascade down one side. In the foreground, he introduced a Bösendorfer grand piano, whilst the rocking chair sat at the other side of the open floor area. Mike's tape recorder was alongside.

Lawson also used the two ends of the transept to good effect. In one, he created a lounge area, complete with two settees, and discretely positioned a painting of his own on the wall. The other became Mike's dining room. Lawson envisaged a fully laid-out dining table with a series of hand-painted frescos as the interior walls.

The six shows all followed the same pattern. Mike opened each one with a chorus of 'Nothin' To Do' before going into an uptempo number, followed by a more conventional ballad. Each show had one featured guest plus a regular dance spot involving Mike and Denny Bettis. In another change, Bernard Herrmann led the full weight of the Northern Dance Orchestra to accompany Mike and take one solo spot.

Mike's opening lines in the first show added to the sense of a comeback. 'Just in case you've been wondering where I've been for the past few months,' he said looking straight to the camera, 'I've been touring just about all over the world and I finished up in South Africa.' Dickie Valentine was the featured guest and the highspot of the show was intended to be a medley of their respective hits. Once again, however, the tape recorder stole the show.

Mike had scripted a clever piece of dialogue in which the tape recorder voice expressed a concern about 'the rumours that were going around':

Mike: Rumours, what kind of rumours?
Other Fella: Well, people have been saying that I'm using
             somebody else's voice.
Mike: No!

Other Fella:	Yes. The story is that it's really the voice of a very well-known American crooner.
Mike:	Don't worry, my friend. They say the same about me. Are you ready for a song...?

The next five shows featured guests such as the Vernon Girls, ventriloquist Denis Spicer and violinist Max Jaffa. Other regulars were four girl dancers – Mavis Ascott, Elaine Carr, Jackie Poole and Patsie Porter – all picked for their dancing talents plus their lack of inches.

The shows benefited from a considerable publicity push, with a strong theme of Mike's 'return'. Only one preview rattled the skeleton in the closet with a comment that the series 'puts an end to those rumourmongers who said he was ill and forced to pack in the business'. The after-show reviews, though, were more mixed. Whilst the relaxed Michael Holliday was welcomed back, the new features went down less well. Mike was 'slapdash' said one; 'under-rehearsed' said another; a third drew attention to Mike's self-consciousness, attributing it to the presence of a studio audience.

Much of what the reviewers saw was true. Ken Lawson recalled Mike's constant uncertainty about his performance. With the shows filmed in short sections to accommodate the scene changes, there were frequent, lengthy breaks in the shooting. Mike, said Lawson, was constantly seeking feedback and encouragement at every break. On some mornings, it was difficult to prise Mike from his dressing room. Lawson recalled John Ammonds asking him to go down and talk to Mike 'because he says he's not in a singing mood today'. Lawson's approach was not to try to get to the source of Mike's worries; he talked to him about everyday things. Lawson's painting was a particular interest for Mike and after a while, it freed him sufficiently from his depression so that the work could begin.

John Ammonds also witnessed some out-of-character outbursts from Mike. In one duet sequence with Max Jaffa, the two stars needed to don cowboy hats. 'Mike took a liking to Max's hat and said he wanted it,' recalled Ammonds. When Ammonds, keen to just get on with the filming, said that Mike's own hat was fine, Holliday stormed off the set, throwing a brand new radio mike that Ammonds had just obtained onto the ground, smashing it. Ammonds hit the roof. He stormed into Mike's dressing room only to find himself disarmed by one of Mike's 'sorry boss, not cut out for this lark' responses.

Ammonds was both pleased and disappointed with the series. The new concept – the more ambitious set, the guests, the new props – had worked well, but he still felt that Mike could have given more. 'I think John thought he had taken Mike as far he could go,' said Ken Lawson.

Mike's mood swings were almost certainly symptoms of his ongoing illness. Depression now is viewed as a relatively common illness. Research suggests that as many as one in ten of the western world's population suffer from it at some time in their lives and whilst the causes are still not fully understood, the treatments available are many and varied.

When Michael Holliday was suffering from the depths of his depression, it was very different. Depression was often seen as self-inflicted and more a state of mind than an illness. The sufferer's deep self-absorption and lack of response to the world around them were seen as causes rather than symptoms. 'Snap out of it,' was the usual message.

Drug treatment for depression was still in its infancy. None of the modern antidepressant drugs such as Prozac were available to clinicians. What was on offer was a narrow range of barbiturates designed to reduce tension and anxiety, and promote sleep. One such drug prescribed for Mike and which he took each evening was Nembutal.

The commonest medical treatment, however, was electro-convulsive therapy (ECT). This treatment, developed in the late 1930s and still applied to particular conditions today, involved sending a mild electric charge into the brain to attack the same transmitter chemicals that are now targeted by medication. Requiring anaesthesia and muscle relaxants to protect the patient from pain, the treatment involved two or three sessions per week. At the end of the Fifties, it was the standard treatment for depression. Mike underwent regular spells of such treatment during the final months of his life. The treatment itself was a traumatic experience that can only have added to Mike's sense of hopelessness.

Mike was probably suffering from dysthmia – an underlying constant depression, with specific depressive episodes triggered by one particular event compounding it. It was at these moments that Mike increasingly talked about taking his own life. When Margie gave evidence at the inquest, Mike's suicide threats, she said, had become commonplace.

Such threats sometimes had elements of black humour to them. John Ammonds recalled his final conversation with Mike. Despite his misgivings, Ammonds wanted another series. Mike, too, was keen. He called Ammonds to see what the prospects were. The producer said that he was due to discuss it with Tom Sloan next time he was in London. Ammonds was one of the few people who knew that Mike had, by this time, taken two overdoses and he asked him how he was. Mike said that he was depressed. He thought he might 'do himself in', he said. Ammonds' immediate response was to inject some humour into it. 'I said to him "Well don't do it just yet, wait until I've talked to Tom Sloan". We both laughed about it,' said Ammonds.

Mike's second overdose had come within days of the transmission of the sixth and final show in the *Holliday At Home* series. The tax situation triggered it. In January, Mike had finally delivered the final instalment on his surtax debt and the focus had shifted to the £1,500 owed on Michael Holliday Productions. Mike's accountants had been pressing him since December for some indication on how he would meet the demand, and by mid-February were showing increasing signs of frustration. Mike had not responded to their letters. They in turn had made no statement of Mike's intentions to the Revenue. 'I do not think they are going to allow this to remain for much longer,' they told him.

The prediction was correct. In a letter dated 5th March 1963, the Collector of Taxes gave formal notice that unless Mike paid the tax in full within seven days, he would commence distraint proceedings for recovery immediately. Up until that point, Mike with the not inconsiderable help of his accountants had walked a taxation tightrope around the edge of the courtroom. Now it seemed he was finally to end up in the dock. The spectre of bankruptcy loomed large.

The Collector's letter arrived on the Wednesday, in the middle of what should have been a busy week. On the Friday, Mike was due to appear at the Mid-Herts Press Ball in St Albans for which Hal Monty had negotiated a £100 fee for a 30-minute appearance. On the Saturday, he was to appear at Malvern, the spa town in the Midlands, followed by a Sunday concert and then a Monday-night appearance at Les Ambassadeurs in Leicester.

None of the bookings went ahead. On 8th March, Mike was rushed to hospital. Again, he had taken an overdose of sleeping tablets. Mike spent four days in hospital, although this time both his stay and his release attracted the minimum publicity. There was no repeat of the staged photographs with Margie from 18 months ago. Indeed, when Mike headed for Spain for a short holiday in May, Margie was not with him.

Mike's early release from hospital triggered another unusual exchange with the BBC. In February, Mike had booked himself to appear on two radio programmes in late March and early April. Other than an appearance on *Parade Of The Pops* in April 1962, they were Mike's first bookings on any of the BBC's musical magazine programmes since 1960.

With Mike hospitalised, a representative from Hal Monty's company, East and West Promotions, rang the BBC to cancel both engagements. At first, the BBC staff were reluctant to act on Monty's instructions. Mike had given a very clear message to them that Monty's remit extended only to stage work. But with Monty's office having all the correct information about the bookings, they took the message at face value. The news had come as no particular surprise. Those inside the BBC who had dealt with Mike had found their conversations odd to say the least. At least one member of the production staff had offered the view that Mike seemed to be heading for a nervous breakdown.

Within days of the call from Monty's company, Mike himself was back on the phone. He was unaware that Monty had cancelled the bookings. Speaking to Trafford Whitelock, the producer of one of the two shows, Mike told him that he had been in hospital for four days but was out now and available for work. When told of the cancellations, Mike apparently took the news calmly but reiterated that East and West Promotions did not handle his radio work. He had, he said, signed up with them until September but volunteered the view that he would then drop them as they were 'no good at all as agents'.

Mike followed up the call with another off the wall letter a few days later. Seemingly personally typed, the letter was headed 'Dear Gang' and said, 'I still haven't got to the bottom of that Monty affair … but I am working on it' and closed thanking everyone for 'being nice about the whole thing'. Concerned at the letter's strange language, one of the BBC production team called Mike, succeeded only in speaking to Margie who was 'wispily charming'. Mike, she said, had been a 'bit upset' about the dates being cancelled but was sure that he would be happy with the reassurance that the BBC would not henceforth deal with East and West Promotions on his behalf.

Mike returned to work in April with a few low-key live bookings before heading to Majorca for a ten-day holiday in May. Travelling alone, he briefly rubbed shoulders with Adam Faith, posing for photographs beside the pool of the hotel in Arenal. Holliday also bumped into another showbusiness couple. Whilst not close friends, they knew him well. Mike was, they said, intensely unhappy and deeply depressed about the state of his marriage, but made no mention of money trouble or other worries. Mike's problems, it seems, were all from within.

When Mike returned to London, he had time only to fit in a recording session at Abbey Road before heading for the summer season in Jersey. Norrie Paramor had supervised several sessions during the course of 1962 and early 1963, still searching for the

211

sound or indeed the piece of good fortune that would take Mike back into the charts.

In the autumn of 1962, Mike had recorded three songs. The old standard, 'Have I Told You Lately That I Love You', was the main item, getting a country and western treatment and the nod as the next single A side. The other two sides recorded at that session were both products of the songwriting partnership of Mort Shuman and Doc Pomus. The pair were best known for a series of Elvis Presley hits including 'Surrender', plus the Drifters' 'Save The Last Dance For Me'. One of the two sides, 'It Only Takes A Minute' was the B side release. With a strong beat and an unusual vocal style, it was the most un-Michael Holliday like recording of any that he made for EMI. Surprisingly for a song so unfamiliar in style, Mike despatched it in only a handful of takes.

In January 1963, Paramor had Mike try again with a single, this time from the pen of Ben Raleigh and Bernie Wayne. Both were well-known writers in other partnerships, Raleigh having provided the lyric for 'Tell Laura I Love Her', the Ricky Valence hit from 1960, whilst Wayne could claim the melody rights behind the early Fifties hit 'Blue Velvet'. Regrettably, 'Laugh And The World Laughs With You' was a maudlin song that seemed more like a self-help message to Mike than an attempt on the charts. Despite Mike featuring it in his TV series, it made little impact.

The session in May 1963 continued in the same vein. Mike needed 14 takes to get the A side 'Between Hello And Goodbye' to Paramor's satisfaction, although once again there was doubt as to whether he had actually picked the stronger of the two numbers. The song on the B side was Joe South's 'Just To Be With You Again', a stronger beat number but one which nevertheless seemed to sit more easily with Mike's natural style.

Much has been made of the fact that Mike's suicide coincided with the musical revolution of the Sixties. Scrutiny of the charts up until the end of 1963, however, reveals that in overall terms they were still little changed from those of the mid-Fifties. Solo

212

artists and middle-of-the-road singers could still find hits if they had the right material. Frank Sinatra, Matt Monro, Frankie Vaughan, even Harry Secombe, all registered chart hits during 1963. It wasn't until December of that year, when the Beatles had five records in the Top Twenty, one of which was an LP, that the revolution was visible. Mike's lack of success in the charts was still more to do with the material that Norrie Paramor gave him and his own mismanagement of his career, than any musical revolution.

The Abbey Road session in May 1963 was a landmark for another reason. The original three-year contract that Mike had signed in 1957 had expired in 1960 although EMI had exercised each of the three one-year options on it. The last of those was due to expire in August 1963. EMI needed to decide if they wanted to renew.

The initial response from EMI Chairman Len Wood was lukewarm. He suggested to producer George Martin that they might offer Mike a further year, plus two one-year options. It was not an unduly surprising response. Mike had last appeared in the charts three years ago and the sales of his singles in the last two years had deteriorated markedly. Hindsight shows that Mike's future would have been in the album market, but at the time, recording contracts were written as if LPs didn't exist. Singles were everything.

When George Martin broached the matter with Mike, he was surprised to discover a counter-offer on the table from Dick Rowe at Decca (the man forever remembered in music history as having turned down The Beatles). The Decca deal offered Holliday a five-year contract, guaranteeing eight titles per year. It was tempting, even though Mike had no particular wish to leave EMI. In a letter to Norrie Paramor in June, he made his position clear. 'I'm not mad about giving you three years with options,' he told him. 'I think that's a little one-sided. If you can come up with a better deal, I'll be interested – but no options.'

Paramor was keen to hang on to the mercurial character that

he had first come across eight years before. In a note to Wood, he acknowledged that 'Michael's sales have dropped considerably during the last two or three years, although he is still rated ... and an important name. I feel that if he would pull his socks up, which by the way he has promised to do, we could probably get him back into the charts.' Paramor's advice was clear – offer him a flat three-year term or we will lose him to Decca.

The commercial rivalry between Decca and EMI was strong. Wood hated the idea of losing one of their 'names' to their most prominent rival. That was as much a factor in his decision to go with Paramor's advice as any inherent confidence in Mike. Paramor won the day. A new three-year extension to Mike's 1957 contract was prepared, with royalties increased to twopence halfpenny (1p) per side.

Mike signed the new contract in Jersey on 25th July 1963. Paramor was delighted. 'This is a pretty good victory and I imagine Decca will be somewhat disappointed,' he said in a note to Wood, telling him that Mike had signed. Wood added a schoolmasterly scribble. 'Excellent – well done,' he said.

Paramor lined up for the first session under the new contract for when Mike returned from Jersey. No one knew that the first session would also turn out to be the last.

Chapter 21

'Did I Take My Tablets?'

Jersey was a different kind of summer season from the ones that Mike had experienced before. The small Channel Island didn't seek to compete with the 'kiss-me-quick' resorts of Blackpool, Scarborough and the south coast. It offered a more sedate holiday experience, built more around affluence than adolescence. For the top stars a summer in Jersey offered a decent living but probably only half the earning potential from a mainland resort. For most, it was a venue on the way down rather than the way up.

Mike's season was at the Sunshine Hotel. It was one of a dozen or so hotels that offered top rank cabaret. The high admission charge and continuous food and drink service to tables was more akin to a modern club setting, but it meant that the hotels could offer good enough commercial terms to attract the big names. Mike's routine didn't require him to work too hard. His contract demanded a nightly show, doubling up on Fridays and Saturdays. Often on Sundays, the performers on the island would swap around and play a Sunday concert somewhere other than their base hotel.

Mike was a lonely figure. Margie seems not to have made any trips across to join him and whilst Hal Monty made the occasional visit, Mike was still wary. He had hoped that Johnny Wiltshire and the Trebletones would be with him for the summer but that too failed to materialise. The group was committed to a season in Great Yarmouth with Helen Shapiro. There wasn't

215

enough money in Mike's booking, said Wiltshire, to support him and four musicians.

It was against this backcloth that Mike met Basil le Marquand, a local water-skiing instructor. Le Marquand was working at the Olwin Grove Hotel, a short walk from the flat that Hal Monty had arranged for Mike. 'He was there in the bar one night, on his own,' said le Marquand. 'We got chatting and became friends.' At the end of the season, Mike employed le Marquand as his chauffeur-cum-roadie, staying with Mike at Dailson.

In some respects, le Marquand played the role that Johnny Wiltshire held during the 1961 season in Blackpool. Le Marquand was not in any sense a performer, but he provided the companionship that Mike had always sought. Whereas Mike had largely concealed his domestic troubles from Wiltshire, however, they were all too apparent to le Marquand. 'He was very depressed about his marriage,' le Marquand recalled. Mike, he said, wanted no more than to have a home to go back to, with the lights on and food on the table. 'But,' said le Marquand, 'it wasn't there. He had gone home a few times and found the place in darkness.' Despite the apparent longing for domestic tranquillity, le Marquand also witnessed first-hand Mike's constant pursuit of female company. 'He was a very virile man, shall we say,' said le Marquand.

The state of Mike's marriage was still not the only source of worry. Despite the re-establishment of the working relationship with Hal Monty, the debris from the court case refused to go away. The week after Mike's overdose in March, his own solicitors accepted an instalment arrangement for the balance of their fees – the 'see me at my front door' letter – but added that Mike still owed Monty his costs. They could not be sure, they said, that Monty's solicitors would be so accommodating.

Rubinsteins were right. Monty's costs were still unpaid in early March and indeed another trigger of Mike's apparent suicide attempt may have been a demand from Monty's solicitors, dated 4th March 1963, for interest at 4 per cent on the debt unless settled by 'the end of this present week'. When that deadline passed, Rubinsteins wrote to Mike on 13th March saying that Monty's solicitors had indicated that they were under instruction to 'recover the balance forthwith and are taking steps accordingly'. Rubinsteins added their own 'told-you-so', albeit couched in legalese. 'We must assume that they are working on Mr Monty's instructions and find it hard not to make any comment', they said.

The taxman was also still on Mike's back. Whilst the suicide attempt had led the Revenue to back off from its threat of court proceedings, the debts were still there. Baker Todman had succeeded in persuading them to accept monthly instalments of £100 against Mike's personal tax liability for 1961/62 and £200 against the company tax. It meant that yet again, Mike was committed to finding £300 per month, on top of the Hal Monty debt. Mike's debt to Monty and the Revenue was of the order of £2,500, even though he had now sorted out his long-standing surtax problem.

But, as his accountant had implied before Christmas, there was light at the end of the tunnel. Mike's earnings in the year to September 1962 had been significantly down on previous years. His BBC income – almost entirely from *Holliday With Strings* – was only around £1,000. His record sales had dropped to the point where the royalty stream was only a few hundred pounds whilst the only variety income had been the pantomime season in Torquay and the three provincial weeks in the summer of 1962. Mike's accounts for that year were not completed, but it is unlikely that they would have shown gross income much in excess of £5,000. Whilst Mike's drop in earnings was a worry, it did at least mean that any new tax liabilities arising during 1963 would be light. If Mike could maintain the monthly payments through to the autumn, he had the prospect of being clear of debt for the first time in almost three years.

No further correspondence between Mike and his accountants survives, although his final letter to Margie in October 1963 made reference to the income tax 'wanting their money by Wednesday' [30 October] and that 'even my accountant is tired of me and has deserted me'. Any instalments accepted by the Revenue were always on condition that failure to keep to the schedule would render the full amount due. Mike's letter to Margie suggests that he had not kept up the monthly payments and consequently faced another threatening demand.

Whether his accountants had in fact, 'deserted him' would seem questionable. Mike had shown a tendency before to throw the blame on his advisors. What's more, Mike now had more money coming in than at any time in the past 18 months. His BBC series had been worth £2,000 to him, whilst the Jersey booking grossed fees of over £5,000. Both of these contracts were subject to a 10 per cent deduction for Monty's fees and Mike clearly had other outgoings. But there still should have been enough money to clear both the remaining tax debt and any balance due to Monty.

Mike's will supports the view that he had in fact enough cash to settle. When it was published in April 1964, it revealed that Mike died with debts of just under £5,000 outstanding. Half of the debt figure related to the outstanding mortgage on Dailson. Nevertheless, Mike still had sufficient assets – over and above his share of Dailson (which Margie jointly owned) – to clear these and leave a net figure of £4,916. Even though most of that residual figure reflected his share of Dailson, he was not insolvent at the time of his death.

Mike returned home in September at the end of a low-key but successful season in Jersey. Le Marquand came with him, even though, according to the Jerseyman, Mike expected to find Margie still at home. She wasn't. Margie had finally made the break and gone, it seemed, for good. She had rented a small house in Sompting, close to the south coast and close to where their son Michael was at boarding school. She had also instructed solicitors to begin divorce proceedings.

Mike had no work lined up when he came back from the Channel Islands other than the first EMI session under his new contract. Hal Monty, however, had booked a series of international dates, beginning in Frankfurt on 9th November, and then heading

218

to the Far East for Christmas. Mike also had an appointment at the BBC at the end of October to discuss another series of half-hour shows.

His priority, though, was to find Margie. Eventually he tracked her down to the bungalow in Sompting. With le Marquand at the wheel of the Ford Galaxie, a 1962 replacement for the Ford Fairlane, Mike paid his wife an impromptu visit. The ski instructor waited in the car whilst Mike went to the house. He returned half an hour later, saying nothing to le Marquand about what had transpired.

It had been an unhappy and unsuccessful encounter. His arrival was unexpected and Margie refused to allow him inside. They spoke for a while on the doorstep and whilst the content of the conversation was never divulged, the separation continued. 'Maybe some people thought I had walked out on him when he needed me most,' said Margie in an interview six months after his death. 'I hadn't. I helped him for years. It had just reached an impossible stage.'

They had, she said, separated before and each time, she had made it up. 'Who knows what would have happened?' But a close friend of both Mike and Margie said that Mike believed that he had lost her for good.

Mike spent a lonely and troubled few weeks at home in the autumn of 1963. Hal Monty made regular telephone calls from a range of exotic locations that he was visiting to arrange what he referred to as Mike's 'world tour'. Le Marquand remembered Mike being enthusiastic about the tour and often coming out of the calls with Monty saying that they would be on their way soon. The plan was for le Marquand to go along as general factotum. But other than the calls from Monty, Mike had little contact with the show business world in those final weeks.

Norrie Paramor had arranged the recording session at Abbey Road for the evening of 22nd October. Although it was the first session under the new contract, it had a familiar feel to it. The location was the usual Studio Two, Paramor himself was the producer and the familiar figure of Stuart Eltham was once again

219

in the control room. Paramor again, however, continued his policy of pairing Mike with different arrangers and conductors in the search for the missing piece that would turn on the hit stream.

This time, he paired Mike with Ivor Raymonde, the arranger and conductor best known for his work with Billy Fury, the Bachelors and Dusty Springfield. Raymonde was the co-author and arranger of 'I Only Want To Be With You', the single that in November 1963 launched Dusty's solo career.

The selection of Raymonde to handle the arrangements for the October session was a deliberate change of style by Paramor. The dalliance with country and western had got nowhere, nor had the homespun philosophy of 'Laugh And The World Laughs With You'. The Beatles had arrived and whilst no one knew exactly where their influence was going to take pop music, one message was very clear: to have a chance in the charts, the beat was everything.

Paramor came up with two titles that fitted the bill perfectly. The first, 'Drums' had an impeccable pedigree, coming from the pens of Jerry Leiber and Mike Stoller. The Elvis Presley hits, 'Hound Dog' and 'Jailhouse Rock', had already made Lieber and Stoller rock 'n roll legends. Few indeed would ever have expected them to provide the A side to a Michael Holliday single. The second title, 'Dear Heart', was in a similar vein and is not to be confused with the ballad of the same name that provided a big hit for Andy Williams.

Both numbers benefited from an arrangement that relied heavily on strings, although not the lush sounds of Holliday's albums. The eight violins on 'Drums' play allegretto, driven along by a tom-tom drum that provides a hard, driving beat. 'Dear Heart' is much the same, except that the strings are plucked rather than stroked. The fast pace produced two short tracks, neither much over two minutes, but in both cases Mike delivers outstanding vocals. On 'Drums', he took five or six takes to get the feel of the material before settling into a strong and confident delivery, a singer putting 100 per cent trust in a voice that did not let him down.

220

The two titles needed 14 and 10 takes respectively, with the session's third title interspersed between them. Its title was ironic to say the least. 'My Last Date (With You)' had been a US hit for pianist Floyd Cramer in 1960 under the abbreviated title 'Last Date'. With lyrics added, the song became a plaintiff love ballad, requiring a tender reading of the lyric and a wide vocal range. Although Holliday could be heard telling Paramor that he couldn't cope with the range of the song, he nevertheless delivered three flawless performances out of five takes.

The session should have been the most significant of any since 'Starry Eyed'. Mike was in a relaxed good humour, offering impromptu James Cagney impressions between takes. He seemed to enjoy the session and was quick to acknowledge the odd mistake. 'My fault, Ivor, my fault', he called in a strong Scouse voice after having fluffed a line in the penultimate take of 'Drums'. Later in the session, Paramor told him that he wanted to hear more of a sense of fun in Mike's voice. Before the final take of 'Dear Heart', he told him to 'remember the smile'.

'Okay, boss,' said Mike, happily singing the song along to himself whist he waited for the backing singers to regroup. There was no hint to anyone at the session of what was to come seven days later.

When Paramor heard the test pressings, he was delighted. He called Mike at Dailson the following Sunday to tell him. 'Mike was in fine form at that last session,' he later told the press. Both he and Mike agreed that 'Drums' would be the natural A side for Mike's next release.

What should have been the launch of a new Michael Holliday sound instead became a posthumous curiosity. In between taking the call from Paramor, plus another from Hal Monty, Mike sat down and wrote a three-page letter to Margie. It was the letter that two weeks later would be used to tell the world that Michael Holliday had carefully and deliberately planned to take his own life.

221

Dear Margaret

By the time you receive this, I trust that I shall be at the Land Of Nod. I thought it would be better if you found out this way as I am sure that it will get in the papers one way or another.

I am sorry that I had to do this but I am afraid I am so confused. If you could have spoken to me about it, it might have helped a little.

Even my accountants have grown tired of me and deserted me. The income tax want their money by Wednesday or else. I guess I ain't man enough to tackle it alone.

If I can get word to you about the other world – if there is one – you know me, I will find some way of letting you know. I will let you know because a lot of people are curious about going beyond.

It was by any standards, a pathetic letter and yet had all the standard ingredients of a suicide note – the sense of hopelessness, a motive, and a subtle transfer of guilt to the recipient.

Looked at another way however, the letter was no more than an expression of Mike's depressive mental state. All who knew him closely had become accustomed to hearing the threats to take his life.

Even so, Margie took the letter seriously. She received it on Monday, 28th October and passed it straight to her solicitor who in turn passed it to the local police. A local police sergeant visited Dailson. Mike was not there, but there was nothing to indicate that he had carried out his threat.

Later that evening, le Marquand and Mike left to visit the Freddie Mills Nite Spot. It was a new venture for Mills, succeeding the Chinese restaurant that he had opened when he left the boxing ring. Despite stories that described Mike as a regular at the club, it was in fact his first visit – a fact confirmed by Mills in one of a series of press interviews that he gave over the following days, and by le Marquand 40 years on. 'We usually went to the Embassy Club,' said le Marquand.

The chain of events after Mike and le Marquand left Dailson

were described in detail at the inquest a week later. They arrived at the club around 1.30 a.m., possibly having visited another club en route. They stayed for about 90 minutes, leaving between 3.00 and 3.30 a.m. En route back to Dailson, they stopped for a coffee in Leicester Square and arrived home at 4.50 a.m. A girl, Zena, accompanied them back to the house, although most of the press coverage chose to ignore that point of detail.

Freddie Mills's press interviews and evidence at the inquest painted a picture of Mike in the deepest of all depressions. He had told them in a matter-of-fact way, said Mills, that he had had enough. Tonight was his last night. He was, said Mills, so cool about it that at first he thought it was a joke and responded by telling Mike to go ahead – see if anybody cares. Only later, he said, did he realise that Mike was serious. When he did, both he and his wife Chrissie spent time trying to talk him out of his mood.

Le Marquand told the court that he drove the singer, who was 'slightly the worse for drink', home where they retired to their separate rooms. Once there, le Marquand was woken by Mike shouting from outside the house. He had, he said, wanted to retrieve his briefcase from the car and locked himself out.

According to press reports of the hearing, le Marquand came downstairs to let him in and then went back upstairs to get the car keys. Mike followed, tripped on the stairs, bumped his head on the wall, and fell unconscious. Le Marquand immediately called an ambulance that took Mike to Croydon General Hospital, arriving around 7 a.m. On arrival at the hospital, Mike was found to have taken a large overdose of sleeping tablets. Twelve hours later at 5.50 p.m., Michael Holliday passed away.

It seemed an open and shut case. The evidence from Margie presented a picture – entirely true – of someone who had battled depression for almost three years, had a history of suicide attempts, regularly threatened to take his life and was receiving psychiatric treatment. He was in debt, harassed for tax, lonely and unwilling or unable to trust those around him who might help.

The pathologist's report was equally clear. Mike had taken '20

223

to 25 capsules of Nembutal, in a single dose'. It was, said Dr Haler, sufficient to kill him even without the alcohol that he had consumed. The coroner's verdict of suicide was little more than a formality.

But this would not be the complex story of Michael Holliday without a twist at the end.

Despite the evidence presented at the inquest, there were those close to Mike who were nevertheless surprised to hear the news of his death. Norrie Paramor commented that Mike had looked tired at the last session and knew that he was upset over the situation with Margie, but said, 'you wouldn't have thought that he was going to do anything serious'.

Hal Monty, too, was taken aback. Mike, he said, had asked him to come with him to meet Margie and try and persuade her to come back. Margie had agreed and the meeting was set to take place on Tuesday 29th October, the day on which Mike died. On the Thursday, they were due at the BBC for a meeting about another series of half-hour shows.

Others saw the overdose as an attempt to put psychological pressure on Margie – an attempt to frighten her into coming back. There are phrases in the 'Land Of Nod' letter that seem to be written with that in mind. Johnny Wiltshire always found it difficult to believe that Mike would deliberately take his life. 'Mike always took lots of tablets,' he said. 'He knew what he was doing with tablets except that night, he'd had the brandies that he didn't normally have.'

Another close friend of Mike and Margie had doubts too. 'I know he didn't intend to take his life because he told me he never would,' she said.

There is something in both the timing and the apparent precision of Mike's final act that does not seem quite right. Mike was never the most disciplined or orderly character. How, then, could he calmly map out the end of his own life and put it into effect over a 48-hour period – from the letter on Sunday to the tablets in the early hours of Tuesday morning. Such exactitude and cool-headedness was not a normal part of his make-up.

There are also pieces in the jigsaw of the last 48 hours that do not fit as neatly together as the inquest implied. Much significance was attached to the letter to Margie, but it arrived early. Perhaps Mike underestimated the efficiency of the then GPO. With a reconciliation meeting planned for two days' time, the letter was odd – but a decision to commit suicide when Margie had finally agreed to see him later the same week seems odder still.

There is then the reported heart-to-heart conversation with Freddie Mills. It was Mike's first visit to the club. Basil le Marquand recalled no other meeting with Mills in the weeks leading up to Holliday's death, and the extensive body of personal papers that survive contain no indication that Mills and Holliday were especially close. Was Mills the sort of person to whom Mike would open his heart? Le Marquand said that he was never far from Mike during their stay at the Nite Spot and heard nothing of a 'this is my last night' conversation.

The events after Mike left Mills's club also warrant closer scrutiny. Who was Zena? Most reporters at the inquest drew a veil over her existence, but the few that did mention her revealed that Mike had met her only that night. Forty years later, le Marquand chuckled when asked about her. 'She was just a pick-up,' he said, the latest and last in a long line of available girls who had been only too happy to accept Michael Holliday's invitation to bed.

What happened when Mike, Zena and le Marquand returned to Dailson is also open to conjecture. The inquest heard that Mike had suffered a fall and lost consciousness. That was the reason an ambulance had been called – not because he had been found lying on a bed beside an empty bottle of pills. It was only some time later – when Mike arrived at the hospital – that it became apparent he had taken an overdose.

But Mike's behaviour leading up to a 'fall' on the stairs was not that of someone suffering with symptoms of an overdose of sleeping tablets. The poison inside Nembutal is pentobarbital. When taken in excess, it produces an unsteadiness of gait, slurred speech, difficulty in breathing and a drop in pulse rate and blood

225

pressure. The taker initially becomes groggy before dropping into a deep sleep or a coma. In extreme cases, the result is heart failure.

Mike's condition before the collapse does not map against these symptoms. He was sufficiently alert to arouse le Marquand, even though he was outside the house. He was, it seems, also sufficiently coherent to articulate why he had been outside and what he wanted from the car. As reported, his loss of consciousness was sudden. Mike did not, according to press reports, drift into a coma or a deep sleep. Yet despite apparently suffering a fall of sufficient force to knock him unconscious, the post mortem found no trace of it. In his evidence, Dr Haler said he had examined Mike's body and found no evidence of a fall. 'Not even a bruise,' he said.

Basil le Marquand now has only scant recollection of the inquest. He was a young man, caught up in a flood of media activity surrounding the death of one of show business's biggest stars. As the prime witness to Michael Holliday's final hours, he found the experience unsettling and unnerving. The reporters who buzzed around him seemed interested in only one thing – that Mike had a history of suicide attempts.

In contrast to his hazy memories of the inquest, le Marquand's account of the last hours of Mike's life is lucidly clear and differs markedly from that reported at the inquest. He and Mike, with Zena, had returned to Dailson where le Marquand had seen Mike take the usual tablets that he took every night. Half an hour later, Mike reappeared in the lounge and asked le Marquand, 'Did I take my tablets?' When the skiing instructor told him that he had, Mike said, 'Well, I've just taken them again. You'd better get me to hospital.'

There was, in this account, no fall or incident on the stairs, nor any suggestion that Mike had suddenly lost consciousness. Mike was, said le Marquand, showing signs of grogginess by the time the ambulance arrived but knew what was going on. 'He walked out to the ambulance,' said le Marquand.

And Zena? 'She was still there [at Dailson] when the ambulance came,' le Marquand said. 'I went with Mike to the hospital but when I came back mid-morning she was gone.'

Le Marquand spent the rest of the day at Dailson waiting for news. With no business or family ties to Mike, he was an outsider. He listened for news on the radio. Margie, in Sompting, heard from a friend that Mike was in hospital. She too sat by the telephone. It rang in the early evening. The same close friend asked her if she was sitting down. 'He's gone,' she said.

Michael Holliday was dead at the age of 38. The verdict of the inquest was suicide. The death certificate is clear: 'Poisoning by Nembutal. Suicide.'

But was it so clear? There is no doubt that Mike was depressed, massively so, and had pressures on him that he found difficult to handle. He was unstable and prone to sudden changes of mood and he constantly talked of taking his own life. If he had not taken an overdose in the early hours of 29th October 1963, it is entirely possible that he would have done so the next night, or the night after.

But was the overdose that he took *that* night a deliberate and calculated action that was designed to end his life? The verdict of suicide says that it was. But could it have been a tragic accident?

One question still stands out. Was it really Mike's intention to bring a girl home for a one-night stand and then have her wake up next to a corpse?

Chapter 22

'Dear Mike – Beloved By Many'

The inquest delivered its verdict on Guy Fawkes' day. The day after, Mike's body was taken home to Liverpool in preparation for the funeral at Anfield Cemetery on 7th November 1963.

John Ammonds was one of the few people from show business who attended, along with Norrie Paramor. It was a sombre occasion but Ammonds recalled a moment of black humour as he turned the corner into St Agnes Road. It was from the small two-up, two-down where his mother still lived that Mike would make his last journey. 'The hearse was already outside the house with Mike's body inside,' Ammonds recalled. 'I said to myself "Mike, you fool. You forgot the last detail. You could at least have arranged a six foot coffin."' The TV producer allowed himself a quite chuckle, knowing that the thought would have appealed to Mike's sense of humour.

There were few, if any, show business faces at the funeral. The tributes from other stars were of the floral kind. Cliff Richard and Shirley Bassey were amongst those who sent wreaths but a Liverpool rumour that the Beatles were to act as pallbearers proved to be nothing more than that. Nevertheless, it contributed to a large crowd of 3,000 that thronged the cemetery.

The service took place inside the small Catholic chapel that stood inside the grounds. Mike's grave would be at its door. His headstone stood against the chapel wall and reflected both sides of Michael Holliday. The main inscription said: 'In loving memory of my husband – Norman Alexander Milne. Died 29th October

'1963.' Mike's alter ego was reflected just below. 'Dear Mike –
Beloved by Many.'

Dressed all in black, Margie headed an official group of
mourners, family and close friends. Margie broke down several
times during the service and at the graveside. Mike's mother
was distraught. Within two years, she would be buried with her
middle son.

Margie returned to Dailson and gave an interview to the press.
She talked of Mike's constant depression as the thing that had
driven them apart. The following year, she sold Dailson and
moved to a detached house in Haywards Heath in Sussex, making
a home there for herself and Michael junior. She continued to
use the name of Margie Holliday and to promote Mike's memory
whenever she could. In 1974 she appeared on Radio Merseyside
and said she had happy memories of the good days 'before Mike
was ill'. She never remarried and died prematurely, from natural
causes in April 1981. She was 53. Their son briefly sought to
follow his father's footsteps as Michael Holliday Junior, but was
unable to break through.

In November 1963, EMI released the first of the three singles
that Mike had recorded one week before his death. 'Drums', the
song that should have relaunched the singles career of Michael
Holliday, was now his memorial. It sold 5,000 copies on its first
day in the shops. The remaining tracks were issued on further
singles, the last one fittingly being 'My Last Date (With You)'
in July 1964. A special EP and an LP of Mike's hits also came
out, but within a short time they were the only records of Mike's
that EMI kept in its catalogue.

Bing Crosby, like the rest of the show business world, had
been shocked by Mike's death. 'This is really staggering news,'
he said in an interview with *Melody Maker* the day after the
news broke. 'Michael was an extremely close friend and I cannot
bring myself to think that he has died. I was always extremely
flattered that he had based his style of singing on my style of
singing. He's sure got my voice off to the last degree, I guess.'

In a letter to this author in 1973, Crosby still recalled his friendship with Mike with affection. 'Yes, I knew Michael Holliday well,' he said. 'I think he had great potential, this young man. Very appealing personality and a genuinely good singer.'

In 1976, Crosby surprised the entertainment world by making a return to the live stage, playing sell-out seasons on Broadway and at the London Palladium. The following year, he was back again in England for another Palladium fortnight, plus a series of regional one-nighters. Crosby by now was 74 years old and if his voice had retained much of its quality, he was physically frail, having survived a near fatal fall from a stage at a concert in Pasadena earlier in the year.

His final performance of the tour was in Brighton, a short distance from Margie Holliday's home in Haywards Heath. With Michael junior at her side, Margie watched as Crosby gave a virtuoso performance, culminating in a half-hour medley of over 30 of his biggest hits. They were the songs that Mike and Margie had grown up with, and doubtless her mind went back to the sunny afternoon in California some 18 years earlier. It was Bing Crosby's last performance. Five days later, he collapsed and died on a golf course in Spain.

The name of Michael Holliday faded fast. In April 1964, British show business paid one last tribute. Russ Conway organised a memorial concert for Mike to provide funds for Michael junior's education. The concert was held at the Prince Of Wales theatre on 19th April 1964 and the cream of British show business, from Matt Monro to David Frost, and Alma Cogan to Jessie Matthews, gave their services.

Bing Crosby sent a specially recorded message for the memorial concert. 'I am grateful indeed to have this opportunity to pay tribute to Michael Holliday,' he said. 'He was a fine artist and a loyal and true friend and I lament with you, all of you, his premature passing from the scene before he had reached the fulfilment of his considerable talent. I shall miss him.' The BBC broadcast the concert on the Light Programme, with an edited version issued as an LP by EMI.

But when the doors of the theatre closed, the world of show

business turned its back on Michael Holliday. The BBC's policy of the time was to wipe the tapes of its TV and radio broadcasts, with few exceptions. All bar three of Mike's TV appearances on the BBC were destroyed, along with virtually all of his radio appearances. Only the copies held privately by collectors have meant that any kind of catalogue of Mike's work at the BBC survives.

Val Doonican inherited the 1964 slot that would have housed another series of *Holliday At Home*. Doonican has always been quick to acknowledge his debt to Michael Holliday, who created the template for the relaxed image on which the Irish crooner built a 40-year career. Doonican's first rocking chair, rescued from the prop room by John Ammonds and Ken Lawson, was the one that Mike had used in his last series.

EMI saw little potential in Mike's legacy. The Beatles revolution meant that it was hard enough for those solo performers who were still around to survive, let alone those who had gone. In 1966, EMI offered Margie a once and for all payment of £125 in lieu of future royalties. Margie wisely turned down the offer.

Nevertheless, by the end of the Sixties, it was as though Michael Holliday had never existed. Why should this be?

Part of the reason was the suicide verdict. Suicide had at one time been an offence under English law and until 1961 was still viewed by the church as a mortal sin. Had Mike died two years earlier, his grave could not have been within the hallowed ground of a Catholic cemetery. Suicide was one of British society's last taboos. Like homosexuality and teenage pregnancy, it attracted shame. It was something not to be spoken of. Thirty years passed before any reissued album of Mike's explained his death. 'The manner of his passing need not concern us', was a typical euphemism. What happened to Michael Holliday, and why, was best left unsaid.

Then there was Mike's standing in the show business community. Those who knew him as a person remembered the chirpy, dizzy character with a cheeky grin and a great sense of humour. 'He was a naughty boy but he could get away with murder,' said Johnny Pearson in an interview in 1993.

'I liked him because he was himself,' said Pete Murray recently. 'There was none of this "darling" bollocks about him.'

To many others in the business, though, Mike was a reclusive character. They might see him at functions and events, but generally he kept himself to himself. He was never comfortable with the glitz and gloss that goes with the showbiz lifestyle and many took this as a sign of aloofness. That, plus the embarrassment many felt at Mike's open and relentless womanising, meant that there was no shortage of people in the business who were happy to see Michael Holliday forgotten.

But talent does not die so easily. 'The Story Of My Life' alone proved to be one of the most durable of the Fifties records, appearing on almost every EMI Fifties compilation. In the 1990s, it featured prominently in a Guinness TV commercial, whilst another of Mike's records, 'The Runaway Train', was used to sell insurance. With the advent of compact discs, almost all of Mike's recordings have since been digitally remastered and reissued.

In 1993, unreleased session tapes were discovered in the EMI vaults and issued on a special anniversary CD, whilst a BBC Radio 2 tribute on the thirtieth anniversary of his death reawakened interest in a man who had almost disappeared. CD reissues brought his recordings to the ears of a new generation; even BBC TV's populist soap opera *EastEnders* regularly features 'Stairway Of Love' as background scene music. In 2002, an American audience attending the first of a series of events to mark the centenary of Bing Crosby's birth could be heard to gasp audibly when they heard the voice of Michael Holliday, many of them for the first time. In 2003, the *Liverpool Echo* published its list of '100 Greatest Merseysiders' with Mike in the list.

Michael Holliday sold over 2 million records in his eight-year career, with three Top Three hits and two number ones. More than that, he was the first British singer to make his name through the medium of television. Like Perry Como in the USA, Holliday realised the power of the box in the corner of the living room.

He was the first to break the BBC's mould of starchiness and stiffness. The casual style, the open-neck shirt, the tape recorder, the rocking chair and the knowing wink to the camera were all innovations that Michael Holliday brought to British television.

Above all else, though, Michael Holliday was a singer *par excellence*. His greatest asset was his golden voice – mellow, soft, warm, tender. His gift was that he could open his mouth and sing like a bird. But it was a gift given to a tortured soul who found that adulation and anonymity refuse to go hand in hand.

The story of *The Man Who Would Be Bing* is the story of a Liverpool lad who sailed by the North Star and traded it for the bright lights of show business. And who paid for it with his life.

Appendix 1

MICHAEL HOLLIDAY RECORDINGS FOR EMI COLUMBIA 1955–1963

Release details show the original or first single, EP or LP release for each title, plus the most recent CD release.

All sessions held in Abbey Road Studio 2, except where marked

23 August 1955, 9.30 p.m.–0.15 a.m., with Norrie Paramor and his Orchestra (Overdubbed vocal, orchestral track recorded 6.00–8.30 p.m.)

1 The Yellow Rose Of Texas	*Single*	*DB3675*
(All issues take 7)	*LP*	*The Best of Michael Holliday*
	CD	*The Story Of My Life*

2 Stein Song	*Single*	*DB3675*
(All issues take 7)	*LP*	*–*
	CD	*The Story Of My Life*

16 December 1955, 5.30–8.30 p.m., with Norrie Paramor and his Orchestra (Overdubbed vocal, orchestral track recorded 2.00–5.00 p.m.)

3 Sixteen Tons	*Single*	*DB3714 (78) / SCM5221 (45)*
(All issues take 9)	*LP*	*The Story Of My Life*
	CD	*The Story Of My Life*

4 The Rose Tattoo	*Single*	*DB3714 (78) / SCM5221 (45)*
(All issues take 4)	*LP*	*–*
	CD	*The Story Of My Life*

10 February 1956, 4.30–6.15 p.m., with Norrie Paramor and his Orchestra (Overdubbed vocal, orchestral track 2.00–4.30 p.m.)

5 Nothin' To Do	*Single*	*DB3746 (78) / SCM5252 (45)*
(All issues take 14)	*EP*	*Music With Mike*
	LP	*The Best of Michael Holliday*
	CD	*The Story Of My Life*

235

6 Perfume Candy and Flowers   *Single*   *DB3746 (78) / SCM5252 (45)*
(All issues take 11)   *LP*   –
                                  CD   *The Story Of My Life*

28 February 1956, 6.00–9.15 p.m., with guitar accompaniment
7 Darlin' Katie   *Single*   –
(All issues take 2)   *EP*   *My Guitar And Me*
                                  LP   *The EP Collection*
                                  CD   *The EP Collection*

8 Where The River Shannon   *Single*   –
   Flows   *EP*   *My Guitar And Me*
(All issues take 2)   *LP*   –
                                  CD   *The Story Of My Life*

9 With Me Ould Clay Pipe   *Single*   –
(And Me Donkey and Me   *EP*   *My Guitar And Me*
   Cart)   *LP*   –
(All issues take 1)   *CD*   –

10 Marrying For Love   *Single*   –
(All issues take 1)   *EP*   *My Guitar And Me*
                                  LP   –
                                  CD   *The EP Collection*

28 April 1956, 2.30–5.00 p.m., with Norrie Paramor and his Orchestra
11 Hot Diggity   *Single*   *DB3783(78) / SCM5273(45)*
(Dog Diggity Boom)   *LP*   *The Best of Michael Holliday*
(All issues take 6)   *CD*   *The Story Of My Life*

12 Gal With The Yaller Shoes   *Single*   *DB3783(78) / SCM5273(45)*
(All issues take 6)   *EP*   *Music With Mike*
                                  LP   *The Best of Michael Holliday*
                                  CD   *The Story Of My Life*

12 August 1956, 7.00–9.30 p.m., with Norrie Paramor and his Orchestra
13 The Runaway Train   *Single*   *DB3813*
(All issues take 8)   *EP*   *Music With Mike*
                                  LP   *The Very Best of Michael Holliday*
                                  CD   *The Story Of My Life*

14 Ten Thousand Miles	Single	DB3813
(All issues take 5)	LP	*The Best of Michael Holliday*
	CD	*The Story Of My Life*

20 September 1956, 8.00–11.00 p.m., with Norrie Paramor and his Orchestra

15 A Perfect Day	Single	–
(All issues take 6)	EP	*Our Choice*
	LP	–
	CD	*The EP Collection*

16 Good Luck, Good Health,	Single	–
God Bless You (With Eddie	EP	*Our Choice*
Calvert and Ruby Murray)	LP	–
(All issues take 6)	CD	–

4 December 1956, 7.00–10.30 p.m., with Norrie Paramor and his Orchestra

17 I Saw Esau	Single	DB3675
(All issues take 13)	LP	*Sentimental Journey*
	CD	*Michael Holliday and Edna Savage – Together Again*

18 Yaller Yaller Gold	Single	DB3675
(All issues take 15)	EP	*Music With Mike*
	LP	*The EP Collection*
	CD	*The EP Collection*

1956, precise date unknown.
(Recording made for EMI Parlophone EP 'The Good Companions'. The EP purportedly included soundtrack recordings from the film and although no label credit is given, the opening part of the vocal on this track is clearly the voice of Michael Holliday. No recording data exists, although the EP was released in 1957).

19 Where There's You	Single	–
There's Me	EP	*The Good Companions*
(No take information)	CD	*The Story Of My Life*

15 February 1957, 2.00–5.00 p.m., with Norrie Paramor and his Orchestra

20 It's The Good Things We	Single	DB3973
Remember	LP	*Hi*
(All issues take 12)	CD	*The Story Of My Life*

21 I'd Love To Come Home   *Single* –
    To You   *LP*   *Hi*
(All issues take 3)   *CD*   *The Story Of My Life*

11 March 1957, 3.30–5.30 p.m., with Norrie Paramor and his Orchestra (Overdubbed vocal, orchestral tracks recorded 9 March 1957)

22 My House Is Your House   *Single* *DB3919*
(Mi Casa Su Casa)   *LP*   –
(All issues take 23)   *CD*   *Michael Holliday and Edna Savage*
                                  – Together Again

23 Love Is Strange   *Single* *DB3919*
(All issues take 24)   *LP*   –
                        CD   *The Story Of My Life*

24 Just A Wearyin' For You   *Single* –
(All issues take 5)   *EP*   *All Time Favourites*
                        LP   *Hi*
                        CD   *The Story Of My Life*

20 March 1957, 2.00–4.00 p.m., with Norrie Paramor and his Orchestra

25 That's My Heart Strings   *Single* –
(That's My Boy)   *LP*   *Hi*
(All issues take 10)   *CD*   *The Story Of My Life*

26 I'm Old Fashioned   *Single* –
(All issues take 5)   *LP*   *Hi*
                        CD   *The Story Of My Life*

22 March 1957, 6.00–9.00 p.m., with Norrie Paramor and his Orchestra

27 All Of You   *Single* *DB3973*
                        LP   *Hi*
                        CD   *The Story Of My Life*

28 The Lonesome Road   *Single* –
(All issues take 4)   *EP*   *All Time Favourites*
                        LP   *Hi*
                        CD   *The Story Of My Life*

29 We'll Gather Lilacs   *Single* –
(All issues take 15)   *EP*   *All Time Favourites*
                        LP   *Hi*
                        CD   *The Story Of My Life*

23 March 1957, 2.00–4.00 p.m., with Norrie Paramor and his Orchestra

30 Shenandoah	Single	–
(All issues take 10)	LP	Hi
	CD	The Story Of My Life

31 If I Can Help Somebody	Single	–
(All issues take 5)	EP	All Time Favourites
	LP	Hi
	CD	The Story Of My Life

10 May 1957, 6.00–8.00 p.m., with Norrie Paramor and his Orchestra

32 Wringle Wrangle	Single	DB3948
(All issues take 12)	LP	–
	CD	The Story Of My Life

33 Four Walls	Single	DB3948
(All issues take 8)	EP	Memories of Mike (SEG8373)
	LP	–
	CD	The EP Collection

20 August 1957, 10.00–01.00am, with Norrie Paramor and his Orchestra (Orchestral tracks recorded at sessions 14 & 15 August. Michael Holliday's vocals from these sessions were rejected and he overdubbed new vocals 20 August. Because of the lateness of the session and the high number of takes needed for the first three titles, 'Down By The River' was not recorded at the 20 August session. The title is shown on EMI's session sheets and strictly therefore remains unissued, but may have never been recorded.)

34 Love You Darlin'	Single	DB3992
(All issues take 18)	LP	–
	CD	The Best Of Michael Holliday
		(30th Anniversary Collection)

35 May I	Single	DB4121
(All issues take 18)	LP	Sentimental Journey
	CD	The Story Of My Life

36 Old Cape Cod	Single	DB3992
(All issues take 17)	LP	The Best of Michael Holliday
	CD	The Michael Holliday Collection

37 Down By The River (unissued)
(No take information – existence unconfirmed)

15 October 1957, 2.00–5.00 p.m., with instrumental accompaniment

38 Ramblin' Man	Single	–
(All issues take 12)	EP	Relax with Mike
	LP	The EP Collection
	CD	The EP Collection

39 Kentucky Babe	Single	–
(All issues take 5)	EP	Relax with Mike
	LP	The EP Collection
	CD	The EP Collection

40 Billy	Single	–
(All issues take 4)	EP	Relax with Mike
	LP	–
	CD	The Story Of My Life

41 Skye Boat Song	Single	–
(All issues take 3)	EP	Relax with Mike
	LP	The Very Best Of Michael Holliday
	CD	The Michael Holliday Collection

10 December 1957, 7.00–8.00 p.m., with Norrie Paramor and his Orchestra

42 Rooney	Single	DB4087
(All issues take 7)	LP	The Very Best Of Michael Holliday
	CD	Michael Holliday and Edna Savage – Together Again

10 December 1957, 8.00–11.00 p.m., with Ken Jones and his Orchestra

43 The Story Of My Life	Single	DB4058
(All issues take 12)	EP	Melody Mike
	LP	The Best of Michael Holliday
	CD	The Story Of My Life

44 Keep Your Heart	Single	DB4058
(All issues take 10)	LP	–
	CD	The Best Of Michael Holliday (30th Anniversary Collection)

8 February 1958, 8.00–11.00 p.m., with Ken Jones and his Orchestra

45 In Love (rejected)
(No take information)

12 February 1958, 10.30–00.30am, with Ken Jones and his Orchestra

46 In Love   *Single*   DB4087
(All issues take 33)   *LP*   *The Best of Michael Holliday*
                            CD   *The Michael Holliday Collection*

6–7 March 1958, with orchestra conducted by Edwin Braden.
(These tracks all feature duets with Edna Savage for what was planned as a 10-inch LP. Six of the ten tracks however were rejected or not completed. The remaining four tracks were issued on an EP.)

47 I Wished On The Moon (rejected)
(No take information)

48 S'Wonderful   *Single* –
(No take information)   *EP*   *Sentimental Journey*
                            LP   *Sentimental Journey*
                            CD   *Michael Holliday and Edna Savage – Together Again*

49 Make Believe (rejected)
(No take information)

50 When The Children Are Asleep (rejected)
(No take information)

51 Someone To Watch Over Me (rejected)
(No take information)

52 The Folks Who Live On The Hill (rejected)
(No take information)

53 Blue Skies (rejected)
(No take information)

54 Goodnight My Love   *Single* –
(All issues take)   *EP*   *Sentimental Journey*
                            LP   *Sentimental Journey*
                            CD   *Michael Holliday and Edna Savage – Together Again*

55 Tea For Two   *Single* –
(No take information)   *EP*   *Sentimental Journey*
                            LP   *Sentimental Journey*
                            CD   *Michael Holliday and Edna Savage – Together Again*

241

56 Tiptoe Through The Tulips *Single*   –
(No take information)   *EP*   *Sentimental Journey*
                                LP   *Sentimental Journey*
                                CD   *Michael Holliday and Edna Savage – Together Again*

27 March 1958, 10.00–01.15 a.m., with Ken Jones and his Orchestra
57 Stairway Of Love (rejected)
(No take information)

13 April 1958, 7.00–9.00 p.m., with Ken Jones and his Orchestra
58 Stairway Of Love   *Single*   DB4121
(Take 18)   *EP*   *Melody Mike*
                                LP   *The Best Of Michael Holliday*
                                CD   *The Story Of My Life*

3 June 1958, 7.00–10.45 p.m., with Norrie Paramor and his Orchestra
59 I'll Always Be In Love   *Single*   DB4155
With You   *EP*   *Melody Mike*
(Take 7)   *LP*   *The Best of Michael Holliday*
                                CD   *The Michael Holliday Collection*

60 Careless Hands   *Single*   DB4216
(No take information)   *EP*   *Memories of Mike*
                                LP   *The EP Collection*
                                CD   *The EP Collection*

61 I'll Be Lovin' You Too   *Single*   DB4155
(Take 4)   *EP*   *Melody Mike*
                                LP   *The EP Collection*
                                CD   *The EP Collection*

24 August 1958, 4.30–6.45 p.m., with Ken Jones and his Orchestra
(Orchestral tracks and Holliday's backing vocal recorded 2.30–4.30 p.m.)
62 She Was Only Seventeen   *Single*   DB4188
(No take information)   *LP*   –
                                CD   *The Story Of My Life*

63 The Gay Vagabond   *Single*   DB4188
(No take information)   *LP*   –
                                CD   *The Story Of My Life*

2 November 1958, 7.30–9.30 p.m., with Ken Jones and his Orchestra

64 My Heart Is An Open	*Single*	*DB4216*
Book	*LP*	*The Best of Michael Holliday*
(No take information)	*CD*	*The Best Of Michael Holliday (30th Anniversary Collection)*

18 January 1959, 7.00–9.00 p.m., with Norrie Paramor and his Orchestra

65 Palace Of Love	*Single*	*DB4255*
(No take information)	*LP*	*The Best of Michael Holliday*
	CD	*The Michael Holliday Collection*

66 The Girls From The	*Single*	*DB4255*
County Armagh	*LP*	*–*
(No take information)	*CD*	*The Story Of My Life*

19 January 1959, 2.00–4.00 p.m., with Norrie Paramor and his Orchestra

67 Life Is A Circus	*Single*	*DB4336*
(All issues take 6)	*LP*	*–*
	CD	*The Best of Michael Holliday (30th Anniversary Collection)*

68 Dearest	*Single*	*DB4307*
(All issues take 3)	*EP*	*Memories of Mike*
	LP	*The EP Collection*
	CD	*The Story Of My Life*

69 For You	*Single*	*DB4336*
(All issues take 8)	*LP*	*–*
	CD	*The Best Of Michael Holliday (30th Anniversary Collection)*

19 January 1959, 4.00–5.30 p.m., with Norrie Paramor and his Orchestra

70 Strange Music	*Single*	*–*
(All issues take 7)	*EP*	*Mike*
	LP	*Mike*
	CD	*–*

71 The Folks Who Live	*Single*	*–*
On The Hill	*EP*	*Mike*
(All issues take 4)	*LP*	*Mike*
	CD	*The Michael Holliday Collection*

29 January 1959, 2.00–5.30 p.m., with Norrie Paramor and his Orchestra (The EP 'Mike (And The Other Fella)' featured Mike in duet with himself, a routine taken from his BBC television show. Mike recorded 'the other fella's' vocals on 23 January)

72 Show Me The Way To
Go Home
(No take information)

Single	–	
EP	Mike (And The Other Fella)	
LP	The EP Collection	
CD	The EP Collection	

73 Way Back Home
(No take information)

Single	–
EP	Mike (And The Other Fella)
LP	The EP Collection
CD	The EP Collection

74 Side By Side
(No take information)

Single	–
EP	Mike (And The Other Fella)
LP	The EP Collection
CD	The EP Collection

75 Winter Wonderland
(No take information)

Single	–
EP	Mike (And The Other Fella)
LP	–
CD	The EP Collection

26 March 1959, 2.00–5.15 p.m., with Norrie Paramor and his Orchestra

76 Skylark
(All issues take 4)

Single	DB4437
EP	Mike No 3
LP	Mike
CD	The Michael Holliday Collection

77 I'll Be Seeing You
(All issues take 2)

Single	–
EP	Mike No 2
LP	Mike
CD	Michael Holliday and Edna Savage – Together Again

78 The Lamplighter's Serenade
(All issues take 5)

Single	–
EP	Mike No 3
LP	Mike
CD	–

79 A Nightingale Sang In	Single	–
Berkeley Square	EP	Mike No 2
(All issues take 7/9)	LP	Mike
	CD	–

80 Did You Ever See A	Single	–
Dream	EP	Mike No 3
(All issues take 1)	LP	Mike
	CD	The Best of The EMI Years

26 March 1959, 7.00–10.10 p.m., with Norrie Paramor and his Orchestra

81 In The Good Old	Single	–
Summertime	EP	Mike No 2
(All issues take 3)	LP	Mike
	CD	The EP Collection

82 Love Is Just Around The	Single	–
Corner	EP	Mike
(All issues take 5)	LP	Mike
	CD	–

83 Be Careful It's My Heart	Single	–
(All issues take 4)	EP	Mike No 2
	LP	Mike
	CD	–

84 I Can't Give You	Single	–
Anything But Love	EP	Mike
(All issues take 6/7)	LP	Mike
	CD	The EP Collection

85 Ain't She Sweet	Single	–
(All issues take 5/6)	EP	Mike No 3
	LP	Mike
	CD	–

3 May 1959, 6.30–8.30 p.m., with Norrie Paramor and his Orchestra at Record Supervision Studios

86 Moments Of Love	Single	DB4307
(No take information)	LP	–
	CD	The Story Of My Life

*30 October 1959, 7.00–10.00 p.m., with Eric Jupp and his Orchestra
(This session was originally rejected and two of the three titles remade the
following week. The rejected masters were discovered in EMI's vaults in
1993 and issued on the CD shown)*

87 Starry Eyed	Single	–
(All issues take 13)	LP	–
	CD	The Best Of Michael Holliday
		(30th Anniversary Collection)

88 I Have Waited	Single	–
(All issues take 3)	LP	–
	CD	The Best Of Michael Holliday
		(30th Anniversary Collection)

89 The Steady Game	Single	–
(All issues take 8)	LP	–
	CD	The Best Of Michael Holliday
		(30th Anniversary Collection)

*6 November 1959, 7.00–9.00 p.m., with accompaniment directed by Norrie
Paramor*

90 Starry Eyed	Single	DB4378
(No take information)	LP	The Best of Michael Holliday
	CD	The Story Of My Life

91 The Steady Game	Single	DB4378
(No take information)	LP	–
	CD	The Story Of My Life

*30 November 1959, 2.30–5.30 p.m., with orchestra conducted by Barry
Gray*

92 Four Feather Falls	Single	–
(All issues take 1)	EP	Four Feather Falls
	LP	The EP Collection
	CD	The EP Collection

93 Two Gun Tex of Texas	Single	–
(All issues take 5/6)	EP	Four Feather Falls
	LP	–
	CD	–

94 Happy Hearts And	Single	–
Friendly Faces	EP	*Four Feather Falls*
(All issues take 12)	LP	*The EP Collection*
	CD	*The EP Collection*

95 Ric-Ric-A-Rackety Train	Single	–
(All issues take 4)	EP	*Four Feather Falls*
	LP	–
	CD	–

96 The Phantom Rider	Single	–
(All issues take 4)	EP	*Four Feather Falls*
	LP	–
	CD	–

97 Kalla Ma Kooya Kalla	Single	–
(All issues take 4)	EP	*Four Feather Falls*
	LP	–
	CD	–

10 March 1960, 7.00–9.00 p.m., with accompaniment directed by Norrie Paramor
(This session was originally rejected but the unissued master was discovered in 1993 and issued on the CD shown)

98 Dream Talk	Single	–
(No take information)	LP	–
	CD	*The Best Of Michael Holliday (30th Anniversary Collection)*

16 March 1960, 2.30–4.40 p.m., with accompaniment directed by Norrie Paramor

99 Dream Talk	Single	DB4437
(No take information)	LP	*The Best Of Michael Holliday*
	CD	*The Story Of My Life*

30 May 1960, 6.00–9.30 p.m., with Norrie Paramor and his Orchestra

100 The One Finger	Single	DB4475
Symphony	LP	–
(No take information)	CD	*The Best Of Michael Holliday (30th Anniversary Collection)*

247

101 Little Boy Lost	Single	DB4475
(No take information)	LP	–
	CD	The Michael Holliday Collection

1 June 1960, 2.30–5.30 p.m., with Norrie Paramor and his Orchestra

102 Like Someone In Love	Single	–
(All issues take 6)	EP	–
	LP	Holliday Mixture
	CD	–

103 Bluebird Singing In My	Single	–
Heart	EP	–
(All issues take 7)	LP	Holliday Mixture
	CD	–

104 I Promise You	Single	–
(All issues take 12/14/16)	EP	–
	LP	Holliday Mixture
	CD	Michael Holliday and Edna Savage – Together Again

105 I Can't Begin To Tell You	Single	–
(All issues take 13/15)	EP	Mike In A Sentimental Mood
	LP	Holliday Mixture
	CD	The EP Collection

2 June 1960, 2.30–5.30 p.m., with Norrie Paramor and his Orchestra

106 Just A Prayer Away	Single	–
(All issues take 6)	EP	Mike In A Sentimental Mood
	LP	Holliday Mixture
	CD	The EP Collection

107 Long Ago And Far Away	Single	–
(All issues take 9)	EP	Mike In A Sentimental Mood
	LP	Holliday Mixture
	CD	Michael Holliday and Edna Savage – Together Again

108 Amor Amor	Single	–
(All issues take 9)	EP	–
	LP	Holliday Mixture
	CD	–

3 June 1960, 2.30–6.00 p.m., with Norrie Paramor and his Orchestra

109 Alexander's Ragtime Band   *Single*   –
(All issues take 2)   *EP*   *Mike Sings Ragtime*
                                 LP   *Holliday Mixture*
                                 CD   *The EP Collection*

110 Swanee   *Single*   –
(All issues take 10)   *EP*   *Mike Sings Ragtime*
                                 LP   *Holliday Mixture*
                                 CD   –

111 Margie   *Single*   –
(All issues take 13)   *EP*   *Mike Sings Ragtime*
                                 LP   *Holliday Mixture*
                                 CD   *The EP Collection*

112 One Sweet Letter From   *Single*   –
You   *EP*   *Mike In a Sentimental Mood*
(All issues take 6)   *LP*   *Holliday Mixture*
                                 CD   –

113 That's My Weakness Now   *Single*   –
(All issues take 3)   *EP*   *Mike Sings Ragtime*
                                 LP   *Holliday Mixture*
                                 CD   –

14 September 1960, 7.00–9.00 p.m., with accompaniment directed by Norrie Paramor

114 Young In Love   *Single*   –
(All issues take 7)   *LP*   –
                                 CD   *The Michael Holliday Collection*

115 My Year Of Love   *Single*   DB7265
(All issues take 5)   *LP*   –
                                 CD   *The Story Of My Life*

4 November 1960, 2.30–5.30 p.m., with accompaniment directed by Johnny Pearson

116 (Will You) Stay In Love   *Single*   DB4548
(All issues take 17)   *LP*   –
                                 CD   *The Story Of My Life*

117 I Wonder Who's Kissing   *Single* DB4663
Her Now   *LP*   –
(All issues take 13)   *CD*   The Michael Holliday Collection

118 Catch Me A Kiss   *Single* DB4548
(All issues take 10)   *LP*   –
                              CD   The Story Of My Life

9 February 1961, 7.00–9.00 p.m., with accompaniment directed by Norrie Paramor
119 The Miracle Of Monday   *Single* DB4604
Morning   *LP*   –
(No take information)   *CD*   The Best Of Michael Holliday
                                        (30th Anniversary Collection)

120 (Remember Me) I'm   *Single* DB4604
The One Who Loves You   *LP*   –
(No take information)   *CD*   The Best Of Michael Holliday
                                        (30th Anniversary Collection)

10 March 1961, 7.00–10.00 p.m., with the George Chisholm All-Stars
121 Alabamy Bound (rejected)
(No take information)

122 Between The Devil And The Deep Blue Sea (rejected)
(No take information)

123 When You Wore A Tulip   *Single* –
(All issues take 10/12)   *EP*   –
                              LP   Happy Holliday
                              CD   The Story Of My Life

124 Gone Fishin'   *Single* –
(All issues take 3)   *EP*   Happy Holliday
                              LP   Happy Holliday
                              CD   The Story Of My Life

16 March 1961, 2.00–5.45 p.m., with the George Chisholm All-Stars
125 Alabamy Bound*   *Single* –
(All issues take 16)   *EP*   More Happy Holliday
                              LP   Happy Holliday
                              CD   The Story Of My Life

250

126 Get Happy	Single	–
(All issues take 17)	EP	–
	LP	Happy Holliday
	CD	The Story Of My Life

127 The Best Things In Life	Single	–
Are Free	EP	Happy Holliday
(All issues take 4/6)	LP	Happy Holliday
	CD	The Story Of My Life

128 Lazy	Single	–
(All issues take 4)	EP	More Happy Holliday
	LP	Happy Holliday
	CD	The Story Of My Life

129 I've Got The World On	Single	–
A String	EP	Happy Holliday
(All issues take 6)	LP	Happy Holliday
	CD	The Story Of My Life

17 March 1961, 2.00–5.30 p.m., with the George Chisholm All-Stars

130 Between The Devil And	Single	–
The Deep Blue Sea*	EP	More Happy Holliday
(All issues take 12/13)	LP	Happy Holliday
	CD	The Story Of My Life

131 My Heart Is A Hobo	Single	–
(All issues take 2)	EP	–
	LP	Happy Holliday
	CD	The Story Of My Life

132 Sing A Song Of	Single	–
Sunbeams	EP	–
(All issues take 8/9)	LP	Happy Holliday
	CD	The Story Of My Life

133 Singin' In The Rain	Single	–
(All issues take 9)	EP	Happy Holliday
	LP	Happy Holliday
	CD	The Story Of My Life

(Vocals marked * superimposed on 10 March orchestral track)

251

134 I Got Rhythm	Single	–
(All issues take 5)	EP	More Happy Holliday
	LP	Happy Holliday
	CD	The Story Of My Life

15 May 1961, 7.00–9.00 p.m., with accompaniment directed by Norrie Paramor

135 Dream Boy Dream	Single	DB4663
(No take information)	LP	–
	CD	The Magic Of Michael Holliday

7 February 1962, 7.00–10.30 p.m., with Norrie Paramor and his Orchestra and featuring the Mike Sammes Singers

136 Ain't Got A Dime To My Name	Single	–
	EP	–
(All issues take 7)	LP	To Bing From Mike
	CD	The Story Of My Life

137 Swinging On A Star	Single	–
(All issues take 2)	EP	–
	LP	To Bing From Mike
	CD	The Story Of My Life

138 You Are My Sunshine	Single	–
(All issues take 11)	EP	Mike Sings C&W style
	LP	To Bing From Mike
	CD	The Story Of My Life

139 Home Cookin'	Single	–
(All issues take 3)	EP	Mike Sings C&W style
	LP	To Bing From Mike
	CD	The Story Of My Life

140 I Didn't Slip, I Wasn't Pushed, I Fell	Single	–
	EP	–
(All issues take 5)	LP	To Bing From Mike
	CD	The Story Of My Life

8 February 1962, 7.00–10.30 p.m., with Norrie Paramor and his Orchestra and featuring the Mike Sammes Singers

141 Dear Hearts And Gentle People *(All issues take 7)*	*Single*	–
	EP	*Mike Sings C&W style*
	LP	*To Bing From Mike*
	CD	*The Story Of My Life*

142 I Don't Want To Walk Without You *(All issues take 2/4)*	*Single*	–
	EP	–
	LP	*To Bing From Mike*
	CD	*The Story Of My Life*

143 Be Honest With Me *(All issues take 14)*	*Single*	–
	EP	*Mike Sings C&W style*
	LP	*To Bing From Mike*
	CD	*The Story Of My Life*

144 San Fernando Valley *(All issues take 4/6)*	*Single*	–
	EP	*Mike Sings C&W style*
	LP	*To Bing From Mike*
	CD	*The Story Of My Life*

9 February 1962, 7.00–10.00 p.m., with Norrie Paramor and his Orchestra and featuring the Mike Sammes Singers

145 Moonlight Becomes You *(All issues take 2)*	*Single*	–
	EP	–
	LP	*To Bing From Mike*
	CD	*The Story Of My Life*

146 Sunday Monday Or Always *(All issues take 4)*	*Single*	–
	EP	–
	LP	*To Bing From Mike*
	CD	*The Story Of My Life*

147 Can I Forget You *(All issues take 5)*	*Single*	*DB7171*
	EP	–
	LP	*To Bing From Mike*
	CD	*The Story Of My Life*

148 Moonlight Cocktail *(All issues take 4/2)*	*Single*	–
	EP	–
	LP	*To Bing From Mike*
	CD	*The Story Of My Life*

253

149 It's Been A Long Long Time   *Single*   –
(All issues take 5)   *EP*   –
    LP   *To Bing From Mike*
    CD   *The Story Of My Life*

15 March 1962, 7.00–9.30 p.m., with Norrie Paramor and his Orchestra
150 Wishin' On A Rainbow   *Single*   DB4819
(All issues take 4/5)   *LP*   –
    CD   *The Best Of Michael Holliday*
      (30th Anniversary Collection)

151 I Don't Want You To See Me Cry   *Single*   DB4819 (take 6)
    LP   –
Takes as shown against releases   *CD*   *The Best Of Michael Holliday*
      (30th Anniversary Collection)
      (take 5)

1 August 1962, 2.30–6.00 p.m., with accompaniment directed by Frank Barber
152 Always Is A Long Long Time   *Single*   DB7327
(All issues take 10)   *LP*   –
    CD   *The Story Of My Life*

153 It Only Takes A Minute   *Single*   DB4890
(All issues take 4)   *LP*   –
    CD   *The Story Of My Life*

154 Have I Told You Lately That I Love You   *Single*   DB4890
    LP   *The Story Of My Life*
(All issues take 5)   *CD*   *The Michael Holliday Collection*

November 1962, with orchestral accompaniment, in EMI Studios, South Africa
155 Trane In Mi Hart   *Single*   45-DE 390 (South Africa)
(No take information)   *LP*   –
    CD   *The Story Of My Life*

156 My Blinde Hart   *Single*   45-DE 390 (South Africa)
(No take information)   *LP*   –
    CD   *The Story Of My Life*

157 Tears*
(No take information)

Single	–
LP	–
CD	*The Magic Of Michael Holliday*

158 I Just Can't Win*
(No take information)

Single	–
LP	–
CD	*The Best Of Michael Holliday (30th Anniversary Collection)*

22 January 1963, 7.00–10.30 p.m., with Norrie Paramor and his Orchestra
159 Laugh And The World
Laughs With You
(No take information)

Single	DB4976
LP	–
CD	*The Best Of Michael Holliday (30th Anniversary Collection)*

160 Iron Fence
(No take information)

Single	DB4976
LP	–
CD	*The Story Of My Life*

28 May 1963, 7.00–10.00 p.m., with orchestra arranged and conducted by Frank Barber
161 Just To Be With You
Again
(All issues take 10)

Single	DB7080
LP	–
CD	*The Best Of Michael Holliday (30th Anniversary Collection)*

162 Between Hello And
Goodbye
(All issues take 4)

Single	DB7080
EP	*Memories Of Mike*
LP	–
CD	*The EP Collection*

22 October 1963, 7.00–10.30 p.m., with orchestra arranged and conducted by Ivor Raymonde
163 Drums
(All issues take 14)

Single	DB7171
LP	*The Story Of My Life*
CD	*The Story Of My Life*

(* Tracks marked have English language versions dubbed over same backing as the two previous tracks, which were sung in Afrikaans.)

255

164 My Last Date (With You)	Single	DB7327 (take 6)
(Takes as shown against	LP	*The Best Of The EMI*
releases)		*years (take 6)*
	CD	*The Story Of My Life*
		(take 6)
		The Magic Of Michael Holliday
		(take 5)

165 Dear Heart	Single	DB7265
(All issues take 11)	LP	*The Best Of The EMI Years*
	CD	*The Story Of My Life*

RECORD RELEASES

Catalogue Number	*Title(s)*	*Release Date*

SINGLES

Columbia 78 rpm only

| DB3657 | The Yellow Rose Of Texas | September 1955 |
| | Stein Song | |

Columbia 45 and 78 r.p.m.

| SCM 5221 (45)/ | Sixteen Tons | January 1956 |
| DB3714 (78) | The Rose Tattoo | |

| SCM 5252 (45)/ | Nothin' To Do | March 1956 |
| DB3746 (78) | Perfume, Candy And Flowers | |

| SCM 5273 (45)/ | Hot Diggity (Dog Diggity Boom) | June 1956 |
| DB3783 (78) | The Gal With The Yaller Shoes | |

Note: From hereon, all Columbia 78 and 45 r.p.m. records were issued with the same catalogue number, the 45 issues prefixed by (45).

| (45)DB3813 | Ten Thousand Miles | September 1956 |
| | The Runaway Train | |

| (45)DB3871 | I Saw Esau | January 1957 |
| | Yaller Yaller Gold | |

256

(45)DB3919	My House Is Your House Love Is Strange	March 1957
(45)DB3948	Four Walls Wringle Wrangle	May 1957
(45)DB3973	All Of You It's The Good Things We Remember	July 1957
(45)DB3992	Old Cape Cod Love You Darlin'	September 1957
(45)DB4058	The Story Of My Life Keep Your Heart	January 1958
(45)DB4087	In Love Rooney	February 1958
(45)DB4121	Stairway Of Love May I?	May 1958
(45)DB4155	I'll Always Be In Love With You I'll Be Lovin' You Too	June 1958
(45)DB4188	She Was Only Seventeen The Gay Vagabond	September 1958
(45)DB4216	My Heart Is An Open Book Careless Hands	November 1958
(45)DB4255	Palace Of Love The Girls From The County Armagh	February 1959
(45)DB4307	Moments Of Love Dearest	May 1959
(45)DB4336	Life Is A Circus For You For You	August 1959
(45)DB4378	Starry Eyed The Steady Game	November 1959

Columbia 45 r.p.m. only

DB4437	Dream Talk Skylark	March 1960
DB4475	Little Boy Lost The One Finger Symphony	June 1960
DB4548	Catch Me A Kiss Stay In Love	November 1960
DB4604	The Miracle Of Monday Morning Remember Me (I'm The One Who Loves You)	February 1961
DB4663	Dream Boy Dream I Wonder Who's Kissing Her Now	June 1961
DB4819	Wishin' On A Rainbow I Don't Want You To See Me Cry	April 1962
DB4890	Have I Told You Lately That I Love You It Only Takes A Minute	September 1962
DB4976	Laugh And The World Laughs With You Iron Fence	February 1963
DB7080	Between Hello And Goodbye Just To Be With You Again	July 1963
DB7171	Drums Can I Forget You	November 1963
DB7265	Dear Heart My Year Of Love	March 1964
DB7327	My Last Date (With You) Always Is A Long Long Time	June 1964

EXTENDED PLAY
Columbia 45 r.p.m.

SEG7638	My Guitar And Me	June 1956
SEG7669	Our Choice	November 1956
SEG7683	Music With Mike	March 1957
SEG7752	Relax With Mike	December 1957
SEG7761	All Time Favourites	February 1958
SEG7818	Melody Mike	September 1958
SEG7836	Sentimental Journey	October 1958
SEG7892	Mike (And The Other Fella)	June 1959
SEG7972/ESG7784(stereo)	Mike!	January 1960
SEG7986/ESG7793(stereo)	Four Feather Falls	February 1960
SEG7996/ESG7803(stereo)	Mike! No 2	April 1960
SEG8074/ESG7842(stereo)	Mike! No 3	March 1961
SEG8101/ESG7856(stereo)	Mike Sings Ragtime	September 1961
SEG8115/ESG7864(stereo)	Mike In A Sentimental Mood	November 1961
SEG8161	Happy Holliday	May 1962
SEG8186	More Happy Holliday	October 1962
SEG8242	Mike Sings C&W style	May 1963
SEG8373	Memories Of Mike	December 1964

Parlophone 45 r.p.m.

GEP 8604	The Good Companions	1957

10-inch LP ALBUMS
Columbia 33S Series

33S1114	Hi!	June 1957

12-inch LP ALBUMS
Columbia

33SX1170	Mike! (see note 1)	September 1959
33SX1262/SCX3331 (stereo)	Holliday Mixture (see note 2)	October 1960
33SX1354/SCX3398 (stereo)	Happy Holliday	October 1961
33SX1426/SCX3441 (stereo)	To Bing – From Mike	June 1962
33SX1586	The Best Of Michael Holliday	January 1964
33SX1635	Tribute to Michael Holliday (see note 3)	June 1964

259

EMI World Record Club

WRC T508/ST508 (stereo)	Holliday Mixture	1965
WRC T792/ST792 (stereo)	To Bing – From Mike	1966

EMI One Up Series

OU 2014	The Story Of My Life	April 1974
OU 2205	A Tribute to Bing – From Mike	November 1977

Music For Pleasure

MFP4156461	The Very Best Of Michael Holliday	March 1984

Memoir

MOIR 208	Mike!	July 1988

EMI – The Best Of The EMI Years

EMS1329	The Best Of The EMI Years	April 1989

See For Miles Records

SEE255	Sentimental Journey	May 1989
SEE311	The EP Collection	March 1991

Note 1: The working title for the album *Mike!* was *Takin' It Easy*. Some copies of the album were pressed with labels showing this title.

Note 2: The working title for this album was *Mike Sings And Swings* and was changed prior to release to *Holliday Mixture*.

Note 3: This album features a recording of the concert held in memory of Michael Holliday at the Prince of Wales Theatre, 19 April 1964. It does not feature any Michael Holliday recordings.

COMPACT DISCS

EMI – The Best Of The EMI Years

CDP792260 2	The Best Of The EMI Years	April 1989

EMI Compacts For Pleasure

CDB752032 2	Michael Holliday and Edna Savage – Together Again	April 1990

See For Miles Records
SEECD 311   The EP Collection   March 1991

EMI

7243 8 27740 2 0	The Best Of Michael Holliday (The 30th Anniversary Collection)	April 1994
7243 5 29443 2 3	The Michael Holliday Collection	April 2000
7243 8 55080 2 8	The Magic of Michael Holliday	February 2001
7243 5 97484 2 9	The Story Of My Life (3 CD set)	April 2004

Appendix 2

MICHAEL HOLLIDAY ON BBC TELEVISION

Broadcast Date	Details	Songs (Michael Holliday only)	Recording Details
22 July 1955	THE CENTRE SHOW	My Baby Said Yes Marrying For Love	Live
14 December 1955	MORE CONTRARY	I Whistle A Happy Tune Eileen	Live
18 January 1956	MORE CONTRARY	Sixteen Tons Darlin' Katie	Live
15 February 1956	LESS CONTRARY	Nothin' To Do	Live
14 March 1956	MORE CONTRARY	Marrying For Love Nothin' To Do	Live
18 May 1956	MUSIC FOR A MELLOW MOOD	Nothin' To Do	Live
23 May 1956	HOPSCOTCH	The Yellow Rose Of Texas Blue Shadows On The Trail	Live
29 August 1956	SUMMER SERENADE	The Wayward Wind People Will Say We're In Love	Live
23 September 1956	THE SHOW BAND SHOW	Ten Thousand Miles	Live
26 September 1956	CRACKERJACK	The Runaway Train Ten Thousand Miles	Live

263

18 January 1957	A MUSICAL NIGHTCAP Produced by Eric Miller	Nothin' To Do Gal With The Yaller Shoes I Promise You I Whistle A Happy Tune Kentucky Babe Nothin' To Do	Pre-recorded, date unknown
16 February 1957	6.5 SPECIAL	Ten Thousand Miles Marrying For Love	Pre-recorded, date unknown
25 February 1957	MONDAY MELODY	Yaller Yaller Gold Who Wants To Be A Millionaire (w. Lorrae Desmond, Dudley Savage, Doyer and Ravel)	Live
30 April 1957	STARLIGHT Produced by John Ammonds	You Sang My Love Song To Somebody Else Ramblin' Man My House Is Your House Nine Pound Hammer You Sang My Love Song To Somebody Else	Live
31 May 1957	PLEASUREBOAT	Down By The River Nothin' To Do	Pre-recorded, date unknown
14 June 1957	PLEASUREBOAT	Smile Right Back At The Sun Around The World	Pre-recorded, date unknown
20 June 1957	CAROLE'S COUNTRY CLUB (Carole Carr Show)	Kisses Sweeter Than Wine (w.Carole Carr) With Me Ould Clay Pipe	Pre-recorded, date unknown
28 June 1957	PLEASUREBOAT	Marrying For Love I'm Old Fashioned	Pre-recorded, date unknown

264

12 July 1957	PLEASUREBOAT	Loch Lomond My Little Baby O'er The Hills To Ardentinny	Pre-recorded, date unknown
9 August 1957	PLEASUREBOAT	I've Got Bluebirds In My Heart We Will Make Love	Pre-recorded, date unknown
23 August 1957	PLEASUREBOAT	Love You Darlin' Down By The River	Pre-recorded, date unknown
31 August 1957	6.5 SPECIAL	Old Cape Cod Love You Darlin'	Pre-recorded, date unknown
11 September 1957	NOW	Love You Darlin' The Lonesome Road Wringle Wrangle My Old Man Said Follow The Van	Live

4 October 1957	THOSE
	BEVERLEY
	SISTERS
		I Like Your Kind Of
		    Love (w. Beverley
		    Sisters)
		Eileen
			Pre-recorded,
			date unknown

5 October 1957	6.5 SPECIAL	Dinah I Can't Believe That You're In Love With Me I'll Be Around Blue Skies	Pre-recorded, date unknown
29 November 1957	OFF THE RECORD	Old Cape Cod	No details available

7 December 1957	6.5 SPECIAL	I'm In The Mood
		    For Love
		They Can't Take That
		    Away From Me
		Love You Darlin'
			Pre-recorded,
			date unknown

265

| 21 December 1957 | 6.5 SPECIAL | Remember You're Mine | Pre-recorded, date unknown |
| | | Kisses Sweeter Than Wine | |

| 10 January 1958 | RELAX WITH MICHAEL HOLLIDAY Series produced by John Ammonds | Getting To Know You Billy How About You Goodnight Wherever You Are The Story Of My Life Nothin' To Do | Live |

| 17 January 1958 | RELAX WITH MICHAEL HOLLIDAY | Nothin' To Do Love You Darlin' Just Between You And Me (tape recorder duet) Kisses Sweeter Than Wine Kentucky Babe I'll Be Seeing You | Live |

| 24 January 1958 | RELAX WITH MICHAEL HOLLIDAY | Nothin' To Do When I Take My Sugar To Tea Magic Moments Tiptoe Through The Tulips (tape recorder duet) I'm Old Fashioned Keep Your Heart | Live |

| 25 January 1958 | 6.5 SPECIAL | The Story Of My Life | Pre-recorded, date unknown |

| 31 January 1958 | RELAX WITH MICHAEL HOLLIDAY | Nothin' To Do Blue Skies Winter Wonderland (tape recorder duet) Remember You're Mine Marrying For Love I'll Be Around | Live |

7 February 1958	RELAX WITH MICHAEL HOLLIDAY	Nothin' To Do The Gal With The Yaller Shoes My Blue Heaven (tape recorder duet) I Can't Believe That You're In Love With Me Where The River Shannon Flows Keep Your Heart	Live
14 February 1958	RELAX WITH MICHAEL HOLLIDAY	Nothin' To Do Smile Right Back At The Sun Side By Side (tape recorder duet) The Story Of My Life Skye Boat Song Goodnight My Love	Live
5 March 1958	CRACKERJACK	The Story Of My Life Gal With The Yaller Shoes John Henry	Live
8 March 1958	6.5 SPECIAL	In Love 'Deed I Do	Pre-recorded, date unknown
17 May 1958	RECORD ROUNDABOUT	Stairway Of Love	Live
24 May 1958	6.5 SPECIAL	Stairway of Love Alexander's Ragtime Band (w. Humphrey Lyttleton and his Band)	Pre-recorded, date unknown
7 July 1958	RELAX WITH MICHAEL HOLLIDAY Series produced by John Ammonds	Nothin' To Do Who's Sorry Now Side By Side (tape recorder duet) Stairway Of Love Old Cape Cod Keep Your Heart	Recorded 22 June 1958

267

14 July 1958	RELAX WITH MICHAEL HOLLIDAY	Nothin' To Do
		Gal With The
		  Yaller Shoes
		I Can't Give You Anything
		  But Love
		Tiptoe Through The Tulips
		  (tape recorder duet)
		I'll Always Be In Love With You
		Goodnight, Wherever You Are
			Recorded
			9 July 1958

21 July 1958	RELAX WITH MICHAEL HOLLIDAY	Nothin' To Do
		Smile Right Back
		  At The Sun
		Show Me The Way To
		  Go Home (tape recorder duet)
		On The Street Where You Live
		Blue Moon
		I'll Be Seeing You
			Recorded
			13 July 1958

28 July 1958	RELAX WITH MICHAEL HOLLIDAY	Nothin' To Do
		When I Take My
		  Sugar To Tea
		By The Light Of The
		  Silvery Moon (tape
		  recorder duet)
		I Can't Believe That
		  You're In Love With Me
		Eileen
		I'll See You In My Dreams
			Recorded
			18 July 1958

11 August 1958	RELAX WITH MICHAEL HOLLIDAY	Nothin' To Do
		I Whistle A Happy
		  Tune
		For Me And My Gal
		  (tape recorder duet)
		How About You
		Marrying For Love
		Remember You're Mine
			Recorded
			23 July 1958

18 August 1958	RELAX WITH MICHAEL HOLLIDAY	Nothin' To Do I'll Always Be In Love With You Dinah (tape recorder duet) Blue Shadows On The Trail In Love (mimed to record) I'll Be Around	Recorded 1 August 1958

25 August 1958	RELAX WITH MICHAEL HOLLIDAY	Nothin' To Do
		I'll Be Lovin' You
		   Too
		Tallahassee (tape recorder
		   duet)
		The Story Of My Life
		Kentucky Babe
		Count Your Blessings
			Recorded 15 August 1958

1 September 1958	RELAX WITH MICHAEL HOLLIDAY	Nothin' To Do Blue Skies Winter Wonderland (tape recorder duet) Getting Nowhere Where The River Shannon Flows Keep Your Heart	Recorded 24 August 1958

8 September 1958	RELAX WITH MICHAEL HOLLIDAY	Nothin' To Do
		Sixteen Tons
		Show Me The Way To
		   Go Home (tape recorder
		   duet)
		I'm Old Fashioned
		I Know Where I'm Going
		The Best Things In Life
		   Are Free
			Recorded 29 August 1958

15 September 1958	RELAX WITH MICHAEL HOLLIDAY	Nothin' To Do Getting To Know You The Roving Gambler Way Back Home (tape recorder duet) I Promise You A Perfect Day	Recorded 7 September 1958

269

22 September 1958	RELAX WITH MICHAEL HOLLIDAY	Nothin' To Do
		Stairway Of Love
		She Was Only
		  Seventeen
		Back In The Old Routine
		  (tape recorder duet)
		Getting Nowhere
		Keep Your Heart
			Recorded 17 September 1958

27 December 1958	6.5 SPECIAL	Careless Hands My Heart Is An Open Book	Pre-recorded, date unknown
21 January 1959	THE A–Z OF SHOWBUSINESS	Strange Music The Girls From The County Armagh	Pre-recorded, date unknown

9 February 1959	RELAX WITH MICHAEL HOLLIDAY
	Series produced by John Ammonds
		Nothin' To Do
		Let A Smile Be Your
		  Umbrella
		There's A Goldmine In
		  The Sky
		Bye Bye Blackbird
		  (tape recorder duet)
		Palace Of Love
		Dream
			Live

16 February 1959	RELAX WITH MICHAEL HOLLIDAY	Nothin' To Do
		The Girls From The
		  County Armagh
		Thank Heaven For
		  Little Girls
		My Baby Said Yes
		  (tape recorder duet)
		Last Night On The Back
		  Porch
		The Best Things In Life
		  Are Free
			Live

270

23 February 1959	RELAX WITH MICHAEL HOLLIDAY	Nothin' To Do
		In The Good Old
		   Summertime
		A Little Kiss Each Morning
		Back In The Old Routine
		   (tape recorder duet)
		I'm An Old Cowhand
		I'll See You In My Dreams
			Live

2 March 1959	RELAX WITH MICHAEL HOLLIDAY	Nothin' To Do Some Sunny Day Getting Nowhere Dinah (tape recorder duet) Eileen Remember You're Mine	Live

16 March 1959	RELAX WITH MICHAEL HOLLIDAY	Nothin' To Do
		Palace Of Love
		Thank Heaven For Little
		   Girls
		Tiptoe Through The Tulips
		   (tape recorder duet)
		Dear Old Donegal
		Whispering
			Live

6 April 1959	RELAX WITH MICHAEL HOLLIDAY	Nothin' To Do Surrey With The Fringe On Top It Could Happen To You Nellie Dean (tape recorder duet) Sixteen Tons Darlin' Katie	Recorded 24 February 1959
13 April 1959	RELAX WITH MICHAEL HOLLIDAY	Nothin' To Do Margie John Henry When The Red Red Robin (tape recorder duet) That's My Heart Strings Moonlight Cocktail	Recorded 3 March 1959

271

20 April 1959	RELAX WITH
	MICHAEL
	HOLLIDAY
		Nothin' To Do
		Smile Right Back At
		  The Sun
		September Song
		Winter Wonderland
		  (tape recorder duet)
		Nine Pound Hammer
		Along The Way To Waikiki
			Recorded
			9 March 1959

27 April 1959	RELAX WITH MICHAEL HOLLIDAY	Nothin' To Do Love You Darlin' If I Can Help Somebody Side By Side (tape recorder duet) Mountain Greenery Keep Your Heart	Recorded 10 March 1959
31 July 1959	STARS AT SCARBOROUGH	Let A Smile Be Your Umbrella Ain't She Sweet Dinah (tape recorder duet)	Recorded 29 July 1959
07 December 1959	THIS IS YOUR LIFE (Russ Conway featured)		No details available

5 April 1960	HOLLIDAY AT
	HOME
	(with Dave King
	and Sheila Buxton)
	Produced by
	John Ammonds
		Dream
		Mr Gallagher and
		  Mr Shean (w. King)
		Tea For Two
		  (w. Buxton)
		(other songs not known)
			Recorded
			3 December
			1959

3 September 1960	DICKIE
	VALENTINE
	SHOW
	Produced by
	John Ammonds
		Eileen
		Show Me The Way
		  To Go Home
		  (tape recorder duet)
		Back In the Good Old Days
		  (duet medley with Valentine)
			Recorded 14
			August 1960

22 July 1962	THE SATURDAY SHOW Produced by John Ammonds	Alexander's Ragtime Band Tiptoe Through The Tulips (tape recorder duet) Tea For Two (with Sheila Buxton)	Pre-recorded, date unknown
29 September 1962	THE SATURDAY SHOW Produced by John Ammonds	In The Good Old Summertime Show Me The Way To Go Home (tape recorder duet) Girls Medley – Thank Heaven For Little Girls / Margie / I Love You Samantha / Mary's A Grand Old Name / Dinah / Thank Heaven'	Recorded 19 August 1962
25 January 1963	HOLLIDAY AT HOME (with Dickie Valentine) Series produced by John Ammonds All shows featured Denny Bettis plus Northern Dance Orchestra led by Bernard Herrmann	Let A Smile Be Your Umbrella Moonlight Becomes You Make 'Em Laugh (w. Bettis) Hits Medley (w. Valentine) – The Story Of My Life / Mr Sandman / Starry Eyed / All The Time And Everywhere / The Runaway Train / The Finger Of Suspicion / Stairway Of Love / Old Pianna Rag That Old Black Magic (w. Valentine) Nonsense Medley (tape recorder duet) – Mairzy Doates / Abadaba Honeymoon / Open The Door Richard / Animal Crackers / Constantinople / Crazy Tunes / Ain't Gonna Rain No More / I Scream You Scream / Run Rabbit Run / Bless 'Em All I'll Be Seeing You	Recorded 2 January 1963

1 February 1963	HOLLIDAY AT HOME (with The Vernon Girls)	Dear Hearts and Gentle People
		Technique
		Bing Crosby Medley –
		  Some Of These Days /
		  Where The Blue Of The
		  Night / Mule Train / True
		  Love / Now You Has Jazz
		  Ida, Sweet As Apple Cider
		  (w. Bettis)
		Liverpool Medley –
		  (w. The Vernon Girls):
		  Things / Johnny Todd /
		  Maggie May
		Sleep Medley (tape
		  recorder duet) – Wrap Your
		  Troubles In Dreams /
		  Goodnight Sweetheart /
		  Bye Bye Blackbird / Hit
		  The Road To Dreamland /
		  Show Me The Way To Go
		  Home / Two Sleepy People /
		  Let's Put Out The Lights
			Recorded 10
			January 1963

8 February 1963	HOLLIDAY AT HOME (with The King Brothers)	Have I Told You
		  Lately That I Love
		  You
		Busy Doin' Nothin'
		  (w. Bettis)
		Back In Your Own Backyard
		Dream
		Dinah (tape recorder duet)
		It's A Good Day
			Recorded 17
			January 1963

15 February 1963	HOLLIDAY AT HOME (with Denis Spicer)	The Main Attraction
		Getting Nowhere
		I've Got You Under
		  My Skin
		A Couple Of Song And
		  Dance Men (w. Bettis)
		The Ugly Duckling
		  (w. Spicer doll)
			Recorded 5
			February 1963

274

Lazy Medley (tape
   recorder duet) – It's My
   Lazy Day / Lazybones /
   Oh How I Hate To Get
   Up In The Morning / Lazy /
   Mountain Greenery

| 22 February 1963 | HOLLIDAY AT HOME (with Max Jaffa) | Donkey Serenade
Song And Dance
  Man (w. Bettis)
Tiptoe Through The
  Tulips (tape recorder duet)
Marrying For Love
On The Sunny Side Of The Street
Cradle Song (w. Jaffa)
Y'All Come
Cowboy Medley (w. Jaffa) –
  I'm An Old Cowhand / Wagon
  Wheels / Home On The Range /
  Ghost Riders In The Sky | Recorded 13
February 1963 |
| 1 March 1963 | HOLLIDAY AT HOME (with The Barry Sisters) | If You Knew Susie
Laugh And The World
  Laughs With You
The Lonesomest Man
  In Town (w. Bettis)
Night And Day
Side By Side (tape
recorder duet)
Irish Medley (w. The
  Barry Sisters) – Top O'
  The Morning / Dear Old
  Donegal? Are You Right There,
  Michael / When Irish Eyes
  Are Smiling / MacNamara's Band
The Story Of My Life | Recorded 25
February 1963 |

Appendix 3

MICHAEL HOLLIDAY ON BBC RADIO

Broadcast Date	Details	Songs (Michael Holliday only)	Recording Details
11 March 1956	SAY IT WITH MUSIC	Sixteen Tons	Recorded 11 February 1956
9 April 1956	MIDDAY MUSIC HALL	Perfume, Candy and Flowers Nothin' To Do	Live
15 May 1956	WORKERS' PLAYTIME	Perfume, Candy and Flowers The Best Way To Hold A Girl Nothin' To Do	Live
21 May 1956	BANK HOLIDAY MATINEE	Hot Diggity Where The River Shannon Flows	Recorded 16 May 1956
11 June 1956	TAKE IT EASY	Let's Take It Easy (theme) I Whistle A Happy Tune All By Myself I Can't Believe That You're In Love With Me Darlin' Katie Please Don't Talk About Me When I'm Gone I Promise You	Recorded 1 June 1956

5 August 1956	TAKE IT EASY	Let's Take It Easy Gal With The Yaller Shoes The Wayward Wind Amor With Me Ould Clay Pipe The Birds And The Bees I'll Be Seeing You	Recorded 15 July 1956

12 August 1956	TAKE IT EASY	Let's Take It Easy
		Watching The World
		  Go By
		Little Boy Fishing
		Sweet Genevieve
		Mountain Greenery
		Small Towns Are Smile
		  Towns
		I'll Be Around
			Recorded 10
			August 1956

25 August 1956	VARIETY PLAYHOUSE	Gal With The Yaller Shoes The Birds And The Bees	Recorded 19 August 1956

6 September 1956	WORKERS'
	PLAYTIME
		Mountain Greenery
		Gal With The Yaller
		  Shoes
		Where The River Shannon
		  Flows
			Live

17 September 1956	MIDDAY MUSIC HALL	Ten Thousand Miles Glendora	Live
30 September 1956	MELODY HOUR	Ten Thousand Miles Strange Music	Recorded 26 September 1956
14 October 1956	MELODY HOUR	The Wind, The Wind Rich In Love Hello Young Lovers I Whistle A Happy Tune	Live

278

21 October 1956	MELODY HOUR	Strange Music A Perfect Day Ten Thousand Miles	Live
29 October 1956	MIDDAY MUSIC HALL	The Wind, The Wind Rich In Love Ten Thousand Miles	Live
15 November 1956	MUSIC ON THE MENU	Amor Little Boy Fishin'	Live
3 December 1956	THE SPICE OF LIFE	The Wind, The Wind Ten Thousand Miles	Recorded 26 November 1956

4 December 1956	TOP OF THE
	POPS
		Gal With The Yaller
		   Shoes
		Where The River
		   Shannon Flows
		Steamboat River Ball
		A Perfect Day
		The Yellow Rose Of Texas
		Nothin' To Do
		I Whistle A Happy Tune
		Ten Thousand Miles
			Recorded 20
			November 1956

10 December 1956	THE SPICE OF LIFE	Gal With The Yaller Shoes Strange Music	Recorded 3 December 1956
17 December 1956	THE SPICE OF LIFE	All Of You	Recorded 10 December 1956
26 December 1956	MIDDAY MUSIC HALL	Yaller Yaller Gold Eileen	Recorded 16 December 1956
31 December 1956	THE SPICE OF LIFE	Nothin' To Do Follow Me	Recorded 17 December 1956
14 January 1957	THE SPICE OF LIFE	Yaller Yaller Gold Hello Young Lovers I Whistle A Happy Tune	Recorded 8 January 1957

279

21 January 1957	THE SPICE OF LIFE	I Saw Esau True Love	Recorded 15 January 1957

28 January 1957	THE SPICE OF LIFE	From The Bottom
		   Of My Heart
		Out Of Sight,
		   Out Of Mind
			Recorded 22
			January 1957

4 February 1957	THE SPICE OF LIFE	Out Of Sight, Out Of Mind John Henry	Recorded 29 January 1957
11 February 1957	THE SPICE OF LIFE	Ten Thousand Miles Where The River Shannon Flows	Recorded 5 February 1957
18 February 1957	THE SPICE OF LIFE	Don't Forbid Me	Recorded 12 February 1957
25 February 1957	THE SPICE OF LIFE	I Saw Esau The Wind, The Wind	Recorded 8 February 1957
4 March 1957	THE SPICE OF LIFE	Strange Music	Recorded 26 February 1957
11 March 1957	THE SPICE OF LIFE	Yaller Yaller Gold	Recorded 5 March 1957
18 March 1957	THE SPICE OF LIFE	Friendly Persuasion Nine Pound Hammer	Recorded 12 March 1957
25 March 1957	THE SPICE OF LIFE	Don't Forbid Me Rovin' Gambler	Recorded 19 March 1957
1 April 1957	THE SPICE OF LIFE	We Will Make Love Mi Casa, Su Casa	Recorded 26 March 1957
19 April 1957	THE GREAT WALTZ	True Love	Recorded 14 April 1957
22 April 1957	EASTER BANDBOX	Love Is Strange Strange Music	Recorded 18 April 1957

28 April 1957	SENTIMENTAL JOURNEY (all programmes with Edna Savage) Series produced by John Hooper	No Strings That's What Makes Paris Paree Would You Like To Take A Walk? How About You (w. ES) J'Attendrai Almost Like Being In Love (w. ES) Where Or When Where Did The Night Go? (w. ES)	Recorded 3 April 1957
5 May 1957	SENTIMENTAL JOURNEY	Blue Skies If I Were You (w. ES) Make Believe Spring Spring Spring I Get A Kick Out Of You (w. ES) People Will Say We're In Love (w. ES) Strange Music Auf Wiedersehen (w. ES)	Recorded 10 April 1957
12 May 1957	SENTIMENTAL JOURNEY	You're Getting To Be A Habit With Me (w. ES) All Of You That's Amore (w. ES) Tea For Two (w. ES) Bella Notte (w. ES) Stay Awhile And Listen To My Song There's No Tomorrow (w. ES) Arriverderchi Darling (w. ES)	Recorded 17 April 1957
14 May 1957	FESTIVAL OF DANCE	The Lonesome Road Let's Do It (w. Lita Roza)	Live

19 May 1957	SENTIMENTAL JOURNEY	I've Got You Under My Skin	Recorded 15 May 1957
		Nothin' To Do	
		They Can't Take That Away From Me (w. ES)	
		I Could Be Happy With You (w. ES)	
		Around The World	
		You Make Me Feel So Young (w. ES)	
		I'm Getting Tired So I Can Sleep (w. ES)	
31 May 1957	MICHAEL HOLLIDAY PROGRAMME	I Haven't Time to Be A Millionaire	Recorded 23 May 1957
		I'm Old Fashioned	
		Four Walls	
		Nine Pound Hammer	
		Nothin' To Do	
		You Sang My Love Song To Somebody Else	
		I Whistle A Happy Tune	
2 June 1957	SENTIMENTAL JOURNEY	A Fine Romance (w. ES)	Recorded 29 May 1957
		That Old Black Magic (w. ES)	
		Cinco Robles	
		Long Ago And Far Away (w. ES)	
		London By Night	
		Where There's You There's Me (w. ES)	
		I Won't Dance (w. ES)	
		My Idea Of Heaven	
		Goodnight My Love (w. ES)	
7 June 1957	MICHAEL HOLLIDAY PROGRAMME	Wringle Wrangle	Recorded 28 May 1957
		The Lonesome Road	
		I Can't Believe That You're In Love With Me	
		John Henry	
		Around The World	

9 June 1957	SENTIMENTAL JOURNEY	S'Wonderful (w. ES)
		No Two People
		  (w. ES)
		Stranger In Paradise (w. ES)
		So Rare (w. ES)
		Younger Than Springtime
		That's What A Rainy
		  Day Is For (w. ES)
		Baby Its Cold Outside (w. ES)
		A Man And His Dream
			Recorded
			5 June 1957

14 June 1957	MICHAEL HOLLIDAY PROGRAMME	Getting To Know You
		That's My Heart
		  Strings
		Smile Right Back At
		  The Sun
		Mr (Miss) Wonderful
		It's Anybody's Spring
			Recorded
			4 June 1957

16 June 1957	SENTIMENTAL JOURNEY	Beyond The Blue
		  Horizon (w. ES)
		A Woman In Love
		There's No Cure For
		  L'amour (w. ES)
		Strolling In The Park (w. ES)
		My Blue Heaven (w. ES)
		Hello Young Lovers (w. ES)
		Marrying For Love
		I'll See You Again
			Recorded
			12 June 1957

21 June 1957	MICHAEL HOLLIDAY PROGRAMME	Gal With The Yaller Shoes We Will Make Love With Me Ould Clay Pipe My Little Baby Blue Shadows On The Trail I'll Be Around	Recorded 17 June 1957
24 June 1957	GALA VARIETY SHOW	Blue Skies Nothin' To Do Yaller Yaller Gold The Lonesome Road	Recorded 23 June 1957

8 July 1957	MIDDAY MUSIC HALL	Four Walls Wringle Wrangle	Live
2 September 1957	MIDDAY MUSIC HALL	Love You Darlin' Old Cape Cod	Live
1 October 1957	SENTIMENTAL JOURNEY	Don't Fence Me In You're Just In Love (w. ES) Our Love Affair (w. ES) Be it Resolved Blue Room (w. ES) The Way You Look Tonight I Love The Way You Say Goodnight (w. ES) Goodnight Angel (w. ES)	Recorded 1 August 1957
8 October 1957	SENTIMENTAL JOURNEY	There's A Rainbow Round My Shoulder Our Love Is Here To Stay (w. ES) I Could Write A Book The Folks Who Live On The Hill (w. ES) Its The Natural Thing To Do (w. ES) They All Laughed Where In The World (w. ES) Close Your Eyes (w. ES)	Recorded 5 September 1957
15 October 1957	SENTIMENTAL JOURNEY	I Have Dreamed If You Were The Only Girl In The World (w. ES) It's Never Too Late To Fall In Love (w. ES) Side By Side (w. ES) Lovely To Look At Let's Face The Music And Dance (w. ES)	Recorded 12 September 1957

This Is A Lovely Way
To Spend An Evening (w. ES)
Shall We Dance? (w. ES)

29 October 1957	SENTIMENTAL JOURNEY	So In Love	Recorded 19 September 1957

29 October 1957   SENTIMENTAL JOURNEY

So In Love   Recorded 19
Why Do I Love   September 1957
    You? (w. ES)
D'Ye Love Me? (w. ES)
When The Children Are
    Asleep (w. ES)
All At Once You Love Her
It Only Happens When
    I Dance With You
The Touch Of Your Lips (w. ES)
Dream (w. ES)

5 November 1957   SENTIMENTAL JOURNEY

I've Got Beginner's   Recorded 26
    Luck (w. ES)   September 1957
You Were Meant For
    Me (w. ES)
As Time Goes By (w. ES)
Love You Darlin'
Tell Me I'm Forgiven
Love Is Just Around
    The Corner (w. ES)
I've Told Every Little Star
How Deep Is The Ocean (w. ES)

12 November 1957   SENTIMENTAL JOURNEY

Red Sky   Recorded 3
East Of The Sun   October 1957
    (w. ES)
Anything Goes (w. ES)
Make Believe (w. ES)
Long Before I Knew You
Too Marvellous For Words
    (w. ES)
Strange Music
In The Still Of The Night
    (w. ES)

19 November 1957	SENTIMENTAL JOURNEY	S'Wonderful (w. ES) A Room In Bloomsbury (w. ES) Just In Time The Nearness Of You (w. ES) My Blue Heaven (w. ES) Winter Wonderland (w. ES) Baby It's Cold Outside (w. ES) Never Say Goodbye (w. ES)	Recorded 10 October 1957

26 November 1957	SENTIMENTAL JOURNEY	I'm In The Mood
		  For Love
		Tea For Two (w. ES)
		Just Between You And
		  Me (w. ES)
		I Can't Believe That
		  You're In Love With Me
		Tell Me, Pretty Maiden
		It's De-Lovely
		All Of You
		People Will Say We're In
		  Love (w. ES)
		The Very Thought Of You
			Recorded 17
			October 1957

3 December 1957	SENTIMENTAL JOURNEY	One, Two, Button
		  Your Shoe
		How About You
		  (w. ES)
		Long Ago And Far
		  Away (w. ES)
		I Get A Kick Out Of You
		Two Silhouettes (w. ES)
		No Two People (w. ES)
		No Other Love (w. ES)
			Recorded
			24 October 1957

10 December 1957	SENTIMENTAL JOURNEY	They Can't Take That
		  Away From Me
		Nothin' To Do
		Blue Skies
		I'll String Along With
		  You (w. ES)
		Too Marvellous For Words (w. ES)
			Recorded 7
			November 1957

So Do I

Goodnight My Love (w. ES)

17 December 1957	SENTIMENTAL JOURNEY	Night And Day	Recorded 14
		I've Got Beginner's Luck (w. ES)	November 1957
		Love Around The World (w. ES)	
		Where In The World (w. ES)	
		Once Upon A Winter Time	
		You Do Something To Me (w. ES)	
		Some Enchanted Evening (w. ES)	
24 December 1957	SENTIMENTAL JOURNEY	Beyond The Blue Horizon (w. ES)	Recorded 21 November 1957
		So Rare (w. ES)	
		You Couldn't Be Cuter (w. ES)	
		Just In Time	
		Embraceable You	
		Dancing In The Dark (w. ES)	
		You'll Never Walk Alone	
14 January 1958	WORKERS' PLAYTIME	The Story Of My Life	Live
		Keep Your Heart	
		Kisses Sweeter Than Wine	
2 February 1958	FOLLOW THE STARS	The Story Of My Life	Recorded same day
10 February 1958	MIDDAY MUSIC HALL	The Story Of My Life	Live
		Keep Your Heart	
		Nothin' To Do	
15 February 1958	SATURDAY NIGHT ON THE LIGHT	The Story Of My Life	Recorded 14 February 1958

24 March 1958	BIGGER BEGGARS Radio play by Caryl Brahms and Ned Sherrin	Far Far Far So She Wears Trousers Bernie & Shirley If You Ain't Got Roots Swing Soft That Cradle I Got A Job It's Advertised All Over O Bernie Boy Jobs Wide Wide Guy Lay Him Down	Recorded 8 December 1957
14 April 1958	STARGAZERS' MUSIC SHOP	Rooney	Recorded 29 March 1958
8 May 1958	WORKERS' PLAYTIME	Love You Darlin' I Can't Believe That You're In Love With Me Stairway Of Love	Live
25 May 1958	FOLLOW THE STARS	Stairway Of Love Night And Day	Recorded same day
6 June 1958	MIDDAY MUSIC HALL	Stairway Of Love Strange Music Where The River Shannon Flows	Live

10 September 1958	BLACKPOOL
	NIGHT
		I'll Always Be In
		  Love With You
		I Know Where I'm
		  Going
		Back In The Old
		  Routine
			Recorded 9
			September 1958

29 November 1958	SATURDAY CLUB	Who's Sorry Now She Was Only Seventeen My Heart Is An Open Book Careless Hands	Recorded 26 November 1958

12 July 1959	ON STAGE SCARBOROUGH	Strange Music Love Is Just Around The Corner Ain't She Sweet	Recorded 8 July
18 January 1960	STRINGALONG	Starry Eyed Among My Souvenirs	Recorded 13 January 1960
25 January 1960	PARADE OF THE POPS	Starry Eyed (record) The Steady Game (record)	
13 February 1960	PETER CALLS THE TUNE	The Story Of My Life (record) Starry Eyed (record)	Recorded 6 February 1960
5 April 1960	WORKERS' PLAYTIME	Let A Smile Be Your Umbrella Why Travellin' Light Starry Eyed	Live
10 September 1960	SATURDAY CLUB	Paper Roses Buttons And Bows I Can't Believe That You're In Love With Me One Finger Symphony Home Cookin'	Recorded 6 September 1960
4 October 1960	HOLLIDAY WITH STRINGS all shows feature Johnny Pearson and his Orchestra Series produced by John Browell	Bluebird Singing In My Heart If She Should Come To You Amor I Promise You It's Anybody's Spring You Make Me Feel So Young	Recorded 26 September 1960

11 October 1960	HOLLIDAY WITH STRINGS	Between The Devil And The Deep Blue Sea	Recorded 3 October 1960
		A Little Kiss Each Morning	
		Getting Nowhere	
		Did You Ever See A Dream Walking	
		Kiddio	
		You Make Me Feel So Young	
18 October 1960	HOLLIDAY WITH STRINGS	Home Cookin'	Recorded 10 October 1960
		The Lamplighter's Serenade	
		I Can't Believe That You're In Love With Me	
		Skylark	
		Just In Time	
		Pass That Peace Pipe	
		You Make Me Feel So Young	
25 October 1960	HOLLIDAY WITH STRINGS	Some Sunny Day	Recorded 17 October 1960
		My Little Corner Of The World	
		Bye Bye Blackbird	
		San Fernando Valley	
		Just A Prayer Away	
		All I Do Is Dream Of You	
		You Make Me Feel So Young	
1 November 1960	HOLLIDAY WITH STRINGS	Nice'n Easy	Recorded 24 October 1960
		I'll Be Seeing You	
		My Heart Is A Hobo	
		When Irish Eyes Are Smiling	
		Surrey With The Fringe On Top	
		They All Laughed	
		You Make Me Feel So Young	

290

8 November 1960	HOLLIDAY WITH STRINGS	Go Fly A Kite Like Someone In Love Dinah (w. tape recorder) Old Cape Cod I Whistle A Happy Tune I Can't Begin To Tell You You Make Me Feel So Young	Recorded 31 October 1960

15 November 1960	HOLLIDAY WITH STRINGS	Getting To Know
		    You
		Night And Day
		Tiptoe Through The
		    Tulips (w. tape recorder)
		Strange Music
		It's Anybody's Spring
		Be Careful It's My Heart
		You Make Me Feel So
		    Young
			Recorded 7
			November 1960

22 November 1960	HOLLIDAY WITH STRINGS	Getting Nowhere
		Gone Fishin'
		Side By Side
		    (w. tape recorder)
		If She Should Come To You
		A Nightingale Sang In
		    Berkeley Square
		Just In Time
		You Make Me Feel So
		    Young
			Recorded 14
			November 1960

29 November 1960	HOLLIDAY WITH STRINGS	Smile Right Back
		    At The Sun
		I Promise You
		That's My Weakness Now
		Lazy
		My Little Corner Of
		    The World
		Bluebird Singing In My
		    Heart
		You Make Me Feel So
		    Young
			Recorded 21
			November 1960

6 December 1960	HOLLIDAY WITH STRINGS	A Little Kiss Each Morning	Recorded 28 November 1960
		Did You Ever See A Dream Walking	
		Sleepy Time Gal	
		Amor	
		The Lamplighter's Serenade	
		Between The Devil And The Deep Blue Sea	
		You Make Me Feel So Young	
13 December 1960	HOLLIDAY WITH STRINGS	I'd Rather Just Be Me	Recorded 5 December 1960
		Folks Who Live On The Hill	
		When I Take My Sugar To Tea	
		The Last Round Up	
		Kiddio	
		Home Cookin'	
		You Make Me Feel So Young	
20 December 1960	HOLLIDAY WITH STRINGS	Some Sunny Day Dreamin'	Recorded 12 December 1960
		Show Me The Way To Go Home (w. tape recorder)	
		Little Donkey	
		Quizas, Quizas, Quizas	
		Pass That Peace Pipe	
		You Make Me Feel So Young	
27 December 1960	HOLLIDAY WITH STRINGS	Have You Ever Been Lonely?	Recorded 19 December 1960
		A Nightingale Sang In Berkeley Square	
		Winter Wonderland (w. tape recorder)	
		I Love You, Samantha	
		A Fella With An Umbrella